Survivor Criminology

THE APPLIED CRIMINOLOGY
ACROSS THE GLOBE SERIES

Series Editor

Kimberly A. McCabe, University of Lynchburg, mccabe@lynchburg.edu

Crime and safety continue to be among the top issues facing the global world and the discipline of applied criminology addresses those issues. *The Applied Criminology across the Globe* series is designed to address the ever-growing need for current and accurate information on a variety of subjects as related to applied criminology. The books in this series provide the readers with monographs that are able to inform and educate individuals on crime and criminal behaviors.

Books in the Series

Survivor Criminology: A Radical Act of Hope, edited by Kimberly J. Cook, Jason M. Williams, Reneè D. Lamphere, Stacy L. Mallicoat, and Alissa R. Ackerman
Sex Trafficking of Children Online: Modern Slavery in Cyberspace, by Beatriz Susana Uitts
Policing and Public Trust: Exposing the Inner Uniform, by Eccy de Jonge

Survivor Criminology

A Radical Act of Hope

Edited by

Kimberly J. Cook
Jason M. Williams
Reneè D. Lamphere
Stacy L. Mallicoat
Alissa R. Ackerman

ROWMAN & LITTLEFIELD
Lanham • Boulder • New York • London

Published by Rowman & Littlefield
An imprint of The Rowman & Littlefield Publishing Group, Inc.
4501 Forbes Boulevard, Suite 200, Lanham, Maryland 20706
www.rowman.com

86-90 Paul Street, London EC2A 4NE, United Kingdom

British Library Cataloguing in Publication Information Available

Library of Congress Cataloging-in-Publication Data

Names: Cook, Kimberly J., 1961- editor.
Title: Survivor criminology : a radical act of hope / edited by Kimberly J. Cook, Jason
   M. Williams, Reneè D. Lamphere, Stacy L. Mallicoat, Alissa R. Ackerman.
Description: Lanham : Rowman & Littlefield, [2022] | Series: Applied criminology
   across the globe | Includes bibliographical references and index. | Summary: "Survivor
   Criminology explores how one's status as a survivor has informed their journey
   and commitment to research, teaching, and activism. It provides a both a greater
   understanding to issues of victimization and gives a voice to those experiences as their
   foundation for criminological research, advocacy, and policy development"—Provided
   by publisher.
Identifiers: LCCN 2022013357 (print) | LCCN 2022013358 (ebook) | ISBN
   9781538151693 (cloth ; alk. paper) | ISBN 9781538161333 (paperback) |
   ISBN 9781538151709 (epub)
Subjects: LCSH: Victims of crimes. | Criminology.
Classification: LCC HV6250.25 .S84 2022 (print) | LCC HV6250.25 (ebook) | DDC
   362.88—dc23/eng/20220621
LC record available at https://lccn.loc.gov/2022013357
LC ebook record available at https://lccn.loc.gov/2022013358

♾️™ The paper used in this publication meets the minimum requirements of American
National Standard for Information Sciences—Permanence of Paper for Printed Library
Materials, ANSI/NISO Z39.48-1992.

Contents

Foreword to Survivor Criminology

A Radical Act of Hope

Elizabeth A. Stanko

LIVED EXPERIENCE

I rarely talk about my young self. During the surround sound of #metoo over the past few years, I listened to the debates about sexual harassment. What bothered me was the astonishing lack of historical connection with the early feminist activism from the early to mid-1970s onward. For me, awareness of sexual harassment arose from exposure to a women's studies course in my undergraduate sociology degree (around 1970). I was motivated to participate in early protests. I proudly remember walking up 5th Avenue in New York City for my first feminist march in 1971. We didn't have pussy hats then (I do love them), and besides, it was summer.

Throughout my postgraduate and early research experience, as I largely had my head down on completing my Ph.D. I landed my first university assistant professor appointment at Clark University, in the United States, at age 26. I had never taught a university course before, as I supported myself through graduate school with a full-time research post. Clark University is a small university in Worcester, Massachusetts. I worked in a university department of five people (three men and two women) where there was an atmosphere in the department that permitted the sexual harassment of students and colleagues. Had there been a #metoo in those days I'm certain two of my colleagues would have been outed. It wasn't long, however, before it happened. In 1979, the department hired a dynamic anthropologist, Ximena

Bunster Burotto, a Chilean exile, and within months, she had had enough of this sexualized atmosphere (Enloe, 2017).

For me, working in a sexualized environment wasn't unfamiliar. I had managed sexual harassment on several jobs already—as a waitress (from the manager and sometimes from the clients), as a young woman researcher travelling New York State collecting data for my second research job, and as an assistant professor in that very department at Clark University. Ximena was able to stand up to the sexual innuendo and propositions, where I dodged and tried to find a way of not getting struck by its backlash. The backlash commonly comes when you decide not to play the sexualized games present in the workplace. One usually learns about who holds the power of the game when you won't play, or say no, or say no more. The difference between flirting and sexual harassment is felt through the punishment for not playing along with the sexualized games or when you think that leaving the game altogether is better for your mental health. Sometimes you only learn that it wasn't "just" flirting when you get fired for not enjoying the unspoken rules of the game.

Ximena endured the backlash I had been evading (or at least I thought I was evading it). For me, it was time to #metoo, but there was no Twitter to join (1978) and very few public "me's." In the early months of Ximena's university complaint process, I gave statements to her lawyers supporting Ximena's experiences, and was advised (to my own surprise) that I too was being subjected to the same "hostile atmosphere" that permeated the department. It should not have been a surprise. Perhaps I was too good at dodging and needed to stand ground to help change the unspoken rules. I was willing to testify to the university grievance process not only on Ximena's behalf, but on mine too, and for a number of past and present students who confidentially reported experiences to me. So, for the countless number of women students who told me in person that "they too" were objects of the professors' harassing ways, I felt I owed them a duty of care. The hostility of the atmosphere in the university escalated during the four years it took to wind through the university's complaints process and the courts (there were two lawsuits)—and eventually to a negotiated settlement. We received a public apology. I stood my ground, as did Ximena. It often felt though as if the ground was engulfing me. Newspapers, *MS. Magazine*, and TV talk shows featured the case, and we were our own spokespeople facing a salacious, curious media.

The university complaints process, the lawsuit by Sid Peck for defamation of character (where Ximena, myself and three others were sued for $23,710,000), and the Title IX lawsuit (*Stanko v. Clark* 1981) had me breaking out in hives every day. I was exhausted in 1982 and moved to London for a much-earned university sabbatical.[1] This experience was fundamental to the start of my academic career and underpins my academic scholarship on violence against women. And in 2019, surrounded by account after account of #metoo, I felt the return of PTSD (irritation, flashbacks, tearfulness) that I now remember as the daily reality of living through a high-profile sexual harassment case in the 1970s/early 1980s (Baker, 2008).

LIVED EXPERIENCE AND ACADEMIC CURIOSITY

In my own professional experience, challenging the master narrative of criminology (as taught to me in the early 1970s), required molding a new narrative drawn from a feminist standpoint. This evolving narrative centered around naming women's experiences of men's violence as harmful, grounding my academic writing in the emotions and wisdom gleaned from the four-year struggle to challenge sexual harassment in my own workplace. I never really wrote about that time, nor did I wish to speak about it in public past the first-year post settlement. Silence fed my need to heal. But I clearly infused this experience into an academic narrative that set out dilemmas for women "managing" men's violence. In those days, speaking about my own experience felt too intrusive. Being able to write about women's experience enabled me to develop novel ways of trying to document, in a systematic (and scholarly) way how much and to what effect men's violence intruded into women's everyday lives, running through the veins of life's routine. In many ways, my scholarship benefited from insight that only came from the experiences of pain brought by the sexual harassment case.

My ability to harness my lived experience *as insight* enabled me to articulate processes of victimization, power, the way coercive control works, the way the silencing of harm works, and the gaps in understanding that drive the silencing of violence against women in a professional discipline. Together with other feminist scholars, I began to demonstrate how and why scholarship on crime, criminality, victimization, professional practice, or imprisonment misses the mark. Not only did criminology fail to see the harm of large swathes of victimization of women and girls, but it also actively supported its exclusion from justice. Law and its application blamed the victims for their own harm. The struggle to recognize the harm of sexual violence in many ways is still at its infancy. Criminal law and appeals to justice are still difficult for many as the lived experience of violence is so often integrated into the *being of the harmed*. That intersectional, lived being—in our current political orders regardless of nation-state—is subject to the filters and layers of belief, disbelief, and social respectability founded on colonial, racialized, monied, male privilege. Judge, lawyer, victim, or thief (Rafter & Stanko, 1982), being female involved in the interstices of criminal justice mattered, and its consequences often unsupportive in the various roles working in, appealing to, and being "processed" by the system. It wasn't just the "system" where these consequences lie; the consequences meant that there was no protection under law in an advanced, democratic state should a female participant ask for parity of treatment or respect.

Criminology in the mid- to late-1970s, and through the 1980s largely ignored women and focused its attention on what men did to break some forms of (largely traditional) criminal laws. A boy's profession, criminology studied crime at arm's length, portraying violent criminality as committed by those "other" men. Criminals were the bad apples; racialized imagines of criminality abounded, dominated by presumptions of containment and confinement as state solutions. My first academic conference—the American Society of Criminology (ASC) in 1977—was a shock for me. I was one of those few women at the conference that huddled together in a room to talk about what it felt like to be a woman at the conference, and that small gathering sowed the seeds for the Women and Crime Division in the ASC today. Not only was the profession dominated by men, but the early ASC conferences felt like attending a boys club, with all the bad behavior associated with sexual harassment and inappropriate professionalism. My early lived experiences as an academic was accompanied by reminders that I was *other* in the profession.

The times though were changing. A critique of the state was rising through academia and elsewhere in the 1970s, and through these critical lenses women's voices were slowly beginning to be raised too. The small number of university scholars who began to study women, and the few criminologists who studied women in crime and justice began to grow larger. Activism, which was always an integral part of my academic practice, was also sowing the seeds of challenge and creating new spaces where academic curiosity could shine its light. Throughout the four decades since my sexual harassment case I am unable to separate what I have learned from my lived experience from my academic writing, and I use this aged wisdom in my personal and policy influence today in confronting the way policing and justice is done and experienced by those within its tenacles and without its protection.

SO FAST FORWARD A NUMBER OF DECADES . . .

Today the silence within the profession of criminology is beginning to break. This edited collection offers us insight and reflection about the impact of lived experiences on our work as scholars, activists, and practitioners in the field of criminology. So highly personal, these chapters lay bare parts of the self that are supposed to be removed from professional practice and judgment. Social science—science—prides itself on its "objectivity." As so many of the authors of these chapters attest, objectivity in criminology itself often turns

out to reflect (usually) the accumulated perspective of privileged, white men. Does that make any difference to our theorizing about victimization? Or the application or absence of law? Or indeed the impact of imprisonment? The activism needed to challenge criminal harm? For those working and studying criminology, is the very act of locating lived experience within a systematic professional body of knowledge recognized as scholarship?

The contributions to this volume have much to say about how we, as people with life experience, integrate *ourselves* into professional lives or into the knowledge of the profession as described and studied by it. Our lives do not always fit with the official or scholarly to narratives or its underpinning theory, as it portrays and publishes criminological truths, which have profound implications for law, policy, and best practice. Today, including lived experience is a recognized part of reviewing best practice for many professional decisions and reviews of policy. Methodological tools, such as observation and surveys, need people (and their lived experiences) to tell us about the practice of law and policy. Open government and professional consultation require understanding people's lived experience of governance, of policy, of social change, and of human rights. I am not naïve to believe this happens systematically across the board or such consultations are listened to or even heard. Nor do I believe we currently live in a world that practices equal justice and respect for all peoples.

As some in this volume say, the ability to challenge accepted wisdom requires a person to raise their head above the parapet to say their experience is not as portrayed. Moreover, harnessing the insight of victimization does not negate one's ability to be an expert. Drawing on one's lived experience, living through the PTSD that you document in your research still demands emotional toil and takes an emotional toll. And doing so, as some in this volume say, takes courage. And has personal consequences. It is not only a stance that is risky personally; it is risky professionally. And sometimes, within this profession, being that someone whose experience of criminology's narrative does not fit with the accepted wisdom of many traditional scholars requires living with cognitive dissonance.

And as the authors in this collection demonstrate, the experience of being treated as other, as being removed from the experience of the narrative most in the profession accepted as "fact" and as "theory" jarred their personal and professional journeys (which are inevitably filled with bumpiness, not uncommonly accompanied by bullying, hostility, disadvantage, and invisibility). My hope is that the reader of this volume can learn that all of us have lived experiences. Those lived experiences are valuable resources in understanding and promoting a more rounded accumulation of professional knowledge.

REFERENCES

Baker, C. N. (2008). *The Women's Movement against Sexual Harassment.* New York: Cambridge University Press.

Enloe, C. (2017). *The Big Push: Exposing and Challenging the Persistence of Patriarchy.* Oakland: University of California Press.

Rafter, N., & Stanko, E. A. (1982). *Judge, Lawyer, Victim, Thief: Women, Gender Roles, and Criminal Justice.* Boston: Northeastern University Press.

NOTE

1. Where I wrote *Intimate Intrusions: Women's Experience of Male Violence* (1985).

Introduction

A Call for Survivor Criminology

Kimberly J. Cook, Reneè D. Lamphere, Jason M. Williams, Stacy L. Mallicoat, and Alissa R. Ackerman

THE RELEVANCE OF CRIMINOLOGY

Most people do not have direct experiences with the criminal justice and legal systems. Therefore, the images and ideas that come to mind are mainly influenced by what we've seen on television or in the movies. Within these stories, a crime happens, someone is harmed, and the police, courts, and prisons are here to fix things. What these portrayals generally don't show is the limitations of these processes and the trauma that can occur as a result of the crime and during the legal system process.

Criminologists often ponder whether justice is served by our criminal justice and legal systems. To explore this issue, we ask if justice is a fair process, regardless of the outcome? Is it ensuring that someone is punished for the injury or harm that they have caused, or something else? Who defines what justice is, the victims, the state, or the person responsible for the harmful behavior? A key criticism of our criminal legal system observes that it was not built to serve the needs of victims or offenders of crime. The system, and its processes, represent an administrative approach to dealing with conflict whereby the state serves as a proxy for the victim, and in turn, supersedes the victim's identity. The problem is that justice-related entertainment programming fuels the cultural lore that the justice system and the state is your dependable partner in finding justice. This portrayal obscures a significant disservice for victims and survivors, who often end up voiceless and marginalized as a result. As Nils Christie (1977) suggests:

> The [criminal] proceeding is converted from something between the concrete parties into a conflict between one of the parties and the state. . . . [Thus], the [victim] is a sort of a double loser; first, *vis-à-vis* the offender, but secondly and often in a more crippling manner by being denied rights to full participation in what might have been one of the more important ritual encounters in life. The victim has lost the case to the state. (p. 3)

As criminologists, we are a bridge between the public and the academic research community because we empirically study and explain issues of crime, law, and justice. As faculty, the public is represented by our students in our classrooms. Who are our students when they first come to the classroom? Perhaps they are curious about the world in which they live? Some may embrace criminology to provide answers for their personal experiences. Yet others may be resistant to various research and knowledge because it challenges their truth. Criminology and criminal justice students tend to be punitive towards offenders and have higher support for harsh punishments (Courtright, Mackey, & Packard, 2005; Stringer & Murphy, 2020). Like the general public, students arrive in classes with views about crime and justice that are heavily influenced by crime entertainment. They think they know what they are getting into. They expect to see *Law and Order*, where by the end of the episode, or semester, they will know who all the bad guys are, and how to fight crime and find justice. We also know that television shows about crime and justice are a significant factor when students choose their major (Barthe, Leone, & Lateano, 2013; Ridener, Kuehn, & Scott, 2020; Sarver, Sarver, & Dobbs, 2010). But most examples of crime entertainment do not present a realistic understanding of the criminal justice system (Rafter, 2006). The problem is that these shows pretend to be victim centered without addressing the needs of trauma survivors at large; they present a distorted—and in some cases a propagandized—impression that the legal process is clear, unblemished, and fair, and that it produces resolution, or possibly even healing.

While many students are drawn to criminology and criminal justice from a law-and-order perspective, Eren, Leyro, and Disha (2019) highlight that victimization can also be a driving force in how students think about crime and justice. Students who have either direct or vicarious crime victimization, are more likely to hold negative views about the criminal justice process. Vicarious trauma is also a strong predictor in the decision to major in the field—in particular, this desire is driven by an interest to protect people from oppression and make a difference in their community (Trebilcock & Griffiths, 2021).

When students arrive in criminology classrooms they may be exposed to some unexpected realities, such as miscarriages of justice, evidence of historically targeted minoritized groups being funneled into the prison systems, paltry victims services, and appalling victim-blaming messages from classmates, popular culture, the legal system officials, and perhaps their professors, to name a few. While these realities are exposed in many criminology classes, students may not be encouraged to consider the human dimensions of their professors or the people whose lives they document in research. Minoritized students may not see themselves or their realities reflected in the curriculum, and students who have survived some of the crimes we typically research or teach about may feel alienated from the lessons on that topic if/when the lesson is presented in an "objective" manner. This may result in students with lived experiences being repelled from criminology, or it may result in such students becoming determined to add their insights to the disciplinary canon. Can criminology build a container large enough for the voices of survivors in our midst? Can criminology become a more inclusive field by listening to those whose lives are impacted by crime or exclusion? It is our goal in this volume to say "yes, it can" and even more powerfully: "yes, it must."

CRIMINOLOGY AS INCLUSIVE?

Criminology is the study of crime and criminal behavior: who engages in crime and why, how communities are impacted by crime, how systems respond to crime, and how we can reduce or prevent crime. Ultimately, crime is inherently a complex issue. Criminology has many subfields and specializations through which research, advocacy, and policy can be represented. Many of these subfields highlight the voices of scholars who have been historically silenced or minimized by mainstream approaches. Consider the emergence of perspectives such as feminist criminology, convict criminology, queer criminology, and intersectional criminology. Each of these subfields emerged from relationships between one's personal identity, lived experiences, academic scholarship, and activism. Feminist criminology has contributed deeper and richer understandings of criminal offending (i.e., Chesney-Lind, 1997), criminal victimization (i.e., Fisher et al., 2010; Renzetti, 2013), and gendered social responses to crime (i.e., Sharp, 2014; Daly & Maher, 1998), and may be informed by the personal experiences of the authors (Stanko, 1985; Silver, 2015). Convict criminology (Jones, Richards, Ross, & Murphy, 2009; Richards & Ross, 2001) draws upon formerly incarcerated scholars who write about their experiences in prisons as it relates to penal policy and practice.

Queer criminology challenges the heteronormative perspectives within criminology and sheds light on the unique perspectives and issues that LGBTQ+ communities face within the criminal legal system (Buist & Lenning, 2016). Finally, intersectional criminology focuses on the role of power and the multiple and tangled identities of gender, race, class, and sexuality (Ritchie, 1996, 2018; Potter, 2013, 2015). Indeed, criminology benefits greatly from these areas of scholarship and the voices they bring. Thus, criminology continues to expand and develop and there are areas that are underrepresented.

THE (IN)VISIBILITY OF SURVIVORS IN CRIMINOLOGY

While a number of different policies at the federal level have focused on expanding the rights of victims, the criminal justice system has minimized the voice and needs of victims in many ways. The decision to file charges or prosecute an offender is left entirely with the prosecutor and governed by law. Victims may be notified of any proceedings and have the right to be present. Victims may also make a statement at a sentencing hearing, though they are rarely consulted about their views of punishment. However, this experience is limited to a small proportion of victims. Most crime victims do not have "their day in court." Some may find themselves retraumatized by the very processes within the criminal justice system that are thought to bring about "justice" and "closure" for victims, creating an entirely new experience of victimization (secondary victimization). Many victims choose not to report to official authorities, and may or may not seek out help from family and friends, informal networks, or community support resources. These challenges can impact one's ability to find closure and healing from this trauma.

It is time for a new subfield within criminology: survivor criminology. Survivor Criminology is a trauma-informed approach to the study of crime and justice, stems from the lived experiences of crime survivors, and explores how one's status as a "survivor" has informed a journey and commitment to research and teaching. As feminist criminology provides context to understanding issues of gender and crime, or as convict criminologists provide a lens through which we view and understand issues in incarceration, a spotlight on survivor criminology both provides a greater understanding to issues of victimization and gives a voice to those experiences as their foundation for criminological research, advocacy, and policy development.

One might ask, how does survivor criminology differ from the established field of victimology, which is the scientific study of the relationships between victims and offenders? Research in victimology focuses on questions such as did the perpetrator know their victim, or were they a stranger? Why was this particular person targeted? What sorts of injuries or harm was experienced as a result of this victimization? In addressing these questions, early theories of victimization focused largely on the role of victim culpability and suggested that crime victims were partially to blame for their trauma as a result of decision making and personal factors (von Hentig, 1948; Mendelsohn, 1956). Modern paradigms such as lifestyle theory (Hindelang, Gottfredson, & Garofalo, 1978), deviant place theory (Stark, 1987), and routine activities theory (Cohen & Felson, 1979) also center their discussions on victimization risk based on factors such as personal choice and social environment. In contrast, survivor criminology centers on the traumagenic conditions of society that are created by and sustain our academic field of study and the criminal legal systems.

Just as many feminist, queer, and critical race scholars have pushed mainstream criminology to consider the effects of a racist, sexist, classist, and homophobic understanding of crime, the development of survivor criminology further pushes these boundaries to develop a conversation on how trauma can be an added lens through which we see and understand criminal behavior and victimization. However, it is crucial to note that the identity of *survivor* does not stand alone, separated from other identities. At its inception, we define survivor criminology as an intersectional paradigm. Just as Crewshaw (1991) noted that "contemporary feminist and anti-racist discourses have failed to consider intersectional identities such as women of color" (p. 1246), survivor criminology is rooted in the understanding that survival is not a solitary journey absent from the rest of our identities. The identity of a survivor is intersectional, and incorporates gender, race, social class, sexuality, and other vectors of marginalization that represent many lived realities that are complex, layered, and nuanced.

DISRUPTING CRIMINOLOGY

Cook (2016) suggested that the development of survivor criminology is necessary in order to "cultivate more trauma-informed research" (p. 348). She adds:

> Feminist criminologists, to varying individual degrees, are committed to conducting research that helps to push the policy arena farther along toward human rights without apologizing for the portion of feminist work that is politically relevant as well as empirically researched. Arguably, many of us in feminist criminology are already "survivors" and thus already engage in "survivor criminology." After all, our lives are deeply influenced by the same sexism, racism, classism, and homophobia that has influenced the field in which we work; to ignore that our personal experiences are also political would require us to

amputate a significant part of our analytical capacity, a specious separation that
I am not willing, like many other feminists, to endure. (p. 348)

Judith Herman's groundbreaking work (1997) illuminates many of the
challenges that exist when recovering from traumatic life events. She defines
and explores the experiences of trauma that "overwhelm the ordinary human
adaptations to life" in the wake of events that "generally involve threats to
life or bodily integrity, or a close personal encounter with violence and death"
(p. 33). When a person survives such encounters, they confront the process
of recovering from the physical, emotional, psychological, and social harms
that result from those events.

For the purposes of this collection, we define "survivors" as people who
have had close personal encounters with violence and death, and who have
had close personal encounters with institutionalized oppressions based on
racism, heterosexism, sexism, and poverty—all of which include tentacles
that are life threatening such as lynching, gay-bashing, sexual harassment,
police brutality, and other forms of exclusions. One aspect of recovery that
may be part of a survivor's experience is to embark on a "survivor mission"
(Herman, 1997, p. 207–211), where survivors translate their close encounters
with trauma into a platform for advocacy. Herman writes that "[s]ocial action
offers the survivor a source of power that draws upon her own initiative,
energy, and resourcefulness but that magnifies these qualities [. . . and . . .]
offers her an alliance with others based on cooperation and shared purpose"
(1997, p. 207).

This book begins a conversation about survivor criminology as a body
of work that is devoted to the expression of crime, victimization, and the
criminal legal system through the lens of a survivor. The chapters within this
book explore our authors'—who are scholars, professors, practitioners, and
students in the field—lived experiences with crime and criminal justice and
how these experiences have shaped their research, teaching, and advocacy
work. We were drawn to criminology initially to make sense of our own
lived experiences. Our voices represent experiences that are intersectional,
multigenerational, global, trauma-informed, and resiliency focused. We are
deliberately and decidedly anti-racist, and our experiences acknowledge the
harm that has resulted from institutionalized and structural trauma. Most
importantly, our stories are grounded in our lived experiences. As editors of
this collection, we see survivor criminology as a gathering of voices, from a
heretofore distant place, that stand up against these traumas. In the words of
author Brene Brown:

There will be times when standing alone feels too hard, too scary, and we'll
make our way through the uncertainty. Someone, somewhere will say, "Don't

do it. You don't have what it takes to survive the wilderness." This is when you reach deep into your wild heart and remind yourself . . . I am the wilderness. (Brown, 2017 p. 163)

Our first chapter introduces the work of Dr. Alissa Ackerman and Dr. Alexa Sardina, who are the only two known sex crimes policy experts who are also public rape survivors. Their chapter highlights how collaborative autoethnography can be used as a methodology to study sexually based violence from a survivor lens.

Dr. Reneè D. Lamphere is a survivor of sexual violence and is the author of the second chapter of this volume. She highlights how her experiences of trauma led her to higher education and transformed her teaching and research. Her work focuses on the intersection of sexual violence survivorship and mental health. She suggests that the lived experience of trauma can create meaningful learning experiences for our students.

Chapter 3 shares the story of Dr. Jason M. Williams, a Black male critical criminologist. His presence in the field has been shaped by surviving poverty and structural inequality throughout his youth, and his experience in academia where the shadows of a white, male-dominated infrastructure of traditional criminology has shaped his voice and positionality in criminology.

Our fourth chapter shares Dr. Kimberly J. Cook's personal reflection of her experiences as a formerly battered woman seeking to become a professor. Her chapter provides a deep exploration of her experiences as a survivor of intimate partner violence, particularly as it relates to traumatic aftermath, and her story of resilience provides some discipline-specific insights and lessons learned from criminology.

Chapter 5 is an autoethnographic exploration of Dr. Jennifer Ortiz's history with structural and physical violence. She discusses how her experiences with poverty, harassment by law enforcement, and oppression within academia help her develop research and service agendas that reject mainstream criminological thought and the elitism of academia. Her chapter further explores how her position as a member of the organization Asociación Ñeta, a gang that originated in the prisons of Puerto Rico, served as the foundation for her research and advocacy on behalf of incarcerated persons.

Our sixth chapter examines the life of Monishia "Moe" Miller and her journey as a throwaway kid in the foster care system to a youth advocate and criminal justice professor. Her story highlights how she transformed her adverse childhood experiences of family dysfunction and sexual abuse into her identity as a defender for protection and survival for her students and herself.

Steven Green was convicted of felony murder and robbery for his role in a January 1992 shooting. Just eighteen years old at the time, he was sentenced to life without the possibility of parole (LWOP). His story is our seventh chapter of this volume where he shares how he spent nearly twenty-eight years behind bars before Gov. Jerry Brown commuted his sentence. His story of survival traces his traumagenic roots of family violence to his experiences of surviving juvenile LWOP.

Our eighth chapter is authored by Dr. Toniqua Mikell, whose work applies Black feminist criminology to understanding the role of interlocking systems of oppression for explaining victimization and social control of Black women. Her chapter shares how her identity as a queer criminologist and survivor shifts her teaching, mentoring, and research. Her story represents how intersectional identities and experiences challenge the tools for change both within criminology and academia in general.

Chapter 9 shares a reflection from a classroom interaction that Babette Boyd had with a student on Black Lives Matter. Her chapter highlights some of the recent social and legal history not just for Black lives, but for the future of democracy. Her poem asks us to consider "when did Black lives ever matter?"

Dr. Lauren Silver is a queer feminist scholar of childhood studies, a journey that was directly impacted by her experience as a survivor of childhood sexual abuse. Her story is the tenth chapter in this volume and presents a retrospective and aspirational approach to how agency, voice, innocence, and children's participation blend into a concept of collective-based agency and transformative justice.

Chapter 11 highlights the work of Meredith G. F. Worthen, who shares what it means to be a scholar activist within the context of survivor criminology. Her chapter shares her personal experience of starting/running the Instagram account #MeTooMeredith and provides students and faculty with a framework for understanding how to connect their own interests with scholar activism and survivor criminology.

Chapter 12 is authored by Stacy Parks Miller and draws upon her twenty years of prosecutorial experience in rural jurisdictions. Her chapter illustrates how the intersection of rurality, racism, sexism, classism, and heterosexism permeates the largely white male criminal justice system and the toll it takes on victims.

Our thirteenth chapter provides a global context for the roots of survivor criminology. The work of Keenan Mundine and Carly Stanley highlights how lived and professional experiences, coupled with the ineffectiveness of Australia's penal systems, inspired them to create an Indigenous-centered organization to address the overrepresentation of First Nations people in the justice and child protective systems. Their chapter provides a brief review of the modern history of Australia and the effects of colonization on Aboriginal communities. In sharing their personal stories, they highlight the nexus between trauma, poverty, and incarceration. Their story concludes with a discussion on the ways that they have used their experiences as survivors to advocate for repair, reform, and support for First Nations people in Australia.

SURVIVOR CRIMINOLOGY AS A RADICAL ACT OF HOPE

Given the multiple realms that exist not only for each of the authors in this volume, but also within the field of survivor criminology at large, it is important to acknowledge the impact of these traumas—physical, psychological, emotional, and spiritual. These traumas are present for both for the storyteller as well as for those viewing them. We acknowledge that each of these stories may be difficult to consume. We encourage our readers to take time and space where needed. This could mean reading chapters in small chunks, reaching out to support networks, or setting the book aside as necessary.

We posit that survivor criminology is a radical act of hope. Our hope comes from the belief that a trauma-centered approach to crime, justice, and healing provides the opportunity for criminology to expand its theoretical and methodological roots. We see this work as transformative for the discipline—for students, scholars, members of the community, and policy makers. Imagine if our classrooms were places where students could learn about the effects of structural and interpersonal violence for crime victims and perpetrators. How do we shift our teaching to be inclusive, not only for those who seek out criminology as a way to understand their own experiences with trauma, but also for those who want to work within the field to address these potential risks for harm? How do we consider the intersectional experience of survival? What does our research look like if we centered lived experiences at the heart of our inquiry? What does it mean to be authentic and vulnerable in our scholarship? What would our justice-oriented policies look like if we considered that the criminal justice system can be both responsive to crime, but also a creator of its own forms of trauma for crime victims, crime perpetrators, and the community as a whole? How can we create justice alternatives that are centered around people whose lives and experiences matter? It is our hope that the stories within this volume will begin to scratch the surface of these questions.

REFERENCES

Barthe, E. P., Leone, M. C., & Lateano, T. A. (2013). Commercializing success: The impact of popular media on the career decisions and perceptual accuracy of criminal justice students. *Teaching in Higher Education* 18(1): 13–26.

Brown, B. (2017). *Braving the Wilderness: The Quest for True Belonging and the Courage to Stand Alone.* London, England: Vermilion.

Buist, C., & E. Lenning. (2016). *Queer Criminology.* (Key Ideas in Criminology Series) New York: Routledge.

Chesney-Lind, M. (1997). *The Female Offender: Girls, Women, and Crime.* Thousand Oaks, CA. Sage.

Christie, N. (1977). Conflicts as property. *The British Journal of Criminology* 17(1): 1–15.

Cohen, L. E., & Felson, M. (1979). Social change and crime rate trends: A routine activity approach. *American Sociological Review,* 44(4): 588–608.

Cook, K. J. (2016). Has criminology awakened from its "androcentric slumber"? *Feminist Criminology* 11(4): 334–353.

Courtright, K. E., & Mackey, D. A. (2004). Job desirability among criminal justice majors: Exploring relationships between personal characteristics and occupational attractiveness. *Journal of Criminal Justice Education* 15(2): 311–326.

Courtright, K. E., Mackey, D. A., & Packard, S. H. (2005). Empathy among college students and criminal justice majors: Identifying predispositional traits and the role of education. *Journal of Criminal Justice Education,* 16(1), 125–144. doi: 10.1080/1051125042000333514

Crenshaw, K. (1991). Mapping the margins: Intersectionality, identity, politics, and violence against women of color. *Stanford Law Review* 43(6): 1241–1299.

Daly, K., & Maher, L. (1998). *Criminology at the Crossroads: Feminist Readings in Crime and Justice.* New York: Oxford University Press.

Eren, C. P., Leyro, S., & Disha, I. (2019). It's personal: The impact of victimization on motivations and career interests among criminal justice majors at diverse urban colleges. *Journal of Criminal Justice Education* 30(4): 510–535.

Fisher, B., Daigle, L. E., & Cullen, F. T. (2010). *Unsafe in the Ivory Tower: The Sexual Victimization of College Women.* Los Angeles: Sage Publications.

Herman, J. (1997). *Trauma and Recovery: The Aftermath of Violence—From Domestic Abuse to Political Terror.* New York: Basic Books.

Hindelang, M. J., Gottfredson, M. R., & Garofalo, J. (1978). *Victims of Personal Crime: An Empirical Foundation for a Theory of Personal Victimization.* Cambridge, MA: Ballinger.

Jones, R. S., Richards, C., Ross, J. I., & Murphy, D. S. (2009). The first dime: A decade of convict criminology. *Prison Journal* 89(2): 151–171.

Mendelsohn, B. (1956). A new branch of bio-psychological science: La Victimology. *Revue Internationale de Criminologie et de Police Technique* 10: 782–789.

Potter, H. (2008). *Battle Cries: Black Women and Intimate Partner Abuse.* New York: New York University Press.

———. (2013). Intersectional criminology: Interrogating identity and power in criminological research and theory. *Critical Criminology,* 21, 305–318. doi: 10.1007/s10612-013-9203-6

———. (2015). *Intersectionality and Criminology: Disrupting and Revolutionizing Studies of Crime.* Hoboken, NJ: Taylor and Francis.

Rafter, N. (2006). *Shots in the Mirror: Crime Films and Society*, 2nd ed. Oxford, UK: Oxford University Press.

Renzetti, C. (2013). *Feminist Criminology*. (Key Ideas in Criminology Series) New York: Routledge.

Richards, S. C., & Ross, J. I. (2001). The new school of convict criminology. *Social Justice* 28: 177–190.

Ridener, R., Kuehn, S., & Scott, P. W. (2020). Why do criminology and criminal justice students choose their major? An examination of parental, personality, and other individual characteristics. *Journal of Criminal Justice Education* 31(1): 1–22.

Ritchie, A. J. (2018). *Invisible No More: Police Violence against Black Women and Women of Color.* Boston: Beacon Press.

Ritchie. B. E. (1996). *Compelled to Crime: The Gender Entrapment of Battered Black Women.* New York: Routledge.

Sarver, R. A., Sarver, M. B., & Dobbs, R. R. (2010). Choosing criminal justice: Factors contributing to the selection of criminal justice as a major. *Journal of Criminal Justice and Law Review* 2: 57–66.

Sharp. S. (2014). *Mean Lives, Mean Laws: Oklahoma's Women Prisoners.* New Brunswick, NJ: Rutgers University Press.

Silver, L. 2015. *System Kids: Adolescent Mothers and the Politics of Regulation.* Chapel Hill: The University of North Carolina Press.

Stanko, E. 1985. *Intimate Intrusions: Women's Experience of Male Violence.* Boston: Routledge and Kegan Paul.

Stark, R. (1987). Deviant places: The theory of the ecology of crime. *Criminology* 25(4): 893–910

Stringer, E. C., & Murphy, J. (2020). Major decisions and career attractiveness among criminal justice students. *Journal of Criminal Justice Education* 31(4): 523–541.

Treblicock, J., & Griffiths, C. (2021). Student motivations for studying criminology: A narrative inquiry. *Criminology & Criminal Justice*. https://doi.org/10.1177/1748895821993843

von Hentig, H. (1948). *The criminal and His Victim: Studies in the Sociobiology of Crime*. Cambridge, MA: Yale University Press.

Chapter 1

Balancing the Dual Roles of Sex Crimes Researcher and Rape Survivor

A Collaborative Autoethnography of Survivor Scholars

Alexa D. Sardina and Alissa R. Ackerman

It was September of 2016 when we walked into a coffee shop on the pictur-esque waterfront in Tacoma, Washington. A mutual friend knew that both of us were living in the Seattle-Tacoma area and that we were both rape survivors. What our mutual friend could not have known was that both of us are criminologists trained as sex crimes experts. In fact, as far as we know, we are the only two sex crimes policy experts who are also public survivors. That first meeting on the Tacoma waterfront has turned into a rewarding and productive professional collaboration and more importantly a deeply intimate friendship. The passion that we both have has always been to bring our story as a way to communicate about sexual violence both outside and within the academic realm.

We experienced rape within four months of each other in 1999. While there are some definitely similarities in our experiences, especially in the consequences that sexual violence has had on our lives, there are distinct dif-ferences that provide for a unique collaborative perspective. Alissa was raped in April of 1999 when she was a sixteen-year-old junior in high school. While attending a house party with her girlfriend on the South Florida coast, she went for a walk on the beach with a young man she had just met at the party. When she asked to walk back to the party, the young man behaved toward her as if he wanted to engage in some kind of sexual act. Alissa refused and it quickly became clear that the young man had seen her kissing her girlfriend earlier in the night and had planned this rape as punishment for her being queer. When she said no again, the young man turned violent. Alexa was raped in August of 1999. She had just graduated from high school and was away at college in Boston. During her first week there, she went to the shared bathroom in the middle of the night and was raped at knifepoint by a man hiding in the shower stall. Alexa had never seen this man before but he told her that if she screamed he would kill her and that he would "kill anybody." After raping her in the shower stall, the stranger asked Alexa where her room was. She tried to dissuade him from going to her room because her roommate was there sleeping. But he insisted. He held the knife to Alexa's back as she led the way to her dorm room. He then raped her again on the floor of her dorm room.

Our immediate reactions to sexual violence were drastically different, but the long-term consequences were and remain strikingly similar. Despite visible signs that Alissa had experienced a violent assault, she did not disclose to anyone, telling people she had taken a fall on the rocks on the beach. She did not report to the police or tell anyone close to her for fear they would not believe her. After all, she told herself, she had lied to her parents about being at the party and she had left with a man she had just met and went walking on a dark secluded beach after midnight while her girlfriend was back at the party. Alexa's response was distinctly different from Alissa's. After the rape, Alexa immediately reported what had happened. She was taken from her dorm to the emergency room and examined by a Sexual Assault Nurse Examiner (SANE). While at the hospital, the police came and told her that the man had been apprehended. Alexa agreed to testify during the criminal trial, and ultimately, the man who raped her was sentenced to several decades in prison.

The consequences have been a point of connection for us both and are very consistent with what we know about how survivors experience the aftermath of rape. The psychological consequences for us both have been profound. In the direct aftermath of her rape, Alissa began drinking heavily and engaging in self-harm. She also began experiencing severe anxiety. She distinctly remembers a major panic attack that occurred the day she interviewed for her place in her doctoral program at John Jay College of Criminal Justice/CUNY Graduate Center. After her interview, overwhelmed by how far she had come, she ended up curled in the fetal position on the bathroom floor of the public bathroom at the college enduring a full blown flashback to her rape. Although Alexa believed that testifying and a guilty verdict would "heal" the wounds that her rape had caused, this was not the case. Alexa drank and used drugs before, during, and for many years after the trial and subsequent conviction of the man who raped her. In addition to issues with substance abuse, Alexa also suffered from anorexia coupled with depression and anxiety.

It took Alexa and Alissa years of therapy and resilience to overcome these obstacles. Alexa no longer struggles with substance abuse issues but psychological manifestations persist. She has been diagnosed with bipolar 2 disorder, which is characterized by periods of extreme depression and intermittent manic phases. Alissa struggled on and off with substance abuse, culminating in a decision to live in complete sobriety in 2019. She was also diagnosed with having bipolar 2 disorder after years of psychiatric medications that did not alleviate the mental health symptoms she had struggled with.

Integral to our continued healing has been having this deep and intimate friendship where we can be so completely ourselves. Our personal relationship is so strong that it strengthens our professional collaborations. It is our connection that allows us to dare so greatly when sharing all aspects of our lives in our public-facing and academic work. As criminologists, both of us were trained to be systematic and objective in our scholarship. However, navigating the academic path is as much about developing a research agenda and honing teaching abilities as it is about cultivating an understanding of how to navigate the world. In this chapter we will discuss how we have collectively done this both within academic and professional spaces, as well as in our public-facing roles. As individuals who use our professional voices to draw attention to sexual violence in public spaces, sharing personal experiences, often stigmatizing, is a professional risk we have endeavored together. Scientific inquiry typically requires us to recognize and then set aside any potential biases, but some researchers, including us, acknowledge that doing so is not always possible.

In this chapter we utilize the "self" as the research subject. Despite the fact that both of us are trained in qualitative and quantitative methodologies, neither of us had given much consideration to conducting research where we utilized ourselves as research subjects. It did not take long for us to recognize that our lived experiences and subsequent career paths were so strikingly similar and unique that a *collaborative autoethnography* was the first and most logical choice. We were both formally trained as generalists with doctoral degrees in criminal justice. We independently chose to research very specific topics: individuals who commit sex crimes and the criminal justice policies used to manage these individuals in the community. Both of us are also survivors of violent rapes that occurred within four months of each other. Finally, and perhaps most relevant, is that we are both public about our dual roles as "survivor scholars."[1]

Participating in our own collaborative autoethnography allowed us to better understand the unique contributions we can make to the literature on sex crimes policy and to our students. The purpose of this chapter is to explore those unique contributions.

LITERATURE REVIEW

Despite decades of research, sexual violence remains an elusive problem to combat. In fact, one in nine girls and one in fifty-three boys will experience sexual abuse or assault by an adult before they turn eighteen (Finklehor et al., 2014). Similarly, one in five women and one in seventy-one men will experience rape in their lifetime (Black et al., 2011). Moreover, one out of every two women and one out of every five men will experience a form of sexual violence or victimization other than rape.

We know that most people have experienced or know someone who has experienced a form of sexual violence, but what is less common is the acknowledgment and understanding of the consequences of these experiences. Over 80 percent of female-identifying survivors report both short- and long-term impacts of sexual violence. The impacts of sexual victimization can be detrimental and lifelong. These damaging consequences often come in the form of physical and mental health issues, including anxiety, depression, suicide attempts, chronic pain, eating disorders, migraines, difficulty sleeping, sexual dysfunction, low self-esteem, and dissociation (Black et al., 2011; Kilpatrick, 2000).

The discourse around sexual victimization is such that society exhibits disgust and outrage at the individuals who commit sex offenses. We expect harsh sentences and punitive measures to combat sex crimes. As such, the two main goals of sex crimes policy are to promote public safety and to articulate public outrage. Despite well-intentioned public outrage, most rape survivors see no reflection of themselves in current public policy (Bandy, 2015). Very few survivors formally report their victimization to law enforcement, and of those that do, only a fraction will receive "justice" (meaning the person who harmed them received a formal punishment from the criminal justice system). In fact, according to the U.S. Department of Justice, for every thousand rapes committed only six people will serve time in prison (Department of Justice, 2015). Public outrage and disgust do not necessarily equate with justice being served.

Public policy related to sexual violence is often void of the lived experiences of everyday survivors. It is our experiences that inform our belief that despite a public discourse on being "victim-centered," public policy does not center on the needs of people like us. To date, only one study has focused on the disjuncture between the needs of survivors and the impacts of current Sex Offender Registration and Notification (SORN) policies (Bandy, 2015). This study reported that most sexual assault survivors see little to no reflection of themselves in public policy. Further, the study finds that current policies may actually have a detrimental impact on survivors because they do not focus on survivors' needs. Most funding to combat or punish sexual violence is ear-marked for those who have offended and there is little funding left over for services for those who have been sexually harmed. Bandy (2015) found that survivors and coalitions against sexual assault (CASAs) articulate the need for supportive disclosure opportunities, accurate public education and aware-ness, access to immediate and long-term victim services, and sustainable access to services and support. The lack of these opportunities and resources can be incredibly detrimental to survivors.

OBJECTIVITY IN RESEARCH

The fields of criminology and criminal justice often rely on bureaucrats and government agencies for both funding and access to various avenues of research. This has commonly resulted in work that sterilizes the complex human relationships, dangerous situations, and emotionally charged topics with which criminologists frequently engage. There is an unspoken under-standing that if we, criminologists, disclose the emotions that underlie our work, our colleagues will question its "validity" and our "objectivity" (Drake & Harvey, 2013). This article questions the favoring of a methodology that minimizes the significance of lived experiences and downplays the experi-ential resources of those of us who are in the unique position of "survivor scholars."

In other social science fields, much has been written about the blurring of professional and personal identities in the research environment and a recognition has emerged that, as a research methodology, ethnography is always partially autobiographical (Jewkes, 2011). For instance, psycho-social approaches highlight that the "inner worlds" of fieldworkers structure their choice of research setting, their experiences in the field, and the research roles they choose (Holloway & Jefferson, 2000; Hunt, 1989). Furthermore, feminist literature has emphasized that drawing on and theorizing about one's personal experience can be valuable for the research process (Oakley, 1981). Indeed, in our lived experience we cannot *not* draw on our own personal experiences.

In some areas of criminology and criminal justice research, there has been a growing recognition that the research process is an inherently personal endeavor and that these unique, personal, and emotional experiences can add, not detract, from research. Ferrell and Hamm (1998) suggest that

As a wealth of fieldwork has demonstrated . . . research methods which stand outside the lived experience of deviance or criminality can perhaps sketch a faint outline of it, but they can never fill that outline with essential dimensions of meaningful understanding. (p. 10)

If we accept that deviance research could be illuminated by the lived experience of deviance (or by using the voice of those labeled as deviants), is it not the next natural step to apply the "lived" experiences of victims to criminal justice policies related to sexual violence? Current sex crimes policies do not protect communities, successfully reintegrate individuals who have offended, or consider the contribution that individuals that have commit sex crimes *or* sexual assault survivors can contribute to this body of knowledge. As "survivor scholars," we are in a unique position to bridge this gap. However, we face a particular challenge. Some researchers may appreciate our experiential knowledge to illuminate the literature, while others may (and have) questioned how we can maintain objectivity when conducting research pertaining to sex crimes.

Convict Criminology

Convict criminology has faced similar challenges to those of "survivor scholars." Convict criminology has encountered verbal and written critiques from well-regarded scholars, who have challenged the group for lacking objectivity, for overgeneralizing about the work of non-convict scholars, and for flaunting their ex-convict status as if it gives them singular insight into the world of ex-offender experiences (Newbold et al., 2014). Despite these criticisms, Phillips and Earle (2010) provide an example of integrating the self into convict criminology research. They offer a reflexive examination of prisoner identities and social relationships. Phillips and Earle (2010) were candid about the ways their own lives, histories, and memories shaped and impacted their study. This included acknowledging and sharing memories of racism experienced as children and time spent in prison for political activities. They recognized and were compelled to acknowledge that their study of prisoner identities could not be separated from an introspective and reflexive engagement with their identities (Phillips & Earle, 2010).

Recently Tarana Burke, the founder of the #MeToo movement, announced her edited book with shame and vulnerability researcher Dr. Brene Brown (Burke & Brown, 2021). In their commentary on the release of the book, Brown says that "In co-creation, lived experience always trumps academic experience." Burke replies, "I agree that you can't make your research useful to people, accessible to people, if you don't prioritize lived experience, relevance, and accessibility." While we were trained to be objective researchers, our time and growth, both as scholars and as survivors, has taught us that lived experience must be honored. We agree wholeheartedly with Tarana Burke and Brene Brown.

We share the belief that in order to be a well-rounded discipline, criminology and criminal justice research in general, and research on sexual violence specifically, would not only benefit from, but requires input and commentary from people who have lived experiences with it. We do not claim to have the last word on people who have sexually offended or represent all who have experienced sexual violence. What we do claim is that the viewpoints of "survivor scholars" become part of the criminological picture as it pertains to sex crimes policies and treatment, not just victimology.

Insider/Outsider Status

Researchers, especially those undertaking qualitative methodologies, often position themselves as "insiders" rather than "outsiders" to their area of research. In this paper, we consider ourselves "insiders" and "outsiders." We are "insiders" as rape survivors while simultaneously holding "insider" status as scholars on sex offenses. However, we realize and suspect that we could also be viewed as "outsiders" by either group: scholars and advocates/survivors. Our colleagues may consider us "outsiders" because as rape survivors, the objectivity of our research regarding sex crimes policy and treatment may be called into question. On the other hand, survivor advocates may also view us as "outsiders" or even traitors because our research could be perceived as overly sympathetic to those who have sexually offended. For example, Wasco and Campbell (2002) conducted research to uncover the emotional reactions of rape survivor advocates to their jobs. The authors found that the rape survivor advocates expressed anger in response to both individual and environmental cues of situational accounts of rape. Specifically, some of the rape survivor advocates perceived their anger as an important part of their work with rape survivors (Wasco & Campbell, 2002). The authors suggest that the intense emotional reactions sometimes felt by advocates can serve as resources working with rape survivors (Wasco & Campbell, 2002). Thus, perhaps, the approach to "insider"/"outsider" status offered by Breen (2007) is best applied here. She suggests that the role of researcher is best conceptualized along a continuum, rather than a dichotomy. She further suggests that simultaneously being neither or both an "insider" and "outsider" can minimize the disadvantages and maximize the advantages of both statuses (Breen, 2007).

METHODOLOGY

Autoethnography is a qualitative methodology that uses the self and the context or culture within which the self is situated as data to gain a better understanding of the connection between the self and others (Ngunjiri, Hernandez, & Chang, 2010). Autoethnography has become a popular methodology in recent years, primarily because social scientists have come to understand that, despite all of our training on remaining objective and impartial, our research interests are extensions of our own lives (Ngunjiri, Hernandez, & Chang, 2010). For instance, several individuals have written about their experiences of the coming-out process while in academic positions (Mitra, 2010; Mizzi, 2010). Edwards (2017) reflects on her experience with sexism in higher education. Similarly, autoethnographies on race and ethnicity in the academy abound (Christian, 2017; Ellison & Langhout, 2016; Griffin, 2013). While most autoethnographies to date have been solo-authored pieces, collaborative autoethnography has become increasingly popular. This method allows two or more individuals with shared or similar lived experiences to co-construct a story and analyze shared themes (Davis & Ellis, 2008).

Collaborative autoethnography can take on many forms. Some authors prefer to engage in a fully collaborative process, while others work together on some portions of the study and work independently on others (Ngunjiri, Hernandez, & Chang, 2010). In this collaborative autoethnography, we engaged in a fully collaborative process throughout. The idea for this collaborative autoethnographic study developed out of our individual and collective recognition that our experiences and our career paths are strikingly similar and distinctly unique. Initially, we met face to face and shared the similarities and differences in our experiences as rape survivors, and the manner in which we navigated our paths to academic researchers specializing in research regarding sex crimes. We are both open and public about our experiences and, to our knowledge, we are the only two sex crimes policy researchers in the United States who are also public rape survivors. We believe this dynamic offers an illuminating and unique opportunity to better understand sex crimes and sex crimes policy from the perspective of "survivor scholars."

During the first meeting we developed a series of questions related to (a) our individual experiences with rape, (b) choosing a career path, (c) similarities and differences with other survivors, (d) objectivity, (e) growth/change as scholars, and (f) navigating the world as "survivor scholars." During our second face-to-face meeting, we considered the questions under each theme and developed writing prompts for each. We determined that for each writing prompt we would meet face to face or over the telephone, set a timer for an allotted amount of time, and answer each prompt individually. Upon completion of the prompt, we would set another timer and read each other's writing, and ask clarifying and probing questions. We would then respond to those comments. Collectively, we spent approximately ten hours over a six-month period answering the prompts and engaging in conversation about them.

Next, we independently reviewed each other's written responses to identify key themes from each prompt and then met in person to compare and discuss them. First, we shared our individual analyses with one another and then discussed where similarities and differences arose. Given that the focus of this chapter is on our experiences of being public rape survivors who study sex crimes policy in academic settings, it is beyond the purview of this paper to discuss our defining experiences beyond what was covered in the introduction. The next section identifies and analyzes the key themes we identified.

Findings/Results

Why This Academic Path?

A central thematic finding that emerged from our writing sessions was that our experiences as rape survivors directly impacted our career paths. Alissa expressed that part of her choice to endeavor on this career path was to make sense of why she was raped, while the other part was to help end sexual assault victimization. She wrote:

> Ultimately, I was interested in decreasing victimization and I learned from my studies that our current policies did nothing to deter, decrease offending, or reduce harm. . . . I have spent my entire career studying these questions—it helped me make sense of my own experience. . . . If we can understand the underlying harm caused by victimization we can begin to stop future offenses.

Alexa, on the other hand, wrote that she found herself in this career in part to address the limitation of the criminal justice system as it pertains to sexual violence. However, like Alissa, she also emphasized that part of her focus was on the prevention of sexual violence:

> After going through the criminal justice process as a rape victim, I knew that the course of my professional life had changed. . . . I began to feel that the way to help victims who come forward to report their assaults, was to conduct research that would have an impact on the way that victims are treated throughout the criminal justice process. . . . As my thoughts turned toward sexual assault prevention . . . I believed, and still do, that studying those who sexually offend lends much to prevention efforts.

*Can You Really Be Objective Working with
People That Have Sexually Harmed?*

Another writing prompt focused on whether we, as "survivor scholars," can remain objective as sex crimes policy researchers. Both of us articulated our fear that others might not take our policy research seriously because we are "survivor scholars." Alexa best summed this up when she wrote that

> Although my objectivity has not been directly challenged, it would not surprise me if it were. Because of the societal constructs of victims and offenders, the normative beliefs about each group would suggest that a victim could never objectively research sex crimes.

Both of us remain firm in our stance that objectivity is a necessity. An integral aspect of our training as scholars was to remain acutely aware of our personal and lived experience with the topic. It was through this training and our realization of the importance of objectivity that we both came to the realization that in order to prevent sexual violence we must work with those who have sexually harmed and those who have experienced it to develop policies that serve both populations. For instance, Alissa wrote:

> At the end of the day, I want to prevent sexual violence and I want to reduce harm; that means I must remain open minded to the possibility that harsh and broad criminal justice policies are not effective. I think that doing work with this population is crucial to our understanding and our implementation of sound and evidence-based policy. I can't think of anyone better to do this work than people who can see it from all sides.

Alexa explained the link between sexual violence prevention and sex crimes research in a similar way. She said:

> Exploring this vein of research has caused me to view interventions with those who have sexually harmed to be imperative to sexual assault treatment and prevention efforts. There is a place in this field of research for all voices. Both can contribute to the other's treatment efforts. By engulfing myself in sex crimes research, I have become acutely aware of this relationship.

How Do We View Ourselves Relative to Other Survivors?

Given our career paths and self-imposed title of "survivor scholars," it was important for us to reflect on the similarities and differences between ourselves and other survivors with similar experiences. Alexa suggested that trauma unites many rape survivors. She said that

Sexual assault survivors share a central part of their experience: trauma. They are uniquely suited to understanding the experiences of other survivors. Perhaps this is why many sexual assault survivor's advocates are survivors themselves. In this way, I believe that I am similar to other survivors. I understand the trauma of sexual victimization. Furthermore, I can understand the drive among some survivors to publicly share their experience specifically to advocate for others.

Alissa noted that survivors usually encounter the same psychological and emotional challenges after their assault. She said:

> In many ways I view myself as similar to other survivors, because the experience of victimization is similar and the aftermath of victimization is too. I read the literature on this topic and find that I am no different than the status quo with regard to both the short- and long-term impacts of rape. The emotions, the mental health issues, the body work, the trauma therapy . . . I am no different.

We also conveyed parallel thoughts when we explored how we may be different from other victims of sexual assault. Alexa emphasized the lack of reporting of sex offenses and her realization that improving sex crimes policy may require the work of those that have experienced sexual offending and sexual victimization.

Many survivors never come forward with their stories at all. Of those that do, only a small number do so in a public space. Not only am I an advocate for sexual assault victims, but I am also an advocate for furthering our understanding of those who sexually offend in order to improve treatment and policy for them as well as improving sexual assault prevention efforts. Treatment and policy should be informed by victims' experiences and sexual assault victim prevention efforts would be greatly improved if the perspective of those who offended were included in prevention efforts.

Alissa conveyed a similar sentiment but emphasized the appreciation of her dual role as "survivor scholar." She said:

> I think of myself as different because . . . of those that speak publicly about it, few have chosen a career path that puts them in direct contact with perpetrators. It is a unique place to be to understand the etiology of offending while also understanding the impact of offending on survivors from a personal and professional level. . . . The only way to move through healing for all involved is dialogue—something that neither camp really wants to entertain. I'll never say I am glad I was raped, but I do feel very privileged to be able to hold this duality. It is a unique and powerful place to be.

DISCUSSION

Prior to writing this chapter, we were both astonished by the similarities in our lived experiences. However, it was the reflection and analysis of our writing that confirmed just how analogous our experiences, belief systems, and values are. For example, we are approximately the same age, our rapes occurred within four months of each other, we experienced many of the same detrimental outcomes in the wake of trauma, and we both chose virtually identical careers and specializations within our field. However, as with the details of any victimization, there were differences in our experiences.

The primary difference had to do with reporting the offense. Alexa's case went through the criminal justice system and her experience led her family to see how it can detrimentally impact survivors who *do* come forward. In the aftermath of the criminal trial, Alexa and her family established a non-profit organization foundation to help other survivors who chose to bring criminal charges against their attacker. Alexa very much became the face of the organization. Alissa, on the other hand, never went public about her rape until long after she was in her career. After going public, Alissa became an activist, merging survivor advocacy with legislative and policy activism. Additionally, our specific scholarship endeavors differ. Most of Alexa's scholarship has focused on women who sexually offend and their treatment needs, while Alissa has focused more broadly on public policy issues and individuals who sexually offend, more generally. Despite these differences, what became apparent to us was our identical views regarding our unique voices as crucial to policy and practice with individuals who have sexually offended. Survivor or "survivor scholar" voices are an integral, but often ignored part of policy creation and implementation.

We began writing this chapter in 2016 and since that time our personal and professional lives have become more public. In 2020 we produced and aired a thirteen episode season of a podcast titled *Beyond Fear: The Sex Crimes Podcast*. It was because of the work we had put into this particular collaborative autoethnography that we decided that sharing our stories and our expertise would provide critical insight into all aspects of sexual violence. We decided that it was crucial that we do this in a public forum as survivor scholars. This has shifted our professional lives, but more importantly it has taught us so much about the value of honoring our stories.

LIMITATIONS

Autoethnography is often dismissed from social scientific standards as being insufficiently rigorous, theoretical, analytical, and too emotional (Ellis, 2009; Hooks, 1994; Keller, 1995). Additionally, by using the self as a topic of research, autoethnographers are often criticized for using biased data (Anderson, 2006; Atkinson, 1997; Gans, 1999). However, we believe that autoethnography as a research methodology can be rigorous, theoretical, and analytical while including personal details to illuminate a social phenomenon such as sexual violence. Criminology's failure to explicate the extent to which those who have experienced sexual violence and those who have sexually offended experience the criminal justice system undermines our ability to effectively critique the system (Jewkes, 2011). Removing the emotion and humanity from the research process and the refusal of researchers to admit to feelings of anger, frustration, fear, and outrage due to their research may represent a missed opportunity to enrich the field.

As previously mentioned, a common criticism of autoethnography is that the objectivity of the researcher, either as participant-observer or as witness, can be compromised through personal bias (Mendez, 2013). In the case of "survivor scholars," we expect that we may be accused of abandoning objectivity by engaging in emotive dialogue regarding our respective sexual assaults. Some colleagues would argue that true impartiality can be maintained by remaining emotionally distant from the subject. However, as some convict criminologists argue, that objectivity often diminishes the observations and experiences of the research (Jewkes, 2011). These observations and experiences often provide academics with important situational contexts that would not have been otherwise garnered.

Many autoethnographers also recognize that what we refer to as "truth" changes in representing these experiences. We acknowledge that memory is fallible and that it is not feasible to retrospectively recall events in a way that represents exactly how those events were experienced. Furthermore, autoethnographic researchers assert that reliability, generalizability, and validity take on different meanings when applied to autoethnographic work (Tullis Owen et al., 2009). However, as this work was a collaborative autoethnography, we strove to hold each other accountable through the manner or process of the research itself. The collaborative nature of this project helped us see beyond ourselves within the research methodology, address points of clarification, and be fully committed to developing a deep understanding of the area of inquiry (Merriweather, 2015). When addressing questions of reliability scholars often refer to the narrator's credibility. However, because sexual assault is still considered an uncomfortable topic that many people, including criminologists, avoid talking openly about, our willingness to share our accounts of sexual violence lends credibility to our accounts.

Generalizability is also important for autoethnographers, though not in the traditional sense. In autoethnography, the focus on generalizability transfers from respondents to readers (Ellis & Bochner, 2000). This generalizability is tested by readers as they determine if the story sheds light on their personal experience, an experience of someone they know, or an experience that they have not directly experienced. The generalizability of this study could thus be judged, according to Ellis and Bochner (2000), by whether we have shed light on an experience that is unfamiliar to most readers.

Our personal authority vis-à-vis our professional expertise and lived experiences provides important additions to the extant literature regarding sex violence. Sex crimes policy and practice claim to be survivor-centered, but in reality, this is not the case. As public "survivor scholars," we can speak to the reasons for this from both perspectives. It creates buy-in from multiple audiences. We are not seen as emotional survivors or out-of-touch academics. We do not divorce who we are from what we do. The joint expertise we have as rape survivors and our academic research places us in a unique position.

One implication of this dual expertise is making connections with people on both side of experiences of sexual violence. The literature is clear: current policies do not reduce sexual violence and do not help survivors in the healing process (Bandy, 2015). One potential opportunity for change is the inclusion of restorative justice programs. Having survivors who, like us, are well equipped to speak with perpetrators can be therapeutic and healing for victims and can promote insight and empathy among those who have sexually offended. This is one form of restorative justice that Ackerman and Levenson (2019) have termed "vicarious restorative justice." In its many forms, restorative justice may have positive benefits (McGlynn, Westmarland, & Godden, 2012). We are committed to future research projects where we engage with individuals who have sexually offended as "survivor scholars."

IMPLICATIONS AND FUTURE RESEARCH

Our respective realities are shaped by the social constructions we collectively and individually hold about the world around us (Crotty, 1996). As "survivor scholars," we present our experiences as a contribution to help others work their way through tragedy. We speak our stories so that others may feel liberated to speak theirs without feeling shame or guilt. We believe that we each need to find personal and collective meaning in violent events. One way we have done so, individually and collectively, is by seeing the humanity in those that victimized us. We tell our story to stimulate dialogue about the ways the criminal justice system deals with sexual violence, a dialogue that must provide a seat at the table for everyone.

Survivors of sexual violence typically do not receive the closure they need or the acknowledgment of wrongdoing that they crave in order to heal from the trauma they experienced. Conversely, individuals who commit sex offenses are not able to express regret for their actions or hear the impact of sexual violence from a victim in a therapeutic environment. This leaves everyone touched by sexual violence with many unresolved and conflicting emotions. We contend the solution to this problem may be opening a dialogue between those who have experienced sexual violence and those who have perpetrated it. As "survivor scholars," we are willing to traverse this path and through the recounting of our positive experiences of sharing our vulnerabilities with groups of individuals in treatment after the commission of a sexual offense, we hope that other survivors may be willing to try the same. If this process helps one person, it would be an experiment well worth it.

Autoethnographers ask: "How useful is this story?" and "To what uses might the story be put?" (Bochner, 2002). Our hope is that this work can be used to inform treatment and begin to build a framework that improves the lives of all people impacted by sexual harm. Currently, our criminal justice system does a disservice to all people because processes lack closure, justice, treatment, reconciliation, rehabilitation, and acknowledgment. This project is a first step toward reconciling the lived realities of these two groups.

Although survivor criminology is an emerging field of research, we believe, as evidenced by the publication of this book and the work of others, that the lived experiences of "survivor scholars" will be crucial to our future understanding of the criminal justice system and integral to informing criminal justice policy in the future.

REFERENCES

Ackerman, A. & Levenson, J. (2019). Healing from sexual violence: The case for vicarious restorative justice. Brandon, VT: Safer Society Press.

Adam Walsh Sex Offender Registration and Notification Act (2006).

Anderson, L. (2006). Analytic autoethnography. *Journal of Contemporary Ethnography, 35*(4), 373–395.

Atkinson, P. (1997). Narrative or blind alley? *Qualitative Health Research, 7*(3), 325–344.

Bailey, D., & Sample, L. (2017). Sex offender supervision in context. *Criminal Justice Policy Review, 28*(2), 176–204.

Bandy, R. (2015). The impact of sex offender policies on victims. In *Sex offender laws: Failed policies, new directions*, 2nd ed., edited by R. Wright. New York: Springer.

Black, M., Basile, K., Breiding, M., Smith, S., Walters, M., Merrick, M., Chen, J., & Stevens, M. (2011). *The national intimate partner and sexual violence survey (NISVS): 2010 summary report*. Atlanta, GA: National Center for Injury Prevention and Control, Centers for Disease Control and Prevention. https://www.cdc.gov/violenceprevention/pdf/nisvs_report2010-a.pdf

Bochner, A. (2002). Perspectives on inquiry III: The moral process of stories. In *Handbook of interpersonal communication*, 3rd ed., edited by M. Knapp and J. Daly, 73–101. Thousand Oaks, CA: Sage.

Breen, L. J. (2007). The researcher 'in the middle': Negotiating the insider/outsider dichotomy. *The Australian Community Psychologist, 19*(1), 163–174.

Burke, T., & Brown, B. (2021). Introduction to *You are your best thing*: A conversation. Retrieved on February 8th, 2021 from https://brenebrown.com/blog/2021/01/25/introduction-to-you-are-your-best-thing-a-conversation/

Christian, M. (2017). From Liverpool to New York City: Behind the veil of a Black British male scholar inside higher education. *Race Ethnicity and Education, 20*(3), 414–428.

Crotty, M. (1996). *The foundations of social research: Meaning and perspective in the research process*. Thousand Oaks, CA: Sage.

Davis, C., & Ellis, C. (2008). Emergent methods in autoethnographic research: Autoethnographic narrative and the multiethnographic turn. In *Handbook of emergent methods*, edited by S. N. Hesse-Biber & P. Leavy. New York: Guilford Press.

Department of Justice (2015). *National Crime Victimization Survey (2010–2014)*. Washington, DC: Author.

Drake, D. H., & Harvey, J. (2013). Performing the role of ethnographer: Processing and managing the emotional dimensions of prison research. *International Journal of Social Research Methodology, 17*(5), 489–501.

Edwards, J. (2017). Narrating experiences of sexism in higher education: A critical feminist autoethnography to make meaning of the past, challenge the status quo and consider the future. *International Journal of Qualitative Studies in Education, 30*, 621–634.

Ellis, C. (2009). *ReVision: Autoethnographic reflections on life and work*. Walnut Creek, CA: Left Coast Press.

Ellis, C. S., & Bochner, A. P. (2000). Analyzing analytic autoethnography: An autopsy. *Journal of Contemporary Ethnography, 35*(4), 429–449.

Ellison, E. R., & Langhout, R. D. (2016). Collaboration across difference: A joint autoethnographic examination of power and whiteness in the higher education anti-cuts movement. *Race Ethnicity and Education, 19*(6), 1319–1334.

Ferrell, J., & Hamm, M. S. (1998). *Ethnography at the edge: Crime, deviance, and field research*. Boston: Northeastern University Press.

Finkelhor, D., Shattuck, A., Turner, H. A., & Hamby, S. L. (2014). The lifetime prevalence of child sexual abuse and sexual assault assessed in late adolescence. *Journal of Adolescent Health, 55*(3), 329–333.

Gans, H. (1999). Participant observation in the era of "ethnography." *Journal of Contemporary Ethnography, 28*, 540–548.

Griffin, K. L. (2013). Pursuing tenure and promotion in the academy: A librarian's cautionary tale. *Negro Educational Review, 64*(1/4), 77.

Hollway, W., & Jefferson, T. (2000). *Doing qualitative research differently: Free association, narrative and the interview method.* London: SAGE.

Hooks, B. (1994). *Teaching to transgress: Education as the practice of freedom.* New York: Routledge.

Hunt, J. C. (1989). *Psychoanalytic aspects of fieldwork.* London: SAGE.

Jacob Wetterling Crimes against Children and Sexually Violent Offender Registration Act, Public Law 103–322. (1994).

Jewkes, Y. (2011). Autoethnography and emotion as intellectual resources: Doing prison research differently. *Qualitative Inquiry, 18*(1), 63–75.

Keller, E. F. (1995). *Reflections on gender and science.* New Haven, CT: Yale University Press.

Kilpatrick, D. (2000). *The mental health impact of rape.* Charleston: Medical University of South Carolina.

Levenson, J. S., Grady, M. D., & Leibowitz, G. (2016). Grand challenges: Social justice and the need for evidence-based sex offender registry reform. *Journal of Sociology & Social Welfare, 43*(2), 3–38.

McGlynn, C., Westmarland, N., & Godden, N. (2012). "I just wanted him to hear me": Sexual violence and the promises of restorative justice. *Journal of Law and Society, 39*, 213–240.

Mendez, M. (2013). Autoethnography as a research method: Advantages, limitations and criticisms. *Colombian Applied Linguistics Journal, 15*, 279–287.

Mercado, C.C., Alvarez, S., & Levenson, J. S. (2008). The impact of specialized sex offender legislation on community re-entry. *Sexual Abuse: Journal of Research & Treatment, 20*(2), 188–205.

Merriweather, L. R. (2015). Changing the "I": Autoethnography and the reflexive self. *JAEPR, 1*(2), 64–69.

Mitra, R. (2010). Doing ethnography, being an ethnographer: The autoethnographic research process and I. *Journal of Research Practice, 6*(1), Article M4. Retrieved July 5, 2017, from http://jrp.icaap.org/index.php/jrp/article/view/184/182/

Mizzi, R. (2010). Unraveling researcher subjectivity through multivocality in autoethnography. *Journal of Research Practice, 6*(1), Article M3. Retrieved July 5, 2017, from http://jrp.icaap.org/index.php/jrp/article/view/201/185

Newbold, G., Ross, J. I., Jones, R. S., Richards, S. C., & Lenza, M. (2014). Prison research from the inside: Convict autoethnography. *Qualitative Inquiry, 20*(4), 439–448.

Ngunjiri, F. W., Hernandez, K. C., & Chang, H. (2010). Living autoethnography: Connecting life and research [Editorial]. *Journal of Research Practice, 6*(1), Article E1. Retrieved July 5, 2017, from http://jrp.icaap.org/index.php/jrp/article/view/241/186

Oakley, A. (1981). Interviewing women: A contradiction in terms. In *Doing feminist research*, edited by H. Roberts. London: Routledge.

Phillips, C., & Earle, R. (2010). Reading difference differently? Identity, epistemology, and prison ethnography. *British Journal of Criminology, 50*(2), 360–378.

Tewksbury, R. (2005). Collateral consequences of sex offender registration. *Journal of Contemporary Criminal Justice, 21*(1), 67–81.

Tullis Owen, J. A., McRae, C., Adams, T. E., & Vitale, A. (2009). Truth troubles. *Qualitative Inquiry, 15*(1), 178–200.

Vandiver, D. M., Cheeseman Dial, K., & Wortley, R. M. (2008). A qualitative assessment of registered female sex offenders. *Criminal Justice Review, 33*, 177–198.

Waldram, J. B. (2012). *Hound pound narrative: Sexual offender habilitation and the anthropology of therapeutic intervention.* Berkeley: University of California Press.

Wasco, S. M., & Campbell, R. (2002). Emotional reactions of rape victim advocates: A multiple case study of anger and fear. *Psychology of Women Quarterly, 26*, 120–130.

NOTE

1. We define a "survivor scholar" as any individual who is both a survivor of sexual violence or victimization and a researcher who studies sexual violence and/or the people who commit sex crimes.

Chapter 2

No More Whispers in Secret

My Journey to Navigating Trauma in Academia

Reneè D. Lamphere

Do you ever find yourself wondering how you got to where you currently are in your life? I have a PhD in criminology and I am an associate professor of criminal justice and sociology. This is very different than my original career goals, as I started off college as a music major with aspirations of becoming a high school band director. The journey from music to criminology centers around an event that occurred in my freshman year of college. It changed the course of my life. This event, and the subsequent events that followed, frame this chapter. This is the first time that I am sharing publicly some of these events. Mine is a story of survivorship. It is about what happens when multiple traumas converge in space and time, and how I navigated that trauma. My hope is that other young academics can resonate with and find strength in my survivorship. I also touch on some of the challenges and implications of disclosing personal information in an academic environment.

BECOMING A SURVIVOR

I cannot tell my story without giving a little insight into the type of person I am. I am an anxious person; my earliest memories are of panic attacks and being worried about everything and nothing all at the same time. I have struggled with anxiety my entire life, and I was diagnosed with generalized anxiety disorder around my eighteenth birthday. I also struggle with bouts of depression. My parents divorced when I was twelve and I had a hard time adjusting to the new situation. Struggling with mental health problems resulted in weight gain that took a toll on my adolescent self-esteem. I was always saying negative things to myself or blaming myself for anything bad that happened. These struggles spilled over into the classroom and my grades suffered as a result. I had a difficult time getting into college and my application was rejected by several universities until I was finally admitted to a college in upstate New York in 2001, which felt great and brought a sense of relief to me. I was feeling better about myself and my future for the first time in a long time. I remained anxious; that was always there. Nonetheless, I was excited at the prospect of getting a higher education and all the new possibilities that college offered. I had a wonderful summer after I graduated high school making memories with my childhood friends. In August, I went to Oswego to start a new chapter in my life.

I was your typical college freshman; I was living away from home the first time and enjoying my time making new friends and attending my classes. In addition to traditional college activities though, I made some friends who liked to party, and I frequently went off campus to drink with my new friends. Not yet twenty-one, we could not get into bars, but for one bar in particular that had a reputation for allowing minors to drink. On a Thursday night in September, some new girl friends and I went to that bar, and sure enough they let us in with an underage ID. We drank and danced until the bar closed; we left there all very intoxicated. A young man there, Victor, was a "townie" (i.e., someone who lived in town but did not go to school there), who one of my friends had met. I had seen him before this night though I did not know him well, especially now in hindsight. He danced and drank and hung out with us all night at the bar. At the end of the night my friends and I were all getting in a cab to go back to campus, and Victor pulled me aside and offered me a ride home. He said it would save me the money of having to pay for the cab. I know if my friends were not so intoxicated, they would have objected, but I told them I had a ride and snuck away before they could even object. I was happy to not spend the money to pay for the cab and in my heart felt that my new "friend" was going to give me a ride home. In the end this ride only saved me $2 in fare; little did I know this moment and decision would change the rest of my life.

As soon as we got in the car, he said he needed to go to his aunt's house to feed her dog. It was 2am, I felt like this was strange, but I ignored that feeling (which I now recognize as my intuition) and went along for the ride. When we got to the house there was a dog, so my mind was reassured at least for a moment. He asked if I wanted to see the house and mentioned that he had a room that he stayed at sometimes at this house. Again, I remember thinking that I did not want to go upstairs in this house, but I ignored that feeling and followed him up the stairs. I walked into the room and was standing with my back to the door when I felt a shove from behind and I was thrown onto the bed. In that moment I knew that I was in a bad situation. In typical fashion, I immediately started blaming myself in that moment for getting myself into this situation.

He raped and sexually assaulted me for the next several hours. I was very inexperienced with sexual activity prior to this; I had only had sex one other time before this incident. I had seen sexual assaults on television and movies but that was the only reference point I had about it; no one in high school or in college had a discussion with me about sexual assault or sexual violence. In the movies I saw people fight back, so in my head I felt like I wanted to fight back, but in that moment where I was being physically overpowered by this person, the more I resisted, the more physically aggressive he became. So I didn't fight. I didn't kick and scream. I didn't do what I thought people were "supposed" to do. I let the moment happen and did what I felt was best to get me out of the situation alive. While he was assaulting me, I just kept telling myself what an idiot I was for going home with someone who I did not know.

By the time he stopped it was daybreak. He told me to put my clothes on and we got in his car so he could drive me back to campus. We sat in silence on the ride to the dorms. As we got close to the dorm, he put his hand on my knee. It is one of the only times I have ever felt like my body was physically rejecting the touch of another person; I will never in my life forget that moment. It was almost like he was trying to apologize for what he did or wanted to make it seem like he had good intentions with me. When we got in front of the dorm, he reminded me that one of my friends had a crush on him, and that she would be mad if she found out that he and I had sex. He said I should keep what happened between us a secret and I agreed. I honestly would have agreed to anything to get me out of the car at that moment. I got out, he drove off, and I sat in front of my dorm smoking a cigarette, trying to process what had just happened to me.

I wish I could say this is where I told someone about what happened, but like most sexual assault victims, I did not. In fact, it is estimated that over 90 percent of victims of sexual assault on college campuses do not report the assault (National Sexual Violence Resource Center, 2015). I had many reasons for not saying anything. I did not want my new friend to know I had sex with her crush; I worried she would no longer want to be my friend. I believed my parents would freak out and withdraw me from college if they knew. I decided to keep it to myself. I knew about Plan-B, the medication that prevents pregnancy, and I wanted to be on the safe side. That morning I talked to the doctor at the student health center. They asked what happened, but I could not say the words. I lied and said the condom broke with my boyfriend (I did not have a boyfriend). They gave me the medication. I decided to keep this to myself.

I tried to put the incident behind me; however, a few weeks afterwards, I began to have pain in my genital area. The local emergency room doctor said I was positive for the herpes simplex virus (HSV). There was medication I could take to help with the outbreaks, but there was no cure for HSV. I immediately went back to my dorm and called my dad, who was the person I was closest to at that time. I told him everything. He replied, "You can't rape the willing, Reneè." Like all victims who experience victim-blaming, I was crushed. Since then, we have talked about this and he has apologized for his reaction. Still, I need to be honest: his reaction really shut me down. I chose not to talk about my sexual assault with anyone to avoid any more negative reactions.

After this happened, I was determined to learn everything I could about rape and sexual assault. I went to the library on campus and researched articles on the topic and read everything I could get my hands on. I became fixated on the criminal justice system and what happened to survivors of sexual assault. Around this time, I had another friend who was sexually assaulted who chose to go through the criminal justice system. Supporting her provided insights into how the system treats survivors. By the end of my freshman year, I changed my major to criminal justice. Though I was not brave enough at that time to report the person who raped me, I knew I could help other rape victims by being an advocate. Ultimately, I determined the best way I could do this was to be a criminal justice professor and do research on rape and sexual assault. My survival became a mission.

In the years following my assault I tried to bury it as much as I could, but the physical harms endure. Initially, I had severe HSV outbreaks, so I took preventative medication to curb them. Still, every morning when I took my pill, I was reminded of what happened to me. Every time I had a new dating partner and had to disclose my HSV, I was reminded of that event. Despite these reminders, I carried on with this trauma always under the surface and tried to live a normal life. My thinking was if I just tried not to think about it or talk about it, that in my mind it might not even be real. I did what I have always done when I do not have control of the environment around me: I poured myself into my education. Sometimes it felt like I could not control the things around me, but I could always control my grades. I graduated with my bachelor's degree in 2006 and I graduated with my PhD in 2012. I took my first teaching job, where I am now a tenured associate professor.

COMING OUT AS A SURVIVOR

My first year at post-graduate school was wonderful: I loved connecting with my students and felt like I was fitting in well at my new university.

That spring, I was honored to be the recipient of the Last Lecture Award, named after Dr. Randy Pausch, a professor at Carnegie Mellon University who passed away but who gave an inspirational lecture to his students prior to his passing (Pausch & Zaslow, 2008). I was asked to give a hypothetical last lecture to current students, where my only prompt was "if this was your last lecture to students, what would you want to say?" I wanted so badly to be honest about the experiences that lead me to become a criminologist, but I was very fearful of the repercussions of public disclosure; it was a struggle. Ultimately, I delivered my last lecture including the disclosure of my sexual assault in April 2013. The audience clapped and applauded, much to my relief. In that moment I felt relieved; however, in the days that followed, I began to hear rumors that some colleagues were saying my disclosure was "inappropriate" and that they would have never disclosed in a public manner. I felt self-conscious and doubted if I made the right decision to disclose. I also received an overwhelming number of messages that praised me for my bravery and strength in disclosing. I tried to focus on the positive and ignore the negative, but it always loomed in the back of my head that people were whispering negative things about my lecture.

My last lecture was recorded, so I was able to share it with my students in subsequent semesters. It became my way to disclose my sexual assault to my students. I felt that I was being inauthentic by not disclosing what happened to me, especially when it literally shaped who I was as an academic. The more I disclosed, the more students began opening up to me. I could hardly go a week or two without a student disclosing their sexual violence victimization to me. I learned early on the importance of having resources on campus, and I quickly got to know the different offices that were available to assist students going through this trauma. The importance of offering services to sexual violence survivors cannot be overstated. Research with sexual violence survivors has shown that having a greater number of post-assault resources results in better outcomes for these individuals (Campbell, 1998; Hayes-Smith & Hayes-Smith, 2009; Wasco, Campbell, Howard, Mason, Staggs, Schewe, & Riger, 2004). However, I felt conflicted about all of the disclosures I was receiving. On one hand I was so glad to be a source of support for young people going through such traumatic events, as I wish I had someone like me to support me when I went through it as a student. On the other hand, it was emotionally exhausting to have to hear traumatic stories over and over again and processing everyone else's trauma while trying to process my own trauma after being so public about it was overwhelming. I now recognize having to manage the feelings of my students as emotional labor. Emotional labor is something that many academics experience but in particular female academics experience at consistently high levels. Further, while both men and women experience lower levels of emotional labor post-tenure, tenured women continue to experience comparable levels of emotional labor despite having received tenure (Tunguz, 2016). As a non-tenured, female professor the emotional labor of my students' trauma was a heavy burden to bear.

A NEW KIND OF SURVIVAL

In the years following my Last Lecture I struggled with my mental health. I did my best to be "normal," but deep down I felt that something was off with me. My family doctor prescribed anti-depressants and medication for my anxiety, which helped some. I thought maybe I was unhappy at work, so I applied for a job at a different institution. I was one of the final candidates in that job search, but ultimately, I was not hired for the position. This took a deeper toll on me than I recognized at the time. I was also dating someone who was unkind to me, and my mental health plummeted in the time I was dating him. In September 2015, he convinced me that the "problem" with me was my mental health medication. He issued an ultimatum: "Stop taking your medication, or I'm dumping you." I stopped taking my medication that day. I didn't talk to a doctor or taper off or anything; I just flat out stopped taking them. Within a few days, I started to feel very bad. I was sad and anxious; I cried a lot too. My partner told me I was feeling that way because the medication was making its way out of my system, and that I would feel better when it was over. I also started to have some passive suicidal thoughts such as "I wouldn't care if a bus hit me today." Then, I started thinking of plans for how I could kill myself, and I told myself no one would care if I died.

On a Friday night in October 2015, we attended a wedding of one of his family members, where we got into an argument. We were both drinking and went home early. When we got home, he announced he was leaving me for good. I did not plead or beg for him to stay, I simply accepted it, and in the back of my head I knew what I was going to do. On his way out the door I told him I would never see him again and to have a nice life. After he left, I drank three shots of vodka. I had decided this was it; this was going to be the moment I did what I had been thinking about doing for weeks. I went in my closet and picked up my strongest leather belt and I hung myself in my closet. What happened after that was a blur to me. I had lost consciousness and woke up to police all around me. When she picked him up, he told his mother that I said I would never see him again. They drove to the gas station a half mile down the road and saw a police officer there. His mom told the officer what I had said to her son, and they immediately dispatched officers to my apartment. I am so thankful they came as I would not be here today if it was not for their swift actions.

I was taken to the local emergency room in an ambulance, and I was admitted to the psychiatric unit in the hospital that evening. Waking up in the hospital was surreal. The first twenty-four hours I slept a lot, but after that was over, I started to become anxious about work. I was on the tenure-track at that time and I felt the uneasiness of not having the security of tenure. To put it plainly, I was afraid I would lose my job. Looking back, I should not have been worrying about my job in those days after that incident. I should have been worried about my mental health and getting better. I was able to contact my immediate supervisors and let them know I would be out for a couple of days at the hospital. I then said everything I could to persuade my doctors and counselors to let me out of the facility. I begged them to let me go back to work. They released me that Tuesday morning. The doctor was hesitant, but I assured her I would be getting follow-up services, and she let me go. To recap, I tried committing suicide on a Friday, and I was back in the classroom the following Wednesday morning. Looking back it all just seems so crazy to me, but again I think it's a testament to the things that people will do to protect their job security.

I remained single after the suicide attempt, and I tried to resume a normal life. I started seeing a new psychiatrist and therapist and I was trying to recover some normalcy. Still, in the months following, I struggled more than I ever have in my entire life. Figuring out the right medications was difficult. Some would have terrible side effects that would affect me at work, things like exhaustion and nausea. I struggled to teach classes and grade assignments and just get out of bed most mornings. After several months of weekly appointments, my psychiatrist suggested an outpatient hospitalization program. He said that would be the best environment for me to get my medication stabilized and also to undergo therapy to try and process what happened to me. He said the minimum amount of time I could expect in the program was four weeks, but that it could last anywhere up to twelve weeks or beyond. Once again, I worried: how could I take weeks off from work without jeopardizing my job security?

While I do not wish to disclose specifics, I will forever be grateful to the human resources staff at my institution and for the Family Medical Leave Act (FMLA). It provided the security to take time off from work to do what was best for my mental health. I do not know if the outcome would have been the same had it not been for the FMLA. I used six weeks of FMLA and I was in treatment Monday through Friday from 9am to 4pm. The specific program was rooted in dialectical behavior therapy (DBT), which has been shown to be effective at decreasing suicidal and self-harm behaviors in randomized clinical trials of adults (Berk, Starace, Black, & Avina, 2020). It combines multiple therapeutic elements, but the one that I found to be most important was the imposition of mindfulness skills. It helped me learn to be more aware of things happening inside of me, such as my thoughts, impulses, and sensations. Rather than avoiding the feeling of anxiety and trauma like I had done my entire life, I learned to use my senses to tune into what was happening around me. I still felt anxious during this process, but I was more aware of my physiological and psychological responses to that. I learned to control the negative thoughts that had taken control of my mind so that they were no longer automatic to me. I learned about self-soothing, and how I could tense and release the pressure in my muscles to help curb panic attacks. I learned more in those six weeks than I had in the twenty years prior to that. It was freeing in a sense; while I was still a trauma survivor, I didn't feel like my trauma had a death grip on my life anymore.

LIFE AFTER SURVIVAL: LEARNING
TO LIVE AS A SURVIVOR

It has been six years since my suicide attempt. I wish I could say that I had my outpatient hospitalization and moved past it and that there were no consequences for me professionally. That, however, is not the case. My suicide attempt has become a "secret"; some people know by my choice, and some people know from gossip. I wish I could say that it has never been used against me in a professional manner but that would also not be the case. And even though time has passed, and it is discussed less frequently, questions surrounding the status of my mental health have come to the surface even within the past few months. I wish I could write this today from a perspective of someone who went through this, but instead I'm writing from the perspective of someone who is actively going through this situation. Much like Erving Goffman (1963) described stigma as a "attribute that is deeply discrediting" (p. 3), I actively feel discredited by the stigma associated with my mental health diagnoses. While I do not know how to overcome stigma associated with a mental health diagnosis, I do know some things that have helped me out over the years that I can share in the hope that it helps others who might be going through a similar situation. I aim these suggestions towards those who are surviving traumas and stigmas while located in higher education.

First, know your resources on campus. Make yourself familiar with your human resources department and the different sources of help that are available to you. I had no idea about enacting the FMLA until I talked to my human resources department. I also got a lot of help through our Employee Assistance Program (EAP). This is a program that was free to me that linked me up with resources in my community to help me after my suicide attempt. I found my current psychiatrist and counselor through the EAP. We got a new director of human resources in the past year. I reached out to them personally to let them know of my situation and what has happened to me in the past, and they assured me that if I needed assistance in the future, they should be the first person I call. The people in human resources are literally paid to be there to help you when you need it. Get to know the resources that are available to you.

Second, always, always prioritize your physical and mental health. I know too well what happens when I did not. Now that I know the importance of therapy I will always be in therapy for the rest of my life. Therapy is not only there for me when things are going wrong, but also there to help me recognize when things are going right. Just having a safe place to process my problems has been so helpful. I have also been focusing on self-care. I am the first person to tell someone to take care of themselves, but I am the last person to take my own advice. Within the past year I have been proactive in doing things that are good for my overall health. I have started exercising again and have lost a considerable amount of weight. I do not make myself available for work 24/7; I have learned to set up healthy boundaries in this regard. Even small things like getting a manicure every few weeks has been good for my mental health. Find the things that make you happy and do them as often as possible. Prioritize your health because at the end of the day, you cannot be the academic that you want to be if your physical or mental health is suffering.

Much like when I was sexually assaulted, I started reading more about mental health in academia. I quickly discovered Katie Rose Guest Pryal (2017), who writes about mental health and disability in academia. As someone who has left academia, her advice and commentary on how her situation in academia impacted her resonated with me. I read her book, *Life of the Mind Interrupted*, as part of a book club put on by my campus's Teaching and Learning Center. We had a video chat with her as well, and it was inspiring to hear her talk about her mental health challenges so openly. They do not define her but rather they are a part of her that she freely recognizes. I have learned many good lessons from Dr. Guest Pryal and I recommend her for those in academia struggling with mental health.

An unexpected source of comfort for me has been my research. In addition to this chapter, I am working on a project with Dr. Shelly Clevenger and Dr. Kim Cook that explores survival experiences of academics. Now that I had disclosed my status as a sexual assault survivor to my students, I became curious about other professors' disclosures of sexual assault with their students. From 2018–2020 we interviewed thirty-three college professors regarding sexual assault disclosures to their students. The majority of participants reported disclosing their survivor status to their students, which is consistent with positionality practices common among feminist scholars (Cook 2016). The context of the disclosure differed depending on many factors; some professors disclose to all students in all classes every semester, and some only disclose at specific times in the semester or with classes where the subject matter fits with their disclosure. We are planning another wave of interviews for this study post-COVID. Doing this study and hearing from others who are also in a similar situation to me was something I found to be healing. It let me know that I am not alone in being a survivor who wants to use their experiences in the classroom. I am looking forward to interviewing more survivors and finding out how the pandemic has impacted their decision to disclose to their students. I did not know that doing research could be something that would help me process my own trauma, but I truly believe it has helped me in this respect.

SOME THOUGHTS ON WRITING THIS CHAPTER

Writing this chapter has been difficult. To be honest, I put off writing this for many months because of the implications of what writing this has for me. This is *my* story, and once it is published, there is no going back. I had to make myself vulnerable in a way that I had not done before, and it scared me. While it was intimidating to write, in the end it was also cathartic; I felt a weight lifted off my shoulders with every paragraph that I wrote. Somewhere inside of me I always felt my mental health problems and my history of trauma were things that I needed to be ashamed of and hide, and there really is power is choosing to no longer hide things that impact me as a person and an academic. In a way I feel that acknowledging these things takes away the secrecy behind them. The title of this paper alludes to this fact. My mental health problems and history as a sexual assault survivor were something that was considered secret, and I know that people whispered in secret about the status of my mental health and questioned my professional competence. People cannot whisper in secret about something that has been shared in a public way through the writing of this paper. This does not mean that these things cannot be used by others to judge me negatively in the future, but if I am upfront about surviving trauma at least it will no longer be a topic of speculation or gossip among other people. I can "beat them to the punch" in a sense. I truly feel there is power in telling your story for others to hear. Looking back, I realize I spent too many years feeling powerless because of the shame and fear that I associated with traumatic events like my sexual assault and suicide attempt. While I feel neither shame nor pride for these events, I feel that I have reclaimed some of my power by writing this chapter. And in reclaiming that, I can also proclaim the resilience being a survivor requires. I am stronger than I ever realized.

While I am certainly glad writing this has been healing for me, I recognize there are some drawbacks to disclosing this information publicly. There are of course going to be people who judge me for the things that happened to me in my past, or even for making the decision to disclose in such a public manner. Again, recalling my Last Lecture and the criticism I received as a result of that, I know too well the fear of judgment looms nearby. But just like I did then, I am going to make a conscious effort to focus on the positive rather than the negative. I continue to use the DBT techniques to help me during hard times. I cannot control the things that happen around me, but I can always control my reaction to them. That is the same approach I am going to take to writing this chapter. I know there are going to be people who will have negative things to say, but I will take that with a grain of salt, as I anticipate most of the feedback to be positive. In my experience, survivors are quick to lift up, not put down other survivors.

After stating all of this I have to recognize that there are many who read this who are not in the same position that I am professionally and do not have the privilege of telling their story without fear of reprisal. I have been in that position of not feeling comfortable disclosing about traumatic experiences. I know that having achieved tenure and having the support of my colleagues puts me in a place of privilege to share my story. Guest Pryal (2017) discussed the privilege of tenure after interviewing other academics who struggle with mental health problems. The tenured professors noted that having achieved tenure made them more willing to be interviewed. Other faculty members, mainly those who were contingent professors, were unwilling to be interviewed for her book due to fear of hurting their job security. She comes to the same conclusion that I have come to, which is that I cannot in good conscious suggest that graduate students, pre-tenured faculty, or contingent faculty disclose details of their trauma and mental health to their colleagues. Stating that though, it is also important to recognize that not every situation is the same, and that there may be some benefit of disclosure for these professors depending on the type of environment they find themselves in. There is no right answer for everyone; much is dependent on the culture of the department someone is working in, so you should always use caution before disclosing personal information.

WHERE DO WE GO FROM HERE?

While I take comfort in the fact that I know I am not alone in suffering from mental health problems as an academic, it still leaves me wondering what is next for us? I believe that rather than individual changes being made, we need structural change if we are truly going to support faculty with mental illness.

In a report by Price and Kerschbaum (2017), they discuss how to promote supportive academic environments for faculty with mental illnesses. They advocate for going beyond passively supporting faculty with mental health problems through things like campus counseling and wellness services. Instead, they encourage all members of the campus community, especially those in leadership roles, to foster access in all aspects of faculty life, including their mental health. Some of their suggestions include promoting access by developing campus mission statements that explicitly state a commitment to faculty with mental disabilities and promoting the use of inclusive language in policies that affect these populations. These suggestions are not just meant to help those currently employed, but also for those who are being recruited to work at the university and those who are newly hired. The ultimate goal would be to think proactively rather than reactively about faculty mental health and access to accommodations, which would demonstrate to faculty that not only are they accepted by the campus community, but they are a vital part of the community and their presence is important to campus life.

My hope in writing this chapter is that it can add a voice to the ongoing discussion surrounding mental health and survivorship in academia. With the COVID-19 pandemic still happening it is impacting professors in ways that are still left to be fully understood. I think now more than ever, those of us who are in a position to advocate for others need to make sure that all faculty, even junior and contingent faculty, have their voices and stories heard. This is my first piece regarding how my mental health impacts me as an academic, but I have promised myself it will not be my last. No matter the consequences of telling my story, I am going to face the world with my head held high because I am a survivor. I am not ashamed to be a survivor. To all survivors and faculty struggling with mental health just know I see you and I will do everything in my power to make your voices heard. You matter. Your struggle matters. Please don't ever forget that.

REFERENCES

Berk, M. S., Starace, N. K., Black, V. P., & Avina, C. (2020). Implementation of dialectical behavior therapy with suicidal and self-harming adolescents in a community clinic. *Archives of Suicide Research, 24*, 64–81.

Campbell, R. (1998). The community response to rape: Victims' experiences with the legal, medical, and mental health systems. *American Journal of Community Psychology, 26*, 355–379.

Cook, K. J. (2016). Has criminology awakened from its "androcentric slumber"? *Feminist Criminology, 11*(4), 334–353.

Goffman, E. (1963). *Stigma: Notes on the management of spoiled identity.* New York: Simon & Schuster.

Guest Pryal, K. R. (2017). *Life of the mind interrupted: Essays on mental health and disability in higher education.* Chapel Hill, NC: Raven Books.

Hayes-Smith, R., & Hayes-Smith, J. (2009). A website content analysis of women's resources and sexual assault literature on college campuses. *Critical Criminology, 17*(2), 109–123.

National Sexual Violence Resource Center (2015). Statistics about sexual violence. Retrieved from https://www.nsvrc.org/sites/default/files/publications_nsvrc_factsheet_media-packet_statistics-about-sexual-violence_0.pdf

Pausch, R., & Zaslow, J. (2008). *The last lecture.* New York: Hyperion.

Price, M., & Kerschbaum, S. L. (2017). *Promoting supportive academic environments for faculty with mental illnesses: Resource guide and suggestions for practice.* Temple University Collaborative. Retrieved from http://tucollaborative.org/wp-content/uploads/2017/05/Faculty-with-Mental-Illness.pdf

Tunguz, S. (2016). In the eye of the beholder: Emotional labor in academia varies with tenure and gender. *Studies in Higher Education, 41*(1), 3–20.

Wasco, S. M., Campbell, R., Howard, A., Mason, G. E., Staggs, S. L., Schewe, P. A., & Riger, S. (2004). A statewide evaluation of services provided to rape survivors. *Journal of Interpersonal Violence, 19,* 252–263.

Chapter 3

I Am Not Supposed to Be Here

Surviving Poverty and Anti-Blackness in Criminology and Academia

Jason M. Williams

Academia prides itself on being a space in which all points of view are appreciated. The cultivation of knowledge is said to know no bounds because science is a democratizing project that embraces all without fear or favor. Nevertheless, as a Black young man just entering criminal justice classes as an undergraduate student, my senses told a quintessentially opposing story. This chapter provides an overview of my journey navigating anti-Blackness in criminology. My journey began first as an undergraduate student before I became a practicing scholar. I share how my positionality is unique toward understanding criminological discourses and the cultivation of knowledge given my background and experiences. The first section underscores my upbringing, where I am from, and why it matters. Although many argue that science is supposed to be objective, I learned that reality and truth always have a subjective component (Collins, 2002; Haraway, 1988; Hill Collins, 2013; Winlow & Hall, 2012). The following section unpacks how I navigated the vicious spaces of academe as a student while trying to hold tight to my ways of knowing. I share lessons I have learned while surviving the multifaceted barriers placed before. I am not supposed to be where I am today, yet I am here, persevering and winning. This story, the maneuvers, and the lessons learned will and must be told.

THE UPBRINGING

As they call it, I was born in the ghetto—a housing project in Northern New Jersey. By the time I was eleven, I had already lost both parents, and my maternal grandmother stepped in to raise me. I was the youngest of two who lived in my household, and I also had an additional, older bi-racial brother who lived across the river in a predominantly white middle-class neighborhood. However, the two I lived with would be the brothers with whom I would experience the challenges of being poor and living in a household with a single Black mom. I can remember as a child how my dad would come and stay with us, but due to changes in social welfare policy, he could not remain permanently. He would often have to take his belongings with him because social workers would come and check to make sure there were no men in the house, or else Mom would no longer receive the benefits she was getting from the state. Due to racism and gender bias, Black fathers could not find work that would allow them to take care of their families fully, so mothers had to rely on the state for benefits. I remember the government butter, cheese, and bread. Moreover, back then, the food stamps were actual coupons, not the plastic cards of today. As kids, we would be happy when we would find abandoned coupon jackets in the exits, hoping like hell there would be coupons in them, but sometimes there was a dollar or two.

Despite the evil and desperate aspirations of the state to break Black families,[1] my father still came around, and we felt like a family. My older brother from across the way would come around too, and from what I hear, he never wanted to leave. He would hide under the bed and in the closets when it was time for him to return home. I can tell from the pictures I have that my older brothers loved me. They still show it today. We were a happy family. Mom was a great cook in every way. She would make the best desserts, and in our project home, we would be in heaven watching television as a family nibbling on her homemade donuts or cakes. When we would want something from the store, she would counter with "Why do you want that?" and "I can make that upstairs." And she was correct. Black moms in poverty had to be stingy with funds; nobody will help them when all else fails. We lived a very happy childhood for the most part, but we could not ignore the influences beyond our apartment. For instance, the constant selling and consumption of drugs, the immeasurable poverty that consumed our lives, and the sustained and coerced social and racialized disorganization in which we lived. These influences hindered everyone in the projects in every way, and nobody's family was immune. Yes, there were some white families around, but not many, and they were just as poor as the rest of us. Despite living in such circumstances, we had tutorial programs that cultivated education in our lives. Then there was Ms. Evelyn, the head of the family and communities division of the housing authority, who took her job seriously. She had an unyielding commitment to us ghettoized children, and fought hard for our betterment. Others and I would often hang around her office, soaking up all that we could because she provided an alternative possibility of the future. Working for her throughout my adolescence is probably what put me on track toward college.

My grandmother would often tell me stories about yesterday, stating how back in the day, Blacks and whites moved into the projects first, and they lived well together. The Italians would let the Blacks walk right into their apartments to use the bathroom. They would play cards or dominoes outside, and instead of waiting for someone to head up to the eighth floor (top floor in the building), someone on the first floor would simply allow their neighbor to use their restroom. Grandmother explains that there was great comradery and love back in the day. However, then came white flight, and most of those whites graduated to mainstream whiteness and never looked back (Woldoff, 2011). Nevertheless, the bulk of my family remained. I also remained until I finished my doctorate at age twenty-six. I had no other way out.

Anyhow, generations later, there was still some connectivity among community members, but not like it used to be. The war on drugs and neoliberalized economic depravity certainly ensured that any sense of organization would be stomped out. There was a tenant council from which I learned a lot about organizing and politics as a youth—but they could only do so much. During the 1990s, we experienced our bout with community policing and the surveillance complex installing cameras outside the complex and in the buildings. Soon people were being arrested for minor infractions, and families were being evicted. Such a swift change in social control strategies would create the harshest living situations we have ever experienced in our complex. Distrust sowed even greater seeds of misery, and while one may think much of this unrest sat among adults, it trickled down to the children.

When I was in kindergarten, my dad had died, and then I lost my mom by fifth grade. I suppose I could have never fully known the impact their deaths had on me, although I did matriculate grade school with behavioral issues. I can recall being labeled delinquent countless times, being taken out of class by juvenile law enforcement, and being scared to death. The process of being abandoned by teachers and school administrators was a daunting experience—and one that, as a kid, I was unable to articulate. The feeling of being quarantined to the undercarriage was visceral and real. As a labeled student, the feeling of not being enough is pungent enough to make one drop out physically and mentally. Even though I was smart, I and others in similar situations began to withdraw from school because discipline seemed to be the main program. I did have one fourth-grade teacher, Ms. L, who understood my situation. She never gave up, even as I left her class. She would still allow me to go on the Student of the Month trips, despite me being horrible in class at times. However, most of the kids where I was from were bringing their imposed baggage with them to class. We have been through and witnessed so much at those young ages, and we had no other way of getting through the pain.

I had known several kids who did not regularly eat breakfast; they depended on the free breakfast program that ran before the start of school. Sometimes they would be so late to school and could not get breakfast, so they had to wait until lunch to eat—after which they were not guaranteed another meal, possibly until the next day at school. Then, social workers from the Division of Youth and Family Services would often come and pull many students from my neighborhood out of class. These visits were often tied to student absences or other concerns/tips given to them by school officials. It was then when I realized how dangerous the school as an institution could be against mostly single Black and Brown mothers. Nevertheless, the pulling out of class by any entity other than school officials would often stick like an unwanted tag that reeked of stigmatization. Teachers, staff, and students talked, so your business got around, and indeed, this affected whether a student could get through the school day. Then when school was over, we would have to go back home to the hood where we would experience the horrors of being marked for the undercarriage before we would wake up the next day to head back to school.

Surviving the school experience also coincided with surviving poverty in the hood. For instance, the schoolhouse served as a meeting place of various socioeconomic personalities and clashes. Children were cruel. Many students from the poorest of neighborhoods were picked on for not having enough. Some kids were laughed at for not being able to afford book covers and were made fun of for creatively using paper bags. Some even arrived at school wearing soiled clothes and reeked of odor. Kids from households known to be inundated with drugs, alcohol, and poverty were specially picked on, and in some cases, teachers were in on the joke. Being so young and having to survive such a violent reality was something no child could make sense of—there was no playbook on how to navigate such a vicious, unforgiving trajectory. Neither society nor the school was willing to save us from the hell in which we found ourselves.[2] As a youth, we did not ask to be born into structural poverty, but here we were, living it at home and seeing its effects at school.

I often felt as if I was being punished, living a life of structural poverty, and having lost both of my parents. I clearly understood that my parents were also victims of circumstance, just as everyone else in our community. It is this very experience that would catapult me into becoming a freethinker. As a youth, I would often ponder about the world's order. I thought deeply about social control mechanisms, how we were controlled in the hood, how our schools were constructed as training camps for the disparaged, and how the curriculum taught us skills we needed to pass standardized exams. This way of living, of having to learn the way of the world, is both cruel and unusual. We are forced to grow up fast while losing our ability to live as a youth. Likewise, authority figures interfaced with us through the lens of adultification (Dumas & Nelson, 2016; Epstein et al., 2017; Ferguson, 2020), limiting their capacity to see and treat us as children. Thus, governing institutions that interfere with our daily lives as Black and Brown kids are acutely aware of their impact and the damage they bestow. Some argued that such vitriol is intentional and necessary to keep the current social, economic, and racial order (Kunjufu, 1985).

Nevertheless, the egregiousness of structural and intentional poverty and its carceral effects on youth of color is rarely identified and unpacked for the danger and violence it poses. In my case, while I was able to make it through K-12 and onto college, I often think about those with whom I grew up and how these structures worked to limit their ability to self-aspire. Navigating poverty meant that I had to grow the will to dream beyond the metal boulders of structural inequality and racism that all but ensured that I would not become successful. To make matters worse, I came from what may be described as a dysfunctional home: I lost both parents and was raised by a single guardian, my grandmother. According to most measures, I should be incarcerated with an extensive criminal record. However, succeeding against such odds does not make me an angel. Also, it does not mean I did not have to engage in street life to survive. To endure the slums, ultimately, most will feel the need to engage in illicit activity. Not engaging in such activity is to be well adapted to your slow state of decay and eventual annihilation. Like anyone else, people in the hood have a will to survive by any means. Sadly, this is the reality society has made for those living in such spaces. Living in the hood meant that you had to develop a Code of the Street (Anderson, 1999) mentality—but this cultural affinity alongside the traditional double consciousness (Du Bois, 1903) any African American develops in white-dominated space severely complicates one's understanding of their positionality in society. For one, you learn that you must behave one way in your neighborhood for survival and another way when traveling in the white space for survival (Anderson, 2011).

For many youths of color navigating this precarious mental terrain, the experience can be daunting. Again, many often feel they have no one they can turn to, especially if they come from dysfunctional homes or communities where the expression of problems or emotions is culturally prohibited. The reality of double consciousness is that it can undoubtedly breed a most unfortunate kind of mental abnormality. As a youth living in a housing project without many resources, it was as if I were locked in solitary confinement. Yes, I was free, but the restriction was still physical based on the structural poverty and racism bestowed upon me. Also, the mental anguish of always wondering what was coming next is an added effect. My apartment complex was separated from a middle-class town by a highway and a river. From our window, we could see the lovely houses in that neighboring locale, and looking over there always gave the impression of the American Dream. Sometimes you could see families on their lawns, getting into their cars, coming and going. And worst, we could also see the New York City skyline—the very essence of American capitalism and success. How could it be that we live so close to the world's capital and yet not have access to any of the resources necessary to become proximate to the success it represented. Encountering the realization of your odds against achieving the success that skyline depicts is piercing enough to force impoverished youth into divergent lifestyles. I saw these capitulations myself. It can be brutal surviving structural poverty and racism. But it is not always easy to take the path of coerced submission either. It is easy to label those who submit without first underscoring the context under which they were made to cave. Nevertheless, this is the setup against which parents try hard to protect their children and often to no avail in the American ghetto.

My mother tried her hardest to provide for my brothers and me—but as any parent learns in the undercarriage, there is very little protection or preparation they can provide to their children in such settings. These spaces are not designed for parenting effectively nor for a human to ever be comfortable or safe. Mothers and fathers may go to great lengths to sacrifice for their children only to find their children taken from them by the state or the streets. Likewise for the children, as parents are taken from kids daily. Our collective misery is the fuel that feeds the criminal legal system and predatory capitalism—supplying jobs to others from the hoods who signed on to become modern-day overseers and to mostly white faraway towns that gain nourishment from our captivity. Still, our bodies are worth so much for the benefit of others but not so much for ourselves.

As a young man, I philosophized much about race and America writ large with friends from my hood. We were smart because we were keenly aware of our positionality compared to our white counterparts (Clark, 1965). However, after my mom died, my maternal grandmother stepped in to raise my two brothers and me. Granny did her best despite the vast age difference between herself and us. As a youth, I could not fully appreciate what my grandmother had given up to raise us, but now I see. She has always engaged in the art of othermothering, helping her daughters and others in the family raise their kids (Collins, 2002). It was not until I reached college that I developed feminist literacies that helped me to better unpack the extreme harms and near criminalization that motherhood bestows onto Black women in particular (Roberts, 1993). In retrospect, I believe my mother also lived with the added pressures of motherhood; after all, she was a single parent. The sacrifice made by my grandmother personifies the very essence of Roberts's (1993) and Collins's (2002) summations about the journey of Black motherhood and its rather dangerous pursuit. For one, its limitations on the self, and particularly how it opens one up to extreme violence at the hands of the state via racialized surveillance tactics designed to diminish the capacity and legitimacy of Black mothers. Despite these threats, my grandmother did what she could, and we were and are grateful. Still, we desperately missed our mother. We were a closely knit little family that did a lot together. We would have family nights on which we would watch our favorite television shows together. Mom would make her homemade desserts. While we lived in the projects, it was as if we lived in the hills for those moments.

The brief backdrop creates the starting point for entering college and the study of criminology and criminal justice.

ENTERING THE GATES OF UNDERGRAD

As an undergraduate student, I initially had a love for the law. I thought I would become a fantastic criminal attorney and possibly delve into international human rights law. However, upon stumbling upon some of the more critical criminal justice courses, my mind began to change my career trajectory. Also, upon finishing undergrad, the chair, Dr. Williams, offered me the graduate fellowship, which paid for my master's degree and provided a stipend. However, the journey through undergrad was quite striking for me. I was a first-generation student and had no actual preparation before attempting this most strenuous task. I had to take an average six classes a semester, sit in classes with those who were, in some cases, more advanced than I on some subjects. I did not have the help of my parents or family members who had been through the process. My grandmother did not know much about college; all she could do was offer emotional support and a few dollars here and there.

My ascendancy to college was exciting and eye-opening. While the university is said to be a place where free thought is initiated and exchanged, these processes are executed with cruel indifference to students whose presence is otherwise unwanted. For instance, I can recall sitting in several classes where topics around poverty and racial minorities arose, and subtle racist and classist statements were made rather plainly. For instance, comments belittling inner cities that were also proxy for race. Or instructors and students outright implying that gangs are synonymous with racial minorities. My undergraduate institution was diverse, but in such spaces, even if there is a good amount of BIPOC in class, their perceived reality may be that these spaces are still white—and they probably are considering power dynamics. The insistence on speaking can often precipitate fierce pushback from faculty, staff, and students during conversations about racism, inequality, or other such factors that BIPOC know all too well as a result of their lived experiences.

I also recall sitting in a course titled "Multiculturalism in Law Enforcement" in which the adjunct professor was a former police leader—but had the niceties game down pat. He knew how to sell the necessity of appearing palatable to each group, especially to racial minorities. However, during class discussion, I critically ascertained that he was not as genuine as he put on when he would allow primarily white students to get away with labeling "up the hill" as a battle zone. "Up the hill" was a geographic location (near campus) known to be crime-ridden. The location was also oppressed, locked off from upward economic mobility, denied equal access to functional educational systems, and most of those who live there are Black Americans. Thus, to me, hearing this in class hit deep. Here I was, once again, surviving circumstances out of my control, but now on a college campus. I was not from this town, yet I identified with those individuals because they looked like me and were experiencing similar circumstances like the ones from which I come. Therefore, in most of my classes, I had to step into battle with fellow students around these issues that were on their face racist. On many occasions, professors such as the one described above would not stop and correct students on their facially racist terminology. Moreover, as a professor now, I understand how those could have been teachable moments too. These professors could have used those instances to delve deeper into sociological contexts of crime and poverty, but this is not the duty of a purely criminal justice program, unfortunately. Often the focus is simply on the role of organizations and the strict adherence to social control.

Many commentators have spoken about the differences between criminology and criminal justice programs, labeling criminal justice as a protective service-oriented program designed to usher state aspirations onto learners so that they could become tomorrow's robots for law enforcement agencies (Frauley, 2005). Such a process necessitates the removal of one's self-awareness of the collective toward one of rugged individualism consistent with neoliberal penality (Williams & Battle, 2017). Under the regime of neoliberal justice, the connection between structural inequality and racism is no longer a factor to individual engagement in crime and how the state responds to those accused of such—or to the functionality of law enforcement more broadly (Hudson, 2007). Instead, citizens are blamed for their shortcomings and negative interactions with the state. This was the type of ideological training against which I was fighting daily in criminal justice classes as an undergraduate student. I always understood the historical oppression under which Black

Americans lived in the United States, and I knew it played a significant role in administering justice (Muhammad, 2010). My participation in classes was always grounded in that lived experience, and it was central to my arguments. Yet the teaching of the criminal justice system seemed to reinforce systems of oppression rather than critically decontextualize the criminal justice system in ways that would allow students to learn about it from various vantage points. It was during these crucial years that I would question the very foundation of education; I learned what it meant to transgress against oppressive pedagogies under the guise of intellectual engagement and "preparedness" for the real world. Frankly, my very existence and mental stability depended upon me being an absolute rebel, and that I indeed became as I moved into graduate studies. My ascendance to graduate studies had much to do with the inaccuracies inherent in my undergraduate experiences. I felt compelled to enter the next stage ready to learn more and to fight. I was utterly empowered despite the horrible experience I would often have in class.

GRAD SCHOOL AND FINDING
MY EPISTEMIC FRAMING

Entering grad school was more daunting of a task than undergrad. In my first year, I do not recall having classes with anyone I knew from undergrad. Therefore, the familiarity of prior years was immediately gone. I had to build my team and sense of sustenance yet again, even though I remained at the same institution. For many first-generation graduate students, the same sense of non-belonging they experience in undergrad returns, but with a vengeance because of differing expectations. It did not take long for me to find someone who was very much like myself. My best friend, Christine, whom I met during these years, was intellectually curious, a native of the town where our school sat, and loved to debate. Both of us attended the same institution as undergrads, but she had finished in an earlier class. She took a brief break before she came back for her graduate degree. We inhabited a similar background of extreme hardship, navigating childhood trauma, schools, and college. Nevertheless, somehow, we made it to this level to earn our master's degrees together.

Christine and I both enrolled in "Research Methods," where we encountered a professor that was extremely hostile to our being in his class. This professor seemed preferential to students who were white (including white Latinxs). We noticed differential treatment based on how he would allocate time toward students outside the classroom. Not only did he appear inaccessible to us, but even when he would cave toward offering help, the time frames would be during the most inopportune moments. Some of us had jobs, other commitments, and could not always meet him at his workplace—a local police station. Yes, he was a police administrator who had earned a doctorate, teaching part-time, possibly hoping for a full-time position in academe. Nevertheless, he ran our class just as he would his police agency. We could not fully engage in his lectures, ask deeply probing questions about methodology, or engage in creative methodologies. He was an absolute dictator and did not shy away from showing it. In this class, Christine and I came together through a medium of oppression, realizing that we both were unhappy and being mistreated. It started with receiving a passing but low grade on our midterm, then realizing that he repeated the same with our final grade. While we knew we were not the top students in this particular class, we certainly knew we deserved better based on the collective of assignments we submitted. Together she and I marched into the chair's office and demanded that something was done about his differential treatment against students of darker skin. Unfortunately, Christine and I were the only two willing to go upstairs on this professor; the others were too afraid. I suppose the professor's positionality as a ranking authority in a local police agency may have played a role, and they wondered if they would be labeled troublemakers. Despite all consequences, Christine and I chose to stand up together, which we continued to do throughout our master's experience. We have much thanks to the former chair who helped us tremendously with our grade complaint, which worked out in our favor.

During this time, I took some of the most radical courses in my college career. I was finally able to take most courses with core faculty. This was a most riveting time for me. My inner intellectual radicalism was activated in ways I could never predict in prior years. Christine and I would spend hours at the library researching topics around race, gender, justice, and international criminal law. We also dove into Black history, making connections between mistreatment in the justice system and broader connections to the Black experience. It was as if we were trying to recapture the education we did not receive in years prior. Most criminal justice curricula lack a concerted concentration on race relations. This gross omission seriously undercut students for both graduate school and the job field. Again, we found ourselves matriculating our master's program, constantly debating issues on race because many of our classmates were agents of the system. Our program was known as a cop shop because many officers attended the program. However, there were people from the courts, social work, and non-profit organizations too. This diversity of backgrounds made for explosive debates in the classroom that more than prepared me for the next level. But once again, I would find myself having to defend that which should be clear to everyone—that race matters in the administration of justice.

During my master's program, I began to tap into standpoint epistemology (Collins, 2002) in ways that allowed me to fully articulate in deeply theoretical frameworks how the system was flawed. Christine and I began to sift through slave narratives and other qualitative works that helped us understand the importance of situated knowledges as viable sources of empirical data (Haraway, 1988). I had always believed that lived experiences matter; however, under the governing ethos of the discipline, they did not seem to hold weight. Debates seemed preferential to quantitative conclusions that always omitted thick description (Bhattacharya, 2017). Meanwhile, context mattered. As a Black American who came up through the literal belly of the beast, I knew for certain that statistics were sorely lacking the human context of structural inequality, racism, heteropatriarchy, and capitalism. Statistics cannot tell that of human suffering and feeling. This was a power dynamic that sought to erase equally other ways of knowing, and this power dynamic served the interest of the state. Those knowledges that challenged quantitative assumptions were deviant (Walters, 2003), somehow less empirical and helpful toward the cause of "alleviating" crime. But what if a scholar's cause is to tell the story of those inflicted by state crime. What if one's standpoint epistemology and situated knowledges place them in opposition with the master narrative indoctrinated into foundation criminal justice curricula? Should they vacate the field or remain and fight? Carol Hanisch said the personal is political (Lee, 2007)—and so is the social sciences. The science of social control in the United States is steeped in histories of white supremacy and Black oppression. Any social science discipline that fails to take this essential truth into account fails to live up to its hype of being an actual science. A scientific discipline is supposed to be democratic and accept all possible variables, data, and ways of knowing. This was and is not the case in criminal justice and criminology. Therefore, the question before me was whether I would accept the norms or rebel.

My master's experience was indeed a moment of mastering as I stepped fully into accepting my radicalism. Luckily, I had some core faculty who were completely supportive, and they nourished my development as a scholar at that time. These professors understood the purpose with which people like Christine and I walked. We always presented passion with our presentations and debates in the classroom, and we never backed down from a challenge. We even challenged professors when we believed assigned literature failed to capture equally other relevant points on a particular issue. This process of persevering was us surviving criminology. This journey continued through my doctoral journey (on an HBCU campus), albeit the curriculum was race-centric and more amenable to topics I preferred to study. However, some of the same power dynamics inherent on PWI campuses and programs were still present. These professors were educated in prominent programs at PWI's and carried some of those same qualities with them. So although students benefited from the race-centric curriculum, radical students faced slight challenges, especially around methodologies.

Nevertheless, my doctoral experience ignited a fire that pushed me deeper into my intellectual development. I took courses with top scholars on race and justice, and these professors did not hold back from telling it like it was while still grounding their lectures in the literature. I knew I had found my people! We unpacked data of all kinds (statistics, textual, etc.). It was a genuinely democratic learning experience that brought together quite an existential breakthrough for me because it was through this process that I became fully emancipated from the white supremacist grip on criminal justice and criminology. During my doctoral program, I began investigating more fully the roots of that governing ethos that commanded so much of the discipline. I questioned who benefited from it and who did not. Relying on much of the sociology of knowledge literature and Black feminism, I began to reject the so-called scientific basis of criminal justice and criminology. The discipline was partial. The way theories have been formulated and taught has been indifferent to marginalized communities. The voices of Black scholars are rarely taught in classrooms or recognized throughout the discipline (Gabbidon et al., 2004; Greene et al., 2018; Young & Sulton, 1991). Thus, a white racial frame (Feagin, 2013) dominated the discipline such that there was no space for other ideas to exist. This meant that I had to develop a profoundly critical and creative means to survive in the discipline. I never had a problem doing what I wanted to do but moving forward in this fashion in academia would be tough, I thought initially. Gatekeeping is serious in academe, and people will push back. Despite the barriers, I vowed not to capitulate to the white frame that dominated the discipline and represent the situated knowledges that I possessed because of my biography. I was fortunate to have attended a doctoral program that nurtured my eclectic academic aspirations, and they chose not to stand in my way. Compared to many stories I have heard from others navigating graduate school, I was fortunate to have been allowed to pursue my scholarly pursuits freely. I left graduate school feeling like my whole self, empowered and prepared to represent those whose voices are purposely omitted.

ENTERING ACADEME

Arriving on the other side was an exciting experience. Once again, I was hit with the first-generation bug, dealing with the newness of my situation. However, having been prepared by my professors at my HBCU, I did not feel like I did not belong. Frankly, I would never give white academe (or any white space) the benefit of thinking I felt such a way. I had worked very hard (as anyone else) to belong, and I did not need anyone's validation. I was not there to make friends, and I did not need anyone's niceties; I was on a mission to educate and conduct research. You learn early that everyone's intentions are not always in your best interest. Academia can be just as cutthroat as any Wall Street bank. My Code of the Street mentality has always kept me safe, and it continues to play an central role in navigating the sociopathic halls of the academe. Navigating this space as an openly Black radical made things more consequential for me, but I was not afraid to let potential adversaries know that I bite back—even before tenure and promotion. The power dynamics on the other side are powerful, so powerful that some people have left the field or fallen sick trying to navigate. For many racial minorities, the university is a very violent and dehumanizing space (Matthew, 2016). It limits our voice, intellectual capacity, and personhood. I figured to myself, if I was going to be taken down, I might as well fight while going down. There are no safe spaces in academe for people like me, so keeping one's mouth shut is a winning strategy for the status quo, not for the individual.

So I arrived on the scene ready to fight no matter what and with an unwavering commitment to the community I represented. I was thoroughly steeped in my standpoint epistemologies, and I knew they were relevant and just as empirical as the alternative. Moreover, I could debate with the best of them on the cultivation of criminological knowledge. So as far as I was concerned, I was geared up and ready for war at any time. However, as a radical Black criminologist, this disposition made me an outlier among other Blacks and scholars of color in the field. While many remained cordial with me at conferences and on social media, I did not receive many invitations to collaborate with other BIPOC criminologists who were well connected and had social capital in the field. Mentorship for junior scholars of my variety is scarce. I could probably count on one hand those senior BIPOC professors in criminal justice and criminology (outside of those who were my professors) who extended a hand to my professional development. Thus, my perception is that I never seemed to fit in with the elite crust of BIPOC criminologists in the discipline. It was as if they were ashamed of me and what I represented. Now, as a tenured associate professor, I still feel this way. It was probably the result of me not being controlled or molded. I was me, and I was not going to change. Also, many Black graduates from HBCUs or so-called lesser ranked programs are underestimated and robbed of opportunities daily. We are denied the chance to self-aspire, thereby creating other discursive power dynamics that evade new streams of knowledge and ways of knowing. This is BIPOC elitism cloaked in whiteness, ensuring its survival to the detriment of those BIPOC scholars deemed inferior. This is a rarely explored truth in academia and especially in criminal justice and criminology. I frankly believe this was done to me as I entered the discipline. Nevertheless, I learned much and made my long hike toward networking, publishing, and creating a career I could stand by. It was the price I had to pay as an openly Black radical in the discipline. And I thank those senior BIPOC criminologist scholars (mostly Black women) who were there to help me on my path. This experience taught me that whiteness and its power to control and influence came in many facets, and I had to be prepared to survive.

Navigating the tenure-track itself was also a vicious cycle. I learned quickly that sometimes having one's own opinion could mean war in some of the most discursive ways. Senior faculty had their agendas for the department, and as a newbie, if you come on board thinking, you will suggest changes that can be an issue to the old guard. Moreover, molding starts immediately upon appointment. Senior faculty often believe they can control and mold junior faculty of color, especially the Academic Karens (Wilson, 2020). For instance, coalition building within departments often puts junior faculty members in quite a bind against those with a higher rank. As a faculty of color who is still looking to develop and secure job security, this is highly compromising. It forces faculty of color into silence during committee meetings of extreme consequence. For instance, hiring, curriculum, bylaws, diversity, and other such committees that profoundly impact the facilitation of department business are very dangerous for junior BIPOC faculty to engage, even though they should have a right to do so. I would argue that junior BIPOC faculty presence on these committees is a strategic must. Predatory senior faculty understand very well the power they hold. I have had to navigate some of these terrains, and these faculty members learned the hard way that I was not the one. I bite back with no regard or respect for their hierarchy of oppression.

But my input on committees of all kinds meant representing those voices not always foregrounded in the university. I was trying to diversify the university's business and ensure that students are introduced to the multitude of perspectives that exist within the discipline and society. I believe the role of the academy is to build new bridges and publics with the community in ways that foregrounds the least among us. However, fighting against the power as I have done has shown me that this is not always the role that people in the university want us to play. After all, it is humans who control the direction of the university—and many of whom may claim to be liberal but walk a different path when the rubber meets the road. Finishing graduate school and entering academe has been a most rewarding effort; however, it has not protected me from the consequences. While my voice is perceived to be loud and powerful, it takes a great deal of inner strength to maintain a sense of self and direction while surviving in a space not designed for the likes of me. Lastly, choosing to sustain the self within such an intentionally violent reality is neither healthy nor necessary, and people must know that too. We do not need the university.

CONCLUSION

I am a person who survived the undercarriage of sustained structural poverty, white supremacy, and a discipline that is unconcerned with the humanity of its subjects. Survival does not always mean a person is OK, as they often persevere to their detriment. As I mentioned above, I lost access to specific spaces within academia. As a divergent, building social capital was much more challenging and scarier. The mental anguish bestowed upon me by other BIPOC scholars was unexpected but also affirmational. I learned that white supremacy governs academe in many ways—and that I had to be prepared beyond just the literature. I had to develop literacies on the functionality of the institution as a whole. Beyond learning these things, I also learned that the fight is never over. Standing up for your values and your perspectives is both noble but also violent. But in the end, I am proud to have traveled the path handed to me, and I would not change it for anything. Growing up as I did prepared me for what I perceive to be a cold, unforgiving world that needs change. However, I learned later that academia was part of that world, and it too needed changing. Until both are transformed for the better, I choose to survive and persevere against the violence each brings against me—but with fight and heart to defend my humanity and others.

REFERENCES

Anderson, E. (1999). *Code of the street: Decency, violence, and the moral life of the inner city.* W. W. Norton & Company.

Anderson, E. (2011). *The cosmopolitan canopy: Race and civility in everyday life.* W. W. Norton & Company.

Bhattacharya, K. (2017). *Fundamentals of qualitative research: A practical guide.* Routledge.

Clark, K. B. (1965). *Dark ghetto: Dilemmas of social power.* Harper & Row.

Collins, P. H. (2002). *Black feminist thought: Knowledge, consciousness, and the politics of empowerment.* Routledge.

Collins, P. H. (2013). *On intellectual activism.* Temple University Press.

Du Bois, W. E. B. (1903). *The souls of Black folk essays and sketches.* A. C. McClurg & Co.

Dumas, M. J., & Nelson, J. D. (2016). (Re)imagining Black boyhood: Toward a critical framework for educational research. *Harvard Educational Review*, 86(1), 27–47. https://doi.org/10.17763/0017-8055.86.1.27

Epstein, R., Blake, J. J., & Gonzalez, T. (2017). *Girlhood interrupted: The erasure of Black girl's childhood.* https://www.law.georgetown.edu/poverty-inequality-center /wp-content/uploads/sites/14/2017/08/girlhood-interrupted.pdf

Feagin, J. R. (2013). *The white racial frame: Centuries of racial framing and counter-framing.* Routledge.

Ferguson, A. A. (2020). *Bad boys: Public schools in the making of Black masculinity.* University of Michigan Press.

Frauley, J. (2005). Representing theory and theorising in criminal justice studies: Practising theory considered. *Critical Criminology, 13*(3), 245–265. https://doi.org /10.1007/s10612-005-3182-1

Gabbidon, S. L., Greene, H. T., & Wilder, K. (2004). Still excluded? An update on the status of African American scholars in the discipline of criminology and criminal justice. *Journal of Research in Crime and Delinquency, 41*(4), 384–406. https://doi .org/10.1177/0022427803260268

Greene, H. T., Gabbidon, S. L., & Wilson, S. K. (2018). Included? The status of African American scholars in the discipline of criminology and criminal justice since 2004. *Journal of Criminal Justice Education, 29*(1), 96–115. https://doi.org /10.1080/10511253.2017.1372497

Haraway, D. (1988). Situated knowledges: The science question in feminism and the privilege of partial perspective. *Feminist Studies, 14*(3), 575–599. https://doi.org /10.2307/3178066

Hudson, B. (2007). *Justice in the risk society challenging and re-affirming justice in late modernity.* Sage.

Kunjufu, J. (1985). *Countering the conspiracy to destroy Black boys: Volume I.* Afro-Am Pub. Co.

Lee, T. M. L. (2007). Rethinking the personal and the political: Feminist activism and civic engagement. *Hypatia, 22*(4), 163–179.

Matthew, P. A. (2016). *Written/unwritten: Diversity and the hidden truths of tenure.* UNC Press Books.

Muhammad, K. G. (2010). *The condemnation of Blackness: Race, crime, and the making of modern urban America.* Harvard University Press.

Roberts, D. (1993). Motherhood and crime. *Iowa Law Review, 79.* https://scholarship .law.upenn.edu/faculty_scholarship/854

Walters, R. (2003). *Deviant knowledge: Criminology, politics, and policy.* Willan.

Williams, J. M., & Battle, N. T. (2017). African Americans and punishment for crime: A critique of mainstream and neoliberal discourses. *Journal of Offender Rehabilitation, 56*(8), 552–566. https://doi.org/10.1080/10509674.2017.1363116

Wilson, S. (2020, September 30). *Surviving academic Karens while Black.* # CrimComm. https://www.crimcomm.net/post/surviving-academic-karens-while -black

Winlow, S., & Hall, S. (2012). What is an "ethics committee"?: Academic gover-nance in an epoch of belief and incredulity. *British Journal of Criminology, 52*(2), 400–416. https://doi.org/10.1093/bjc/azr082

Woldoff, R. A. (2011). *White flight/Black flight: The dynamics of racial change in an American neighborhood.* Cornell University Press.

Young, V. D., & Sulton, A. T. (1991). Excluded: The current status of African-American scholars in the field of criminology and criminal justice. *Journal of Research in Crime and Delinquency*, 28(1), 101–116. https://doi.org/10.1177/0022427891028001006

NOTES

1. See Lee Rainwater, *Behind Ghetto Walls: Black Families in Federal Slum,* 1970.

Chapter 4

From Battered Woman to Professor

A Personal Reflection

Kimberly J. Cook

December 8, 1980. John Lennon was gunned down in Central Park. I heard the tragic news when I was nineteen. I had been beaten by my boyfriend and I could feel the swelling begin to close my left eye. I was trying to keep my lips from drying out because they were split and swelling. My teeth hurt from the punches. My neck hurt; my throat was sore from him strangling me; there were ligature marks on my neck, which I noticed when I went to the bathroom to wash the blood off my face. My body was still aching from the injuries he inflicted the last time he had raped me, so I sat in the chair gingerly. My ribs were also sore. He kicked me so hard that the bruise on my side would be huge and purple by the time I got to my parents' house in Maine. Strawberry Fields forever. John Lennon died. I did not yet know that I was pregnant. The fact that I survived and was in the process of escaping had not yet sunk in—I wanted John Lennon to be alive instead of me. Imagine.

That night is seared into my memory,[1] and the experiences that had brought me to that night shaped me in profound ways, and thus shaped my aspirations and my scholarship. In this chapter, I share what I endured, how I survived, and the impacts on me as a sociological criminologist.

BACKGROUND

As a young woman I had no means to attend college; it was out of my reach. As the youngest of five children from a white working-class family, my parents were clear that if we wanted to attend college, we would need to figure that out on our own. It was an important heads up for us—my parents encouraged us to do well academically and I pursued a college preparation curriculum in high school. I wanted to go to college as soon as I could figure it out. One thing led to another and I took minimum wage jobs and worked in a shirt factory after high school. An opportunity came my way to move from our home in Maine and work on a strawberry farm in Plant City, Florida. My sister and I left for Florida on January 2, 1980, and began working on the farm. We were striking out on our own. We partied. The first few months were fun and the work was grueling. On the weekends, we went to bars to shoot pool.

One night I met a man who challenged me to a game of pool. We played. I won. He bought me a drink. We started dating, and ultimately moved in together after a couple of months. On the first night we were living together he raped me. He had never been violent before and I did not know how to make sense of this violation. I did not use the word "rape" at the time—I knew I had not consented, it was horrendously painful, I screamed for him to stop, and he ignored me. I was sore, bruised, and scared. I was also embarrassed and did not have a voice or vocabulary to describe what he did. Even if I had been able to talk about it, by that time my sister had left Florida and there was no one else I felt I could turn to. Soon he began punching me, kicking me, and choking me, in addition to continuing to force me into sexual activity I did not want. I did not know what to do. He said it was my fault—I believed him.

Few people who know me today—apart from those who have experienced domestic violence themselves—can believe or understand how this happened to me. But it did, and it got worse. He said I needed to do a better job of cooking our meals; I needed to be more aware of what he liked and wanted from me. He told me that if I told anyone about our problems that he would beat me even more because it would cost him his good reputation. He never allowed me to eat outside of his presence because he had strict dietary rules we needed to follow. He would not allow me to eat for days on end. He never allowed me to wear makeup so I would not attract anyone else's attention—except for when I needed to cover up the bruises on my face. He did not allow me to have my own bank account, or even to put my name on a joint account. All my paychecks went into his checking account and he provided me with a meager allowance each week. He was drinking my money away. He had orchestrated a rift between my family and me. My parents were not allowed to call or write to me—he got the mail and intercepted letters. No one in my family knew about the violence; they knew only that I was in Florida living with this man. Eventually, I reached out for help. My co-workers would not help me get away from him because they did not want to get in the middle of it. At that time, I was not aware of any shelters or rape crisis centers in the area. He continued to drink. He lost his job. We moved to Syracuse, New

York, where his father lived. It was early December, and we took Greyhound buses from Tampa—it took us about three days to get to Syracuse. While on the bus, I met a woman who was a Methodist minister going to Syracuse, where her congregation was located. She gave me her phone number and invited me to come to her church once we got settled in New York. I did not tell her about the abuse. On December 8, 1980, we were broke and sharing a tiny apartment with his father. He was belittling me and becoming more and more enraged. He needed money and he said I should go back to Maine, work in the shirt factory again, and send him my paychecks. I agreed; I knew this was my opportunity to get away.

So that afternoon he went out drinking with his cousins, and I called my family from a payphone at a local store. I told them everything and that I wanted to come home for good and never see him again. They wired me a bus ticket to leave the next morning. I just needed a ride to the bus station where I could wait to leave. I called the cops to see if they could help—they refused because there was not a crime in progress. I called the fire department: they refused because their insurance coverage didn't permit that sort of help. I called the Catholic priest: he told me it was my own fault, and he would not shield me from God's judgement. I called the Baptist church and the pastor there told me that I made my bed, and I would have to lie in it. I called that Methodist minister and begged for a ride to the bus station. She refused to help because I was not a member of her congregation.

I went back to the dingy apartment. He returned later that night drunk and angry. While we sat in the tiny living room with his father, I told him that my parents had wired me a bus ticket, that they agreed I could come home to Maine. His rage became even more intense and he screamed that if my parents could afford to buy a bus ticket why can they not send us money instead. I became defiant and shouted back at him that it was not my parents' responsibility to support him. He leapt across the room and started punching me. He beat me severely. His father shouted at me to stop screaming because the neighbors would be upset. During the beating, I somehow managed to see out of the window that a taxi was dropping someone off across the street. I managed to run out into the street to beg the cabby to help me. He agreed—I got in the cab, with my already-packed suitcase, and left. The cab driver was on his final run for the night and he happened to work out of the bus station. It was about a twenty-minute drive. I was bleeding all over—my nose, my split lips, my eyes, and so on. He was an old man and he was kind. He asked me where I was going. I told him. He asked me if I was ok. I said no, not really. I told him I did not have any money to pay him, and he said that was fine. He asked me when was the last time I had eaten—it had been days. I was frail and exhausted. When we arrived at the bus station, he walked me in and showed me where the women's bathroom was so I could wash the blood off my face. He must have gone in to talk to the clerks.

When I came out of the bathroom, the cabby took me into the drivers lounge and told me to stay in there for the night until my bus was boarding the next morning. I would be safe there. He also gave me a dozen donuts and twenty dollars to feed myself on my ride to Maine. He was so kind and thoughtful. I will never know his name, but I will always be grateful for his kindness. I stayed in the drivers lounge. It was about midnight by this time. Eventually, I started paying attention to the music that was playing. The DJ played one Beatles song after another and it was soothing to me. "Yesterday." "Hey Jude." "St. Pepper's Lonely Hearts Club Band." And on and on. I had not been paying attention to the talk in between songs, until the announcement that John Lennon had died. At that point I cried. The world needed John Lennon more than it needed me; could we trade places? Imagine all the people living life in peace.

After two days on the bus, I arrived back in Maine. I was exhausted and tired. I winced when my father hugged me because my ribs hurt so badly; he had never seen me with black eyes and fat lips and strangulation marks on my neck. He wanted to go find the man responsible and kill him—I asked him to stay home and that if he ended up in prison that would be a lot harder on everyone. A few days later, my mom wanted to know if I might be pregnant. I told her I had no idea and that I had lost of track of those details. For about three days straight I slept, ate home-cooked food, went for walks, and slept some more. The shirt factory hired me back. Then on January 2, 1981, my appointment at Planned Parenthood confirmed what my mom suspected; I was pregnant. My parents were so happy that we would "have little feet running around again." My son was born July 30, 1981. I made the choice not to name his father on the birth certificate in order to protect my son from any legal claims/battles that might occur. I did not tell his father about him until years later when I was briefly in phone contact with him again. That did not go well. I have not had further contact with him since then. My son has never met his father.

I hated working in the shirt factory, but I needed a job with health insurance. The factory produced high-end, name-brand, men's and women's dress shirts. Each task was broken down by section; we worked on the assembly line as stitchers (sewing collars, hems, sleeves, and other segments of the shirt process), as inspectors (clipping long threads, ensuring proper stitching), as ironing pressers, as folders (inserting cardboard collars and forms, pinning the cuffs, shoulders and neck around the form). We worked by the dozen and we were paid on a piece rate; we stood all day and were perpetually observed by shift supervisors and plant managers. I worked throughout my pregnancy, and then had about six weeks of maternity leave. It was a union shop, so

I benefited from the collective bargaining protections we got. My son was in daycare, and I went to this job so I could support him. I thought college was beyond my reach at this point. I remember seeing the other women working in the factory, some had been there for thirty years, and I thought, "Is this where I will be in thirty years?" The thought depressed me. When a co-worker quit to enroll in nursing school, she shared with me that there were welfare programs available to help low-income women pursue education and training. This reignited my old desire for a college education. In December 1983 I left the shirt factory. I became a welfare recipient instead of an employed single mother. I had quietly applied for admission and financial aid at the University of Maine. I was admitted and started college in January 1984. I completed my BA in sociology in August 1987, and then started my graduate program at the University of New Hampshire in September 1987, completing my doctorate in July 1994.

CRIMINOLOGY AND ITS DISCONTENTS

The most enduring stance of a scholar is to be curious. An initial foray for many scholars is to find answers to questions that relate to their personal experiences. As an emerging sociologist, I was most interested in sociology of the family, not so much in criminology. As a trauma survivor, I was exploring academic theory and research as possible platforms to understand experiences of battered women. It is normal to connect academic lessons as they relate to our own lived experiences, and then extend to those beyond our experiences, and in truth, the lessons of sociology quickly became a rich avenue for my emotional recovery from the trauma. Sociology was healing my wounds. Criminology in and of itself, while interesting, did not provide me, a crime survivor, with answers to questions I had: Why is domestic violence so common? Why are men allowed to get away with it? Why is it not taken seriously as a crime? Why are its victims mainly women and girls and its perpetrators mainly men and boys? How can it be addressed more successfully? What kinds of supports do battered women need to survive? Where are those supports available? And so on. It was in my sociology classes where explanations based on feminist theory provided important insights, and my personal experience gave birth to a political awakening within me. I began to understand that sexism and institutionalized gender inequality shape our lives in profound ways, such as wage inequality and cultural norms of male dominance, patriarchal religious beliefs and authorization for men to rape and beat "their" women, and shame and victim-blaming in rape culture.

In criminology, I might have learned that my ex would "age out" of violence soon—he was twenty-three when we lived together. I learned he might have benefited from stronger attachments to a church, or to education, and maybe to his family of origin. His religious convictions were dictated by violent patriarchal theology that he used as an excuse to assault me. And his family of origin was a mess—a violent father and a mother who did her best to survive, and after leaving him, to raise her children into adulthood despite the violence seen around them. I learned that, as he did with me, it was typical of abusers to blame the victims for their own acts of violence; the "techniques of neutralization" he used denied the damage that trauma inflicted on me; and combined with feminist theory, I learned about our victim-blaming culture. Critical criminology offered me a bit more understanding of what I had experienced, particularly as it related to aspects of the lived experiences of being in poverty during the traumatic experiences, and then later as a single mother on welfare.

To find answers to the questions I had about abusive men, the feminist theory I learned in my sociology classes proved the most helpful. I learned that the violence I experienced was a consequence of patriarchal social organization (Browne 1987, Dobash & Dobash 1979, Martin 1976). I learned that many men in our society are encouraged to engage in violent behavior to demonstrate their power; I learned about the "power and control wheel" associated with domestic violence that was being developed by sociologist Ellen Pence.[2] I learned in class discussions that questions about abused women such as, "Why doesn't she just leave?" deny the reality of powerlessness and hopelessness that battered women often experience. Just as I was, many of these women are trapped by poverty, isolated by the abuser and kept from friends and family, and ignored or turned away by would-be institutions and "helpers" (recall the response from the Methodist minister to whom I reached out).

In my classes, we also read and discussed books by women of color whose experiences with domestic violence were both similar to and more difficult than mine due to institutionalized racism that impacted their lives (Lorde 1984, hooks 1981, Anzaldua 1983). Criminology offered theoretical and empirical explorations into street crime offending, and relatively little about the "big picture" framework that sociology provided. So I was discontent with criminology. I was fired up by sociology. I was surprised by the pivots during graduate school.

As an undergraduate student at the University of Maine, my sociology professors were kind and compassionate and encouraged examining my life experience using a sociological imagination. When I arrived in graduate school, I quickly learned to become an "objective" scientist by acquiring skills in statistical analysis to test theories. While no one explicitly told me that my life experience was unimportant, some considered it a source of bias that could "contaminate" the analysis. I found that, to do scholarly work, I had to pack away my lived realities as a survivor. Feminist methodology was emerging, and feminist standpoint theory and lived experiences that would shape my work, were not yet articulated (Cook 2016). Therefore, I learned to put that aside for the purposes of completing the curriculum. As Bhattacharya (2015, p. 310) states, "I have often sensed that surviving in academia meant needing to know my place." That place required me to compartmentalize the personal/political in order to pursue the empirical and theoretical content. The methodological education was solid, and the statistical skills were important to learn. I left my personal experiences out of the analysis, as required. To satisfy my feminist leanings, I surreptitiously read emerging feminist theory such as *Black Feminist Thought* by Collins (1991), among others. I found the voices and experiences of women of color to be exceptionally instructive to feminist concerns, especially to understanding the complex layers of harm associated with woman abuse. Combating poverty and sexism was hard in itself, and the ability to survive sexism, racism, and poverty (as battered women of color do) is nothing short of heroic.

Later, in graduate school at the University of New Hampshire, the late Professor Murray Straus served as my main advisor. In 1990, there was an event that would shape my career in fundamental ways. Professor Straus held some controversial views with which he knew I disagreed. Straus is known mainly for his research on "family violence" and specifically his development of the Conflict Tactics Scales (CTS) (Straus, Gelles, & Steinmetz 1980). The CTS is controversial and criticized by feminist scholars for misrepresenting many nuances of violence against women (see Dobash, Dobash, Wilson & Daly 1992 for a full exploration of these critiques). Straus represented his findings as evidence that "women are as violent as men," and that domestic violence is really a matter of "mutual combat" between men and women. In fact, he said that women initiate violence at about the same rate as men do (see Straus 2005 for his review of these claims).

Feminist scholars took issue with his data, and they protested when he was elected president of the Society for the Study of Social Problems (SSSP) in 1990. Straus used his presidency as an opportunity to continue the dialogue. He asked me to help organize a session at the SSSP conference where the speakers would be feminist scholars. He was aware that I had survived domestic violence, and that I found the criticisms of his work very compelling; in fact, I told him that I sided with the critics.

When we arrived for the session, the room was crowded. The audience included some very well-known scholars in this area, many graduate students, and other interested parties. The moderator of the session welcomed everyone, and the speakers shared their comments on the body of Straus's work and their specific points. After some cogent arguments were made about the main issues, the subject of policy implications came up. That is when the mood shifted in the room, and I felt myself becoming increasingly tense and my own trauma was triggered. A critic suggested that one of the policy implications of Straus's research could do real damage to battered women by reducing the level of concern from law enforcement, from legislators debating the passage of new bills, and from funders who provide lifesaving services to battered women. To this point Straus replied, "If women want to stop violence against them, they need to stop being violent towards men." This did me in. I stood up, and, with a shaky voice tinged with frustration and fear, I said, "Professor Straus, you know I respect you and I respect your work, but I think you're wrong. As a formerly battered woman, I never hit my ex, I never attacked him, and he brutalized me in the most vicious ways. I did nothing to deserve how he treated me and all the battered women I have known since have had similar experiences to mine. It was not my fault." And then I walked out of the conference hall, knowing that I had just let the force of my agony explode all over that room. I left feeling shaken, embarrassed, and certain that my time as Straus's graduate student had just ended. I did not see him again for the duration of that conference.

When I returned home, there was a message on my phone answering machine from Straus, asking me to meet with him the next day at 11:00. So I went, expecting to be told to leave the program. But instead, in the quiet of his office, he showed me a list he'd made for our discussion. I didn't quite know what to make of that visual. The first item on his list was simply "SSSP," and then he'd listed two other agenda items below that. We talked for about two hours. I shared in more detail the agony I'd experienced during that session. I told him I felt that he as my mentor did not welcome my subjectivity, my lived experience, as a source of knowledge—and that I was not sure I could simply turn that off. It was too painful and also too important to me; I wanted to use my studies to gain more understanding around it. Had I been trained in the language of "lived experiences" and standpoint theory—a methodology that wouldn't emerge for another few years, and about which I and others would later write (Cook 2016)—I might have been able to persuade him. But at that time, Professor Straus simply listened. He did not tell me to leave the program, nor to find a different mentor. Rather, he talked about how we might continue working together, now that I had finished my MA thesis. He had been set to advise me as I worked on my dissertation on a topic related to domestic violence. But given what I had just expressed to him and at the conference, we agreed instead to work on a topic that would be less emotionally fraught for both of us: public opinion on abortion and the death penalty.

Although I did not completely grasp it at the time, changing my dissertation topic was another unexpected pivot for me: I had planned to specialize in violence against women and to publish in that field.[3] Instead, I had to cope by suppressing this experience, and sharing it only within spaces where I was safe to do so.[4] This pivot changed the course of my career, away from primarily violence against women and towards the sociology of [capital] punishment. Once my dissertation findings were published (Cook 1998a), I quickly launched into a qualitative research project on the same topic, which provided the data for my first book (Cook 1998b). Thus, criminology became my primary focus, and I was pleased with this research area. Feminist criminology helped fuse my scholarly interest with my activism impulse, and it affirmed my lived experience as a trauma survivor.

There are loose parallels to draw. During the time when I was being battered, my ex made it very clear to me that my opinions, feelings, and hopes for the future were immaterial to him, that he was in charge of our life together and I had to get with the program or he would pound it into me, literally. When I said I wanted my own bank account, he told me that as the man of the house it was his right to control the bank account, and that my paycheck had to be part of it. This dehumanizing message made it clear that in order to survive I must submit to his authority.

In some ways, the expectations of "objective" research requires a similar submission process. Whereas I wanted to study woman abuse and use feminist theory as a framework, I also had to submit to the conventions of a field of research that had not yet articulated a way to incorporate lived experiences.[5] In a similar vein, Bhattacharya (2015, p. 312) reflects on her experiences as a woman of color in academia having her presence, her experiences, and her very existence being "dismissed as irrelevant, invisible, and immaterial." So rather than my lived experience becoming a platform for understanding, conventional sociological research training demanded instead that it be compartmentalized to avoid bias.[6]

LIVED EXPERIENCE AND SURVIVING CRIMINOLOGY

Since I could not use my voice in the field of violence against women, and I could not amputate from my existence the stifling pain of victimization, I turned to other areas that have proved to be intellectually lucrative: restorative justice and wrongful convictions. I was fortunate to receive a Senior Scholar award from the Australian-American Fulbright Foundation in 2001; I spent six months in Australia observing the restorative justice (RJ) diversionary program for young people. I was both intrigued by the program and critical of it at the same time. Some of my criticisms have been documented in published research (Cook & Powell 2003, 2006; Cook 2006), and much of my intrigue and ultimately advocacy for RJ has shaped the remainder of my career. As a trauma survivor who internalized so much victim-blaming and silencing, I felt a massive relief when my ex genuinely apologized to me during a brief phone call several years after I escaped. The weight of blame lifted from me in a way that was palpable. If RJ could provide the opportunity for other survivors to experience similar relief, then I wanted to support that. In 2004, I became a certified restorative justice practitioner with a training program by Kay Pranis (Zehr, Amstutz, MacRae, & Pranis 2015).

Being a practitioner of restorative justice satisfies both the intellectual and applied areas of academic life. In many ways, transforming academic lessons into a platform for community healing is extremely appealing. When working with trauma survivors who are pursuing restorative justice resolutions, I am keenly aware of the complex coping strategies that survivors often use to get through each day—both strategies of incorporation and strategies of avoidance (Westervelt & Cook 2012). That is, as fundamentally existential beings, we humans often depend on our ability to "make sense" of our experiences in a way that helps us to resolve the pain we feel from trauma—which is a strategy of incorporation. For many of us, our efforts to "make sense" of it include a desire to have not suffered in vain; we want others to take the lessons of our experiences and transform them into a better future. We therefore engage in social policy reform or efforts to make professional practices more sensitive to the needs of those who are harmed. This quest to make our suffering "count" for something is a source of comfort that can also be palliative to the process of resolving the grief we often feel from our lost sense of security.

Judith Herman (1997, p. 207) explains that some trauma survivors embrace a "survivor mission" and work to cultivate meaning from their painful life experiences. She writes:

> [M]ost survivors seek the resolution of their traumatic experiences within the confines of their personal lives. But a significant minority, as a result of the trauma, feel called upon to engage in the wider world. These survivors recognize a political or religious dimension to their misfortune and discover that they can transform the meaning of their personal tragedy by making it the basis for social action. While there is no way to compensate for the atrocity, there is a way to transcend it, by making it a gift to others.

Part of the experience for trauma survivors is a desire to hold compassionate space for others who have traumatic life experiences. For example, while conducting my research with exonerated death row survivors, I connected with those people as a fellow trauma survivor.[7] I have navigated the contours of trauma: powerlessness, being silenced, being ignored, and then the post-traumatic stress that ensues and does not truly end (Cook and Westervelt 2018, Westervelt & Cook 2010, 2012, 2018). Of the eighteen exonerated death row survivors who participated in our research, seventeen wanted their actual names used in our published research so that their stories would matter to the wider world. Their legal nightmares were part of a public record of having been severely harmed by the state, and to reclaim their identity and innocence they chose for us not to attach a pseudonym to their life experiences. Many trauma survivors also engage in public policy advocacy. For example, many of our exonerated death row survivors are connected to a nonprofit organization, Witness To Innocence,[8] whose mission is to offer peer support to each other and to abolish the death penalty. Their life experiences have been very influential in slowing down the pace of executions across the country, and the abolition of capital punishment in many states in the United States. Acting as a conduit for their stories has been one of the greatest honors of my career.

For scholars who are also survivors, as I am, the experiences we have had inform the field and the research we do, despite our training to consider those experiences a source of bias and contamination for analysis. That is, as a qualitative scholar with the duty to interpret qualitative data for the purposes of constructing grounded theories, my personal life experiences inform my analytical choices. Charmaz (2014, p. 17, emphasis in original) writes, "[W]e are part of the world we study, the data we collect, and the analyses we produce. We *construct* our grounded theories through our past and present involvements and interactions with people, perspectives, and research practices." For those of us with the "both/and" life experience (both survivor and scholar), we should not be expected to amputate the wisdom of our hard-won survival in order to engage in the important work of our science. Bhattacharya (2009, 2015) encourages us to decolonize research away from the oppressive confines of sexism, racism, heternormativity, and economic power. Part of decolonizing criminology involves infiltrating criminology with voices of survivors, and creating a platform for intersectional revolution (Potter 2015). As we pivot towards survivors' voices in our culture (i.e., #BlackLivesMatter, and #MeToo) we need to continue striving towards a more inclusive criminology.

In our book documenting the lived experiences of exonerated death row survivors (Westervelt & Cook 2012, p. 125), we wrote that "'[e]xpertise' comes in many forms, although our academic worlds tend to view scholars as the experts in various fields. It is also true that our exonerees' harrowing experiences of wrongful capital convictions, incarceration, and survival create an expertise with a different set of credentials. Having stared down the barrel of the gun, as it were, and survived, their views on the death penalty as a social policy issue are well informed and compelling." Similarly, I encourage criminologists to embrace the expertise found in the lived experiences of those who have survived the actual ordeals that many of us study. Their survival illuminates strengths, offers insights, and can shape public policy reform in ways that our academic research may not.

The audience I imagine for this chapter is younger scholars coming into the field trying to find where they fit and how their personal life experiences might aid or obstruct their success. In criminology, as a discipline, we deal with extremely difficult aspects of social life—often the most painful life experiences are the topics we study: homicide, rape, sexual and domestic violence, and then how the legal system responds to these tragedies. We study punishment, mass incarceration, executions, wrongful convictions, secondary victimization, victim services, policy reform, juvenile crime and justice, and on and on. It's understandable that people who have personal life experiences with some of these social realities have entered the field of criminology, and those people offer a source of compassion, wisdom, and understanding that remains untapped. In order to tap that wisdom, we must first create a disciplinary platform that acknowledges the importance and accepts the lessons we can draw from that personal material.

But there's a catch: writing this chapter has left me feeling vulnerable and anxious. I know how risky it is to write it. I see in this chapter too many first-person singular pronouns—certainly more than my early mentor Professor Straus and many of my colleagues would condone. Because our scholarly training requires us to push our voices aside in the interest of giving voice to others, the fact that I am publishing my own story for everyone to see risks my reputation within the field. No doubt that some readers will find this chapter self-indulgent and narcissistic. Judith Herman observes that "psychological trauma is an affliction of the powerless. At the moment of trauma, the victim is rendered helpless by overwhelming force. When the force is that of other human beings, we speak of atrocities. Traumatic events overwhelm the ordinary systems of care that give people a sense of control, connection, and meaning" (1997, p. 33).

I know those feelings too well. Citing the *Comprehensive Textbook of Psychiatry* Herman points out that trauma is often accompanied by "intense fear, helplessness, loss of control, and threat of annihilation" (1997, p. 33). Those are the feelings that live in my gut, and I cope with them daily. It has been a painful journey to write this chapter because it required me to excavate memories and emotions that were packed away in the attic of my body and brain. But this is a struggle that has long been with me. As a trauma survivor, I weigh every decision to expose my personal vulnerability, and I gauge the safety of every setting. In the end, I've decided to publish this because I believe the benefit to other trauma survivors, in criminology especially, outweighs the critique I might experience from colleagues.

A major goal of survivor criminology is to support and encourage the field to become more trauma-informed in our methodology, in our theories, and in our practice. Trauma-informed methodology (Newman, Risch, & Kassam-Adams 2006) offers ethical guidelines for conducting research with trauma survivors. Drawing from feminist research methods, I have attempted to apply methodological lessons when interviewing trauma survivors (Westervelt & Cook 2012). My current research involves in-depth interviews with original crime victims, namely homicide victims' family members and rape/sexual assault survivors, in cases where wrongful convictions and exonerations occurred (Cook 2017). To conduct this research, I continue to incorporate lessons from feminist methodologies and to assure the participants that they are in control of the interview setting, location, time, and duration. Criminological theories vary widely in terms of their trauma-awareness, and there is much room for growth, particularly in theories of offending. As a restorative justice practitioner, I try to apply trauma-informed care in all of the cases that I facilitate and in the trainings that I offer to support the use of RJ in my community. Being a survivor of trauma and naming that in those spaces help to ensure both my academic credibility and the lessons drawn from lived experience.

My point is to credit the resiliency and strength survival requires. The pivots in my life were not of my choosing, but the choices I made in light of those unexpected shifts reflect a resiliency that many battered women exhibit (Miller 2018). American culture is infatuated with the "rags to riches" stories and my journey from battered woman to professor invites that trope. Miller points out that the social construction of identity sometimes depends on a "before and after" framework. She writes, "Identity comprises both an internal self-identity and an external identity that is contingent on interactions with others" (Miller 2018, p. 174). As such we are social beings who are shaped by our experiences in fundamental ways, and while some of our experiences are not of our choosing, we do have the agency to respond to those experiences. Resiliency is as simple as breathing and as complex as setting goals and building a plan. It is within that process where new identities are formed; resiliency is a process, not a product. Miller continues to outline three dimensions of "hardiness at the micro level" (2018, p. 176–177) which are (1) finding a meaningful purpose in life, (2) believing that we can influence our surroundings and events, and (3) believing that we can learn and grow from positive and negative experiences.

My personal process toward resilience involved the support of my family (welcoming me home, ensuring that my child and I would have what we needed, etc.), a vision for something different/better, and my own sense of determination. It also has involved a huge dose of support from my professional colleagues, particularly the American Society of Criminology Division on Women and Crime (DWC).[9] I am particularly grateful to the strong feminist empowerment, collaborative ethic, and devotion to intersectional support that is available in the DWC. I am especially grateful to my dear friend Mona Danner,[10] who was sitting with me in that SSSP session in 1990 and immediately offered support. The "sourdough" of feminist praxis is that we take a little for ourselves, and give heartier portions to others and thus create sustenance and vitality in a field we all inform through our research and our lives.

CONCLUSIONS

I offer this chapter as a message to the younger scholars in our field to feel stronger, more secure, and empowered to be a whole person. Understand that there may be times when you need to compartmentalize some aspects of your experiences in order to complete the task before you (qualifying exams, for instance), but please be compassionate with yourself in the learning process. Also, understand that you should not feel the need to suppress your desired field of study, especially if that relates to your personal life experience, as I ended up doing. Criminology needs your passion, your insights, your voices, and your contributions. Your lived experiences matter to the broader world, and to criminology.

Fortunately, as I write this in 2021, criminology has evolved. A student recently came to my office to explain why she had missed so much of the semester and that she had to withdraw from school. This young Latina is a good student who wants to do well: she's smart, kind, and thoughtful. While majoring in criminology she has drawn connections to her own life experiences as an abused child, she has learned where to find resources, she learned to name her experiences for what they were, and she has learned that many women share her painful life experiences. Also, she and her family face the complications associated with varying immigration status, depending on generations, which profoundly impacts her struggle and her coping over the years.

That day in my office, she told me that the criminology and restorative justice classes had given her the courage to share with her family what she needed to say aloud to them. They, particularly her mother, believed her, despite what it would cost her mother personally. They took action to protect her. So, in this regard, I am grateful that we have developed "survivor criminology" to give her the words she needed to say out loud: to claim her truth, to know she is not alone, to know that she can overcome her painful experiences. I dedicate this work to her.

REFERENCES

Anzaldua, G. (1983). *This bridge called my back: Writings by radical women of color.* Latham, NY: The Kitchen Table: Women of Color Press.

Bhattacharya. K. (2009). Othering research, researching the other: De/colonizing approaches to qualitative inquiry. In J. Smart (ed.), *Higher Education: Handbook of Theory and Research* (Vol. XXIV, pp. 105–150). Dordrecht, The Netherlands. Springer

———. (2015). The vulnerable academic: Personal narratives and strategic de/colonizing of academic structures. *Qualitative Inquiry* 22(5): 309–321.

Browne, A. (1987). *When Battered Women Kill.* New York: The Free Press.

Charmaz, K. (2014). *Constructing Grounded Theory,* 2nd edition. Thousand Oaks, CA: Sage.

Collins, P. H. (1991). *Black Feminist Thought: Knowledge, Consciousness, and the Politics of Empowerment.* New York: Routledge.

Cook, K. J. (1998a). A passion to punish: Abortion opponents who favor the death penalty. *Justice Quarterly* 15(2): 329–346.

———. (1998b). *Divided Passions: Public Opinions on Abortion and Death Penalty.* Boston: Northeastern University Press.

———. (2006). Doing difference and accountability in restorative justice conferences. *Theoretical Criminology* 10(1): 107–124.

———. (2016). Has criminology awakened from its "androcentric slumber"? *Feminist Criminology* 11(4): 334–353.

———. (2017). Shattered justice: Original crime victims' experiences with wrongful convictions. American Society of Criminology annual conference, Philadelphia. November 15.

Cook, K. J., & Powell, C. (2003). Unfinished business: Aboriginal reconciliation and restorative justice in Australia. *Contemporary Justice Review* 6:279–291.

———. (2006). Emotionality, rationality, and restorative justice. In W. S. DeKeseredy & B. Perry (eds), *Advancing Critical Criminology: Theory and Application.* New York: Lexington Books.

Cook, K. J., & Westervelt, S. D. (2018). Power and accountability: Life after death row in the United States. In W. DeKeseredy & M. Dragiewicz (eds), *The Routledge Handbook of Critical Criminology,* 2nd edition, 269–279. New York: Routledge.

Dobash, R. E., & Dobash, R. (1979). *Violence against Wives: A Case against the Patriarchy.* New York: The Free Press.

Dobash, R., Dobash, R. E., Wilson, M., & Daly, M. (1992). The myth of sexual symmetry in marital violence. *Social Problems* 39(1): 71–91.

Donnelly, D., Cook, K. J., Van Ausdale, D., & Foley, L. (2005). White privilege, color blindness and services to battered women. *Violence against Women* 11: 6–37.

Donnelly, D., Cook, K. J., & Wilson, L. (1999). Provision and exclusion: The dual face of services to battered women in three deep south states. *Violence against Women* 5(7): 710–741.

Herman, J. L. (1997). *Trauma and Recovery.* New York: Basic Books.

hooks, b. (1981). *Ain't I a Woman: Black Women and Feminism*. Boston: South End Press.

Kaya, Y., &. Cook, K. J. (2010). A cross-national analysis of intimate partner violence against women. *International Journal of Comparative Sociology* 51(6): 423–444.

Lorde, A. (1984). *Sister Outsider: Essays and Speeches*. Trumansburg, NY: Crossing Press.

Martin, D. (1976). *Battered Wives*. San Francisco, CA: Glide Publications.

Miller, S. L. (2018). *Journeys: Resilience and Growth for Survivors of Intimate Partner Abuse*. Oakland: University of California Press.

Moraga, C., & Anzaldua, G. (eds.). (1983). *This Bridge Called My Back: Writings by Radical Women of Color*. Watertown, MA: Persephone Press.

Newman, E., Risch, E., & Kassam-Adams, N. (2006). Ethical issues in trauma-related research: A review. *Journal of Empirical Research on Human Research Ethics* 1(3): 29–46.

Potter, H. (2015). *Intersectionality and Criminology: Disrupting and Revolutionizing Studies of Crime* (Key Ideas in Criminology Series). New York: Routledge.

Stanko, E. (1985). *Intimate Intrusions: Women's Experiences of Male Violence*. Boston: Routledge & Kegan Paul.

Straus, M. A. (2005). Women's violence toward men is a serious social problem. In D. R. Loseke, R. J. Gelles, & M. M Cavanaugh (eds.), *Current Controversies on Family Violence*, (2nd edition, 55–77). Newbury Park, CA: Sage Publications

Straus, M. A., Gelles, R. J., & Steinmetz, S. K. (1980). *Behind Closed Doors: Violence in the American Family*. New York: Doubleday.

Westervelt, S. D., & Cook, K. J. (2007). Feminist research methods in theory and practice: Learning from death row exonerees. In S. Miller (ed.), *Criminal Justice Research and Practice: Diverse Voices from the Field*. Boston: University Press of New England.

———. (2008). Coping with innocence after death row. *Contexts* 7(4): 32–37.

———. (2010). Framing innocents: The wrongly convicted as victims of state harm. *Crime, Law, and Social Change* 53(3): 259–275.

———. (2012). *Life after Death Row: Exonerees Search for Community and Identity*. New Brunswick, NJ: Rutgers University Press.

———. (2018). Continuing trauma and aftermath for exonerated death row survivors. In J. Acker, H. Toch, & V. Bonventre (eds.), *Living on Death Row*. Washington, DC: American Psychological Association.

Zehr, H., Amstutz, L., MacRae, A., & Pranis, K. (2015). *The Big Book of Restorative Justice*. New York: Good Books.

NOTES

1. https://www.psychologicalscience.org/news/indelible-in-the-hippocampus-is
-the-laughter-the-science-behind-christine-blasey-fords-testimony.html "Indelible in
the hippocampus" as Dr. Christine Blasey-Ford said when recounting her own

experience being abused, allegedly by Supreme Court Justice Brett Kavanaugh, during his confirmation hearings, on September 27, 2018.

2. https://www.theduluthmodel.org/wheels/

3. I have published some research in this subject, but not as a main area of specialization. See Donnelly, Cook, and Wilson 1999; Donnelly, Cook, Van Ausdale, and Foley, 2005; and Kaya and Cook, 2010.

4. A significant safe space for me is the American Society of Criminology, Division on Women and Crime. At the annual conference, the DWC hosted informal gatherings for women to share privately our needs, our experiences, and our activist goals within the broader organization. The DWC provided solidarity, support, acceptance, and inspiration throughout my career.

5. For many logistical reasons—time in the program, relocation to a different university with a different mentor would cost time/money I didn't have—I opted to remain at UNH.

6. I am deeply grateful to those pioneering feminists (such as Stanko, 1985) who used her personal experience to inform her research and gave me courage to do so gingerly over the years. I confess to being too cowardly to be more open about it over the years. I have shared bits and pieces in smaller ways when I deemed it was safe for me to do so.

7. My research partner on this project, Dr. Saundra D. Westervelt, is also very compassionate to understanding trauma. Readers of this chapter should not misconstrue my points herein—I do not claim to have a unique capacity for understanding trauma because I have survived, and by implication she does not. She is a very sensitive feminist scholar with a deep commitment to promoting understanding.

8. https://www.witnesstoinnocence.org/

9. See https://ascdwc.com/ for more information.

10. https://www.odu.edu/directory/people/m/mdanner

Chapter 5

From East New York to the Ivory Tower

How Structural Violence and Gang Membership Made Me a Critical Scholar

Jennifer Ortiz

When people hear the word "survivor" they likely picture victims of crime who overcome their trauma. However, as we develop survivor criminology, it is imperative to remember that people who break the law are also victims and survivors. Offenders often endure years or even decades of violence before entering a path of criminality. In this autoethnographic account, I aim to expand the word "survivor" to encompass those who are both victims of violence and perpetrators of crime. In doing so, I hope to shed light on how structural violence perpetuates criminality by marginalizing certain populations. Although criminology often disaggregates structural violence from other forms of violence (or ignores it altogether), I believe this approach is problematic because structural violence begets other forms of violence. Structural violence "refers to the avoidable limitations that society places on groups of people that constrain them from meeting their basic needs and achieving the quality of life that would otherwise be possible. These limitations, which can be political, economic, religious, cultural, or legal in nature, usually originate in institutions that exercise power over particular subjects" (Lee, 2019, p. 123). Thus, social institutions perpetuate oppression and marginalization through structural violence. If survivor criminology seeks to honor survivors, we cannot ignore the plight of offenders like me. I am a survivor of physical and structural violence in my neighborhood, my household, my public-school education, the criminal injustice system, and my doctoral program.

UNCLE APACHE

One of my most vivid early childhood memories was watching my uncle Apache being arrested by officers from the corrupt seventy-fifth precinct[1] in East New York, Brooklyn. Although I was only four years old at the time, thirty years later this memory is permanently etched in my mind. It was 1991 and the United States was nearly two decades into the failed War on Drugs. New York State was leading the misguided charge towards mass incarceration through its disastrous Rockefeller Drug Laws (Kohler-Hausmann, 2010). My uncle Apache was a victim of these oppressive laws and sadly he did not live long enough to become a survivor. Apache was a caring man who battled substance addiction for most of his life. However, even while in an active crack addiction, he tried to be a good uncle. One of my fondest memories was him gifting me a bootleg VHS tape of *Home Alone* for my birthday.

Watching the New York City Police Department (NYPD) hit Apache with a nightstick before handcuffing him and throwing him into a police van, was my first experience with how the criminal injustice system treats people they view as dispensable. If Apache were arrested today, he would be offered treatment through a drug court. In 1991, he was sent to prison like countless other substance-addicted persons of color (Human Rights Watch, 2012). My uncle returned from that incarceration two years later, broken and still addicted to crack. He would continue to battle his addiction until his death in 2001. Apache's life taught me how the criminal injustice system places people into a vicious cycle of incarceration and poverty, which many can never escape (Ortiz & Jackey, 2019). Apache's memory inspires me every day to help men like him escape the grips of addiction and the cruel criminal injustice system.

EAST NEW YORK

I grew up in East New York, Brooklyn during the late 1980s and early 1990s. In 1990, East New York recorded the highest number of murders of any New York City neighborhood (James, 1991). Violent crime in East New York was fueled by extreme poverty. In 1993, the per capita income in East New York was $8,013 (James, 1993). Despite the clear link to poverty, the City responded to violent crime by flooding the streets with more police officers. Ironically, officers from the seventy-fifth precinct were themselves engaged in criminality including extortion, drug dealing, and murder (Holzman,

Saidman, Yellen, & Russell, 2014). For these reasons, my family raised me to never confide in the police because they were only there to harass and arrest us like they did to Apache. My family adhered to the Code of the Streets (Anderson, 1999) whereby street justice was the primary means of solving our problems. Most of the men in my family were gang members who protected the block from crime and violence. Although orthodox gang researchers often portray gang members as savage criminals whose primary focus is committing crime (Brotherton, 2015), that portrayal ignores the role of structural violence.

Gangs often serve a protective function in neighborhoods whereby the gang members ensure that their families and unaffiliated members of the community do not fall prey to crime. In many communities, gangs fill the void created by underfunded social institutions and decades of distrust between the community and law enforcement (Venkatesh, 2008). My gang-affiliated family members filled that void on Dumont Ave in East New York. Because I grew up watching my family protect the community, I was deeply disturbed when later in life a college professor described gangs as neighborhood "infestations." I could not reconcile her dehumanization of gang members with my experiences. I tried to raise my concerns in class to no avail. Although this professor never had direct experience with gang members, she was convinced she knew more about gangs than I did. This class inspired me to study gangs through a critical lens that rejects the pervasive dehumanization and demonization of gang members. My final paper in this course later served as the inspiration for my doctoral dissertation.

Although my family members served a protective function in my community, I will not deny that their street justice often lead to vicious cycles of reprisal. By the age of ten, I had lived through multiple shootouts including one incident where the windows of my grandmother's building were shot out. I recognize that to some criminologists, street justice seems self-destructive, however, the structural and physical violence perpetuated by the NYPD left families with no choice but to fend for themselves. Unlike other communities, we could not call the police because they would not respond or they would take the opportunity to harass our family. Poverty, police harassment, and criminal records created a vicious cycle of failure that kept my family in the margins of society. East New York was a difficult place to grow up and my male relatives offered our family and neighbors the only protection from violence. They offered protection to those of us who could not call the police for help.

MY HOUSEHOLD

In addition to the structural violence in East New York, I lived with structural and physical violence in my home. For the better part of my life, my father was substance addicted. He used drugs and alcohol to numb the post-traumatic stress disorder (PTSD) brought on by his traumatic childhood in the South Bronx neighborhood of New York City. Sadly, my dad was not alone in his suffering. Research indicates that inner-city children have high rates of PTSD due to their exposure to violence and poverty (Mazza & Reynolds, 1999). A recent study found that PTSD rates among inner-city children are comparable to PTSD rates among veterans returning from active war zones (Citizen, 2019). Although my dad never served in the military, his traumatic childhood experiences lead him to develop PTSD that would go undiagnosed for decades.

At a young age, my dad was forced to sell drugs and commit violent crimes to provide for himself. My grandfather was an abusive and unemotional man who believed that men should not say, "I love you," to their children. My dad spent the better part of his childhood seeking love and acceptance while combating the race wars of the 1970s and 1980s. My grandparents were part of the Puerto Rican diaspora that relocated to New York City to escape unemployment and poverty in Puerto Rico (Whalen & Vasquez, 2005). Many Puerto Ricans traveled to the mainland by boat, and thus, many settled in New York City. Between the 1930s and 1970s, Puerto Ricans emigrated to impoverished communities like the South Bronx and Spanish Harlem because they sought manufacturing jobs (Duany, 2012). In 1960, Puerto Ricans made up 8 percent of the New York City population. By 1970, they made up 12 percent of the population (Kaiser, 1976). As the Puerto Rican population increased, they struggled for resources and were met by discrimination (Whalen & Vasquez, 2005) that sparked fights between Puerto Ricans, Italians, and African Americans, especially in the South Bronx neighborhood where my dad lived.

At twelve years old, my dad joined a gang to find the love and protection he needed. This decision would lead to a spiral of destruction. At fourteen years old, a corrupt NYPD officer threatened to arrest my father if he did not sell drugs for the officer. This forced criminality led to many violent confrontations with rival gangs and drug dealers. In the end, my dad turned to alcohol to numb the pain of these experiences, which contributed to years of financial instability. My father's story exemplifies the cyclical nature of structural violence (e.g., poverty and police corruption) and mental health issues. Structural violence can trigger mental health issues that place people into a cycle of poverty, which subsequently leads to criminality (Anakwenze &

Zuberi, 2013). Victims and survivors are transformed into offenders because of the inequality and oppressive social institutions that plague the United States. In my father's case, poverty and corrupt police officers forced him into a cycle of violence and substance abuse.

By the time my father met my mother in 1985, he was an alcoholic. My father supplemented his alcoholism with cocaine and marijuana consumption, which often led to horrific outcomes in our household. He would often spend his paycheck on drugs and alcohol leaving little money for bills and rent. Thus, we moved often during my childhood. I can remember residing in at least ten different addresses between my birth and my fifteenth birthday. My dad's alcoholism also resulted in domestic violence. Some of my most vivid childhood memories are of my mom screaming for help or lying down next to me and crying herself to sleep. By ten years old I had spent dozens of nights comforting my mother, who suffered from her own demons.

My mother suffers from undiagnosed mental illnesses that makes her an unfit mother. When I was fourteen years old, she told me, "If I didn't get pregnant with you, I wouldn't have been stuck with your piece of shit dad for this long." I did not realize it at the time, but my mother's mental health issues led her to inflict physical and psychological abuse against her children, a pattern she learned from her parents. My grandparents were physically abusive, and my grandfather was an alcoholic during my mother's childhood and adolescence. Like many children exposed to violence in the household, my mother learned to normalize domestic violence (Edleson, Ellerton, Seagren, Kirchberg, Schmidt, & Ambrose, 2007), which is why she married a substance addicted man like her father.

When I was fifteen years old, my parents divorced. Ironically, my parents' tumultuous relationship came to an end just as my dad was finding religion and sobriety. Although I recognize that my parents had a dangerously unhealthy marriage, their divorce had negative consequences on their children that are consistent with research. Research indicates that divorce can lead to negative physical, emotional, health, and education outcomes in children (Demir-Dagdas, Isik-Ercan, Intepe-Tingit, & Cava-Tadik, 2018). Prior to my parents' separation, school was my escape from the madness at home. However, after my parents' divorce, I embarked upon my own destructive path.

PUBLIC SCHOOL

My older brother Joseph began school in 1989. My parents enrolled him in Public School 202 in East New York. In the first grade, my brother became ill in school and vomited on his clothing. The school did not notify my parents.

My brother spent the entire day in vomit-stained clothes even though my dad worked within walking distance of my brother's school. When my mother arrived at dismissal time, she was understandably furious and called my father. My father walked to the school and argued with the principal, who attempted to rationalize the school's decision. My father flew into a rage and lifted the principal off of the ground by his neck. While I could never condone my dad's actions that day, I understand now that my dad was responding to structural violence committed against my brother. My brother was traumatized from that incident and my dad handled it in the only way he knew how: violence. After all, violence begets violence. In response to this incident, my dad decided he would not allow me to attend school in East New York.

My dad used a fake address to enroll me in Public School 60 in Woodhaven, Queens. I did not realize it at the time, but my father was committing a felony offense that could have landed him in prison for years (Joldersma & Perhamus, 2020). Growing up I remember my dad saying, "Stay in school so you don't end up like me working in a warehouse." Despite his alcoholism and substance addiction, my dad was determined to see his children escape poverty through education. Given the structural violence that plagued East New York public schools and the poverty that plagued my family, my dad had little choice but to commit a felony offense to ensure we received a high-quality education.

My elementary school offered a phenomenal education that I credit with much of my success today. We had computer classes in the early 1990s, which was nearly unheard of in public schools back then. By the third grade I was learning Italian and volunteering in the school's library. The teachers were phenomenal and offered a reprieve from the violence at home and in my neighborhood. The librarian, Mrs. Brandstatter, once told me, "You can go anywhere in a book." That quote resonated with me as a child and I began escaping reality through books. I was too poor to afford to buy books, so Mrs. Brandstatter instilled in me a love for libraries. At ten years old, I began memorizing the Dewey Decimal System so I could become a librarian like Mrs. Brandstatter.

Although I was attending an excellent school, Woodhaven was a predominately white neighborhood at the time and the student body at P.S. 60 reflected that population. Most of my classmates had middle-class parents who were police officers, doctors, and businesspeople. The students wore name-brand clothes, and many could never dream of eating the free lunch provided by school. I was merely a poor Puerto Rican from East New York wearing my brother's hand-me-down clothes. One of the hardest struggles of my childhood was learning to balance being in a predominately white school while living in a predominately Black neighborhood. I watched as Black and Brown kids in East New York attended underfunded schools riddled with violence and underqualified teachers. All the while I was attending a well-funded school where they constructed a new building to ensure class sizes remained small. At my school, we went on field trips, learned about community service, and were given every advantage to succeed. Attending P.S. 60 made me cognizant of economic inequality.

Prior to attending P.S. 60, I did not realize my family lived in poverty because everyone in East New York was low income. Research asserts that deprivation is relative, meaning that a person's sense of their own poverty occurs by comparing their position to others (Young, 1999). Mass media did not exist in the early 1990s at the same scale as today, so my only points of comparison were other Brooklynites. However, the students at P.S. 60 made me painfully aware of my poverty on a regular basis. By the fourth grade, I was being called "the girl who smells" because at times my family could not afford to wash clothes. My poverty was on full display for all to see and I spent many nights crying myself to sleep over my classmates' comments.

In the sixth grade, several of my classmates would call me a dog and bark at me. One classmate gave me a Christmas card with a picture of a dog barking to represent me. I lashed out and scratched his arm. I went home scared because I thought the school would suspend me. To my surprise, the school called my mother and scheduled a meeting with the boy and his parents. I brought the Christmas card to the meeting and the school mediated the situation. Both of us apologized to each other and the incident was over. I did not have to miss a single day of school. This incident made me aware of the racial and economic disparity in discipline across schools (Morris & Perry, 2016; Irwin, Davidson, & Hall-Sanchez, 2013). A suspension could have been my first step in the school-to-prison pipeline (Mallett, 2016), but instead P.S. 60 allowed me to continue my education uninterrupted. By contrast, students in East New York were often suspended, which led many to drop out of school. In the 1990s, East New York schools had significantly higher dropout rates than other New York City neighborhoods (Berger, 1991), driven in part by zero-tolerance policies that gave rise to the school-to-prison pipeline. Schools like P.S. 60 prepared students for advanced middle school programs while East New York schools prepared students for juvenile detention facilities.

My experience with mediation in elementary school serves as a constant reminder that the education system perpetuates structural violence against students of color and lower-income students, which oftentimes destines them for a life of failure and oppression (Irwin, Davidson, & Hall-Sanchez, 2013). If I had attended school in East New York where the majority of students are people of color, I would not have received mediation or other restorative justice practices (Payne & Welch, 2015). I likely would have fallen prey to the school-to-prison pipeline at an early age. Although I avoided the school-to-prison pipeline, poverty and abandonment would lead me to gang life.

ASOCIACIÓN ÑETA

The high-quality education I received in elementary and middle school led me to attend the third-highest-ranked high school in New York City, Brooklyn Technical High School. At Brooklyn Tech, I met a global studies teacher named Mr. Kivanoski who supervised Progressive Student Awareness, a student organization focused on social justice and activism. Although he did not know it at the time, Mr. Kivanoski sparked the revolutionary flame that burns within me today. He inspired me to fight against structural violence. I remember protesting the school's dress code and staging a walkout to demand contracts for our teachers. My two and a half years at Brooklyn Tech motivated me to fight for marginalized people. Although I was thriving at Brooklyn Tech, by fourteen years old I had to seek full-time employment. My mother's mental illness led her to stop paying utility bills. I remember winters without heat and summers without electricity. I was living two lives, one as a student at an elite high school and one as a poor teenager trying to survive my household. I could not survive both lives simultaneously.

Several weeks before my fifteenth birthday, my parents separated, causing me to enter a spiral of destruction. Initially, my dad paid child support and would pick me and my sister Stephanie up for visits every other weekend. During this time, my mom began visiting nightclubs several times per week. She would take my father's child support money and use it to party, often leaving me and my siblings without food. Eventually my dad stopped paying child support and by my seventeenth birthday he disappeared altogether. My mother was too busy reclaiming her youth to be a parent. We lived in squalor including a barren fridge and a rodent-infested home. As the only other working person in the household, I became fully responsible for Stephanie. I was a fifteen-year-old child trying to figure out how to parent an eight-year-old. I was emotionally broken because I could not comprehend why the people tasked with raising me no longer cared for me. Despite my own emotional trauma, this experience triggered my survival instinct, and I began formulating plans to ensure Stephanie and I would survive.

I knew I could not provide for Stephanie if I was still in high school. In the middle of my junior year of high school, I transferred to Richmond Hill High School, where the educational standards were so low, I could skip my senior year and graduate in four months. I transferred to Richmond Hill as a junior but I was placed into senior-level classes so I could graduate. The education was abysmal compared to Brooklyn Tech. I had classes from

8am to 12pm and I could enter and leave the school as often as I wanted. At Brooklyn Tech, I had classes from 8am to 3:30pm, and the doors were guarded so students could not cut classes. Brooklyn Tech prepared students for college while Richmond Hill High School prepared students for failure. The contrast between these two educational experiences illustrated to me why many inner-city children failed while Tech students excelled. When I started at Richmond Hill High School, I was lost and in need of adult guidance, so I joined Asociación Ñeta. The Ñetas offered me physical, emotional, and financial support. I began selling drugs at my local park while still working full-time as a receptionist at a local real estate office making $5/hour. I did not realize it at the time but the Ñetas would inspire my entire life's work.

When I asked to join Asociación Ñeta, the members provided me with the gang's literature. Through this literature I learned that the original name of the Ñetas was Asociación Pro-Derechos del Confinado or the Association for Prisoner's Rights. This group was founded in Oso Blanco prison in Puerto Rico by incarcerated men combating structural and physical violence perpetuated by correctional officers. These men developed a set of rules to regulate life in prison. These rules are comparable to the Convict Code (Irwin, 1970) in that both ideologies are meant to minimize the suffering of incarcerated people. Although many men in my family experienced incarceration, I remained ignorant to the cruelties that existed behind prison walls because we never spoke about prison in our family. People went to prison and they came home; what happened to them in prison remained shrouded in mystery and shame. I know now that some of the men in my family likely endured sexual and physical violence in prison. Research suggests that 2 to 5 percent of the prison population experience sexual violence and 21 percent experience physical violence during their incarceration (Wolff & Shi, 2009). Research further indicates that violent incidents in prison are underreported because incarcerated persons fear retribution for "snitching" (Fowler, Blackburn, Marquart, & Mullings, 2010). Moreover, victims of sexual assault or abuse often feel a sense of shame, which may cause them to avoid reporting or speaking about their experiences (Weiss, 2010; Dorahy & Clearwater, 2012). While I may never know the true extent of trauma inflicted upon the men in my family, the Ñetas taught me that incarceration was a traumatic experience. The Ñeta literature opened my eyes to the lived realities of incarcerated persons. The leaders of my chapter[2] explained the importance of fighting for our brothers and sisters being held in cages. This experience made me think back to my uncle Apache and everything he must have endured in prison. Today, all my work is focused on alleviating the plight of the incarcerated population and individuals in gangs.

Contrary to popular lore, most gangs do not abide by a blood in, blood out code (Bolden, 2020), and most gang membership is short-lived (Decker &

Lauritsen, 2002). I was only a gang member for four years, but I give credit for my career to the Ñeta teachings. While some criminologists may dismiss the Ñeta teachings as rhetoric that conceals the gang's criminality, those teachings made me a critical scholar. Those teachings took me from East New York to the Ivory Tower of academia. I continue to live by those teachings even though my gang membership ended over fifteen years ago.

REDEMPTION THROUGH EDUCATION

Although I was an active gang member making enough money to provide for Stephanie, I longed for school tremendously. My education was always my escape from the horrors of my life. In 2004, I decided to enroll in college. I had not taken my SAT exam in high school because I graduated in my junior year. No one in my immediate family had ever attended college so I was unsure how to begin the application process. When I was at Brooklyn Tech, I aspired to attend Ohio State University or Stanford University, but those dreams were no longer possible. Although I was raising and supporting Stephanie, legally I had no right to take her across state lines. So I began searching for colleges in New York City where I could study criminal justice. John Jay College of Criminal Justice was the most obvious choice. At the time, John Jay offered an associate degree in police studies that did not require the SATs. I applied and was accepted. On the first day of my freshman year, I met the man who would become my mentor and pseudo-father, Dr. Douglas Thompkins.

Dr. Thompkins was a former gang member who had served time in prison. I could not believe that someone who was like the men in my family was a college professor. Seeing him in front of that classroom was the most powerful and transformative experience of my life up until that point. Dr. Thompkins made me believe I could achieve great things despite being a gang member from East New York. He would have long conversations with me about being in a gang and why I needed to walk away so I could do the work that the Ñetas wrote about in their literature. He never admonished me for being a gang member or a drug dealer like other adults would. Dr. Thompkins offered me undying support. He would let me bring Stephanie to school and occasionally he would feed us. He welcomed us into his family and for the first time in years I felt like I had someone to guide me. Dr. Thompkins told me I should be getting a bachelor's degree instead of an associate degree, so I changed my major to a bachelor of science in criminal justice after that first semester. He helped me stop drinking heavily, and he helped me escape an abusive relationship. He literally saved my life.

In 2006, Dr. Thompkins encouraged me to apply for the joint-degree bachelor-master's program where I could earn two degrees in five years. One semester when I could not afford my tuition, he offered to pay the balance until we could find alternative means. Dr. Thompkins then helped me apply for the John A. Reisenbach Foundation Fellowship, a program that covered my tuition for three semesters. He motivated me to earn a Ph.D., something I never imagined doing when I started college. Dr. Thompkins practiced radical compassion (Van Cleve, 2020) with his students, which inspired my current approach to teaching. I utilize student-centric classroom models that prioritize the needs of students over the institution's needs. My students know that I care for them and I will do anything to see them succeed, just like Dr. Thompkins did for me.

DIRECT EXPERIENCE WITH THE
CRIMINAL INJUSTICE SYSTEM

During my third year of college, I began dating a member of the Bloods gang, which led me to relocate to Bedford-Stuyvesant, Brooklyn. One night the Bloods held a fundraiser for a member who was diagnosed with lupus and did not have health insurance. This fundraiser is a prime example of how gangs fill the void created by structural violence in society (Venkatesh, 2008). The young woman who needed lupus treatment was nineteen years old and could not afford health insurance nor did she qualify for free health insurance. The Bloods were her only option to acquire the money necessary to pay for her healthcare costs.

Because I was good at math, my partner asked me to collect the money at the fundraiser. I was stationed behind the desk at the entrance to the clubhouse we rented for the night. The event began at 9pm, and at 1am, officers from the seventy-fifth precinct raided the clubhouse. When attendees saw the police arriving, they immediately began discarding weapons and drugs they had on their person. The NYPD officers who responded allowed most people in the party to leave but they placed me, my partner, and four other individuals in handcuffs. The officers did not explain why we were being arrested. They confiscated the monies we raised, handcuffed each of us, and chained the six of us together before placing us in a police van.

The officer driving the van asked us, "Are you ready?," which confused us because we were handcuffed and chained together. What choice did we have? The officer then sped away from the scene before slamming on his brakes causing those of us in the van to collide into each other. The officer proceeded to speed up and slam on his brakes another four or five times on the short ride to the precinct. We could hear him laugh every time. Although I did not know the term back then, the officer's actions that night are part of a common practice called "rough-rides" (Correia & Wall, 2018). This term became part of the national discussion of police brutality following the murder of Freddie Gray at the hands of the Baltimore Police Department (Ortiz, 2017). When the Freddie Gray case made national headlines in 2015, I cried because any one of us in that NYPD van could have been Freddie Gray. I was heartbroken and angered when I learned that the officers in the Gray case would face no repercussions. It served as yet another reminder that structural violence not only encourages but commends all forms of violence against groups deemed dispensable by society.

The group of six arrested on that night in 2007 were held in Brooklyn central booking for three days without seeing a judge, despite a landmark New York Court of Appeals case that limited the time from arrest to arraignment to twenty-four hours (*Roundtree v. Brown*, 1991). I was three years into my criminal justice degree, so I knew something was wrong. I sat in the cell unable to eat because I was so angry. I could not understand why we were arrested, and no one offered an explanation. On the third day, I finally met with a public defender who informed me that we were arrested on multiple charges ranging from weapons possession to providing alcohol to a minor. The NYPD had recovered guns and drugs discarded during the raid and were attempting to charge us with those items. I sat in stunned silence as the public defender explained that because I was a first-time offender, the best course of action was to plea to some charges in exchange for a probation sentence. At the time, I aspired to be a criminal defense attorney and I knew all too well the long-term impact of a criminal record. I knew I could not accept a plea to a felony charge. When we finally faced a judge, we were informed that the NYPD had vouchered $143 into evidence. I was furious because we had raised nearly $3,000 at the fundraiser. In that moment it became clear why the police had raided the party: they wanted money.

Eventually I pled guilty to two low-level misdemeanor offenses in exchange for youthful offender status, which meant that my record would be sealed from the public if I stayed out of trouble until the age of twenty-one (see NY CPL 720.35). This experience made me realize how easily someone could be given a criminal record. We were just gang members who the police believed they could destroy without repercussions. We would merely accept plea bargains like 97 percent of people facing charges do (National Association of Criminal Defense Lawyers, 2018). The public defender thought I would just accept a plea deal so she could close the case. Although public defenders are supposed to help clients prove their innocence, most public defenders are saddled with large caseloads that render them incapable of providing adequate defense (Schoneman, 2018). In some jurisdictions, public defenders spend less than five minutes with each client (Weiss, 2019) with most of that time spent trying to convince the defendant to accept a plea deal. Perhaps the most ironic part about my experience is that I was never arrested for the many crimes I *did* commit as a gang member.

My arrest further fueled a desire to critique and dismantle the criminal injustice system. I began to explore the topic of wrongful convictions, which eventually lead me to become a prison abolitionist. Prior to my arrest, I believed we could reform the criminal injustice system and improve prisons so that incarcerated individuals could be rehabilitated. My direct experience with the criminal injustice system taught me that reform is a pipe dream because structural violence is inherent in the criminal injustice system. The criminal injustice system is a self-perpetuating institution that destroys the lives of every person who enters it. The system tried to destroy me, but it failed. In fact, it motivated me to become someone powerful enough to help other people combat the system. I left gang life after that arrest and focused on college.

TOMÁS

In April 2008, I was headed home from work on the J-train in New York City when I set eyes on the man who would become my husband, Tomás. By this time, I was renting a three-bedroom apartment in Queens with two room-mates. When Tomás exited the train at the same station as me, I introduced myself. We started dating and spent many nights bonding over our mutual childhood traumas. Tomás was born and raised in the South Bronx and we shared similar experiences battling poverty, violent households, and over-coming sexual violence. Unbeknownst to me at the time, Tomás was in active heroin addiction and was homeless.

In March 2009, Tomás was arrested while visiting his brothers in Pennsylvania. Tomas and his brothers fought with a man who was sleeping with Tomás's sister-in-law. Tomás had a prior felony record from a 1997 drug charge so the prosecutor was hell-bent on handing him a lengthy sentence (Montalvo & Ortiz, 2020). Tomás battled those charges and after six months in the Luzerne County Jail he was released in September 2009. When he came home, he wrote me a twenty-page letter detailing all the traumas in his life. He confessed to me about his heroin addiction and how he had achieved sobriety while incarcerated because he wanted a better life. He told me about the brutality he faced while incarcerated at eighteen years old at Auburn Correctional Facility in New York State. He was thirty-one years old when he wrote me that letter and it was the first time he ever spoke about the trauma he endured. At first, I was taken aback by the sheer amount of physical, sexual, and structural violence he had endured in his short thirty-one years of life. I was also proud of him for achieving sobriety and wanting to change his life. His story made me wonder if my uncle Apache had similar experiences in prison.

In December 2009, Tomas and I moved into a small one-bedroom basement apartment in Queens. We were ecstatic to start our new life together. However, our dreams were shattered when New York State began garnishing Tomás's paycheck. Tomás had a seven-year-old son named Adam who he loved dearly. During his incarcerations, Tomas accumulated child support debt, which is a common financial barrier among the formerly incarcerated population (Pearson, 2004). The civil court system began garnishing $600 per month from Tomás's salary, leaving him with little to provide for our household. Determined not to let the system destroy him, Tomás decided to acquire a second job. For nearly a year Tomás worked over sixty hours per week at two different jobs to ensure that he could provide for me and Adam. I watched in awe as he battled oppressive parole restrictions and the civil court system. He was working hard at being a good man, but the system was determined to impede him in any way it could.

In 2010, the economy was in shambles. Tomás was laid off from his job in October and he could not locate steady employment. At the time, the unemployment rate for people with felony records was higher than the national unemployment rate during the Great Depression (Prison Policy Initiative, 2018). Tomás was receiving unemployment benefits; however, 50 percent was garnished for child support. Knowing that we could not continue to make the $600 per month child support payments, we decided to petition the court for an adjustment to the child support order. However, I was naïve to the impact Tomas's criminal record would have on his case. The civil court judge treated Tomás like he was a deadbeat junkie who was actively trying to avoid child support payments. The first family court judge refused to give Tomás an adjustment and instead placed him on one year of probation for failure to pay child support. The $600 per month child support order remained in place despite Tomás being unemployed. He was ordered to attend an employment readiness program eight hours per day, five days per week. Although the program claimed to help people locate employment, the program consisted largely of resume and interview preparation, which were of little help to construction workers like Tomás. Tomás could not attempt to locate employment on his own because failure to attend the program was grounds for revoking his probation. He spent a year in the program and in the end he remained unemployed. Tomás would spend another two years trying to locate steady employment (see Montalvo & Ortiz, 2020 for a detailed account of Tomás's experiences).

Witnessing Tomás's struggles with the civil court system made me keenly aware of the collateral consequences of a criminal record. Although there is literature exploring the impact of a criminal record on employment (Pager,

2003; Johnson & Johnson, 2012), education (Stewart & Uggen, 2020), and housing (Thacer, 2008), scholars have not explored the structural violence enacted by the civil court system against people with criminal records. Witnessing Tomás battle both the criminal and civil court systems while trying to rebuild his life post-incarceration motivated me to study reentry. Today, my activism and research center on improving living conditions for formerly incarcerated persons and abolishing prisons. My work as a scholarvist (Green, 2018) centers on helping people like Tomás combat a criminal injustice system that is determined to see them fail. Tomás's experiences inspired my research agenda and were it not for his presence in my life I would not have a doctoral degree. Although I endured physical, sexual, and structural violence throughout my life, nothing could prepare me for the trauma I would endure in my doctoral program.

STRUCTURAL VIOLENCE IN ACADEMIA

When I decided to apply for doctoral programs, I knew I could not leave New York City because Stephanie was still in public school. Given the turbulent nature of our childhood, I did not want to create more instability in her life. Research indicates that transferring schools can negatively affect grades (Schwartz, Stiefel, & Cordes, 2017) and may contribute to high school dropout rates (Gasper, DeLuca, & Estacion, 2012). I was nearing the end of my joint-degree bachelor-master's program so I decided to apply for John Jay's criminal justice doctoral program. When I received my acceptance letter, I was ecstatic. Unbeknownst to me, I was walking into an elitist program riddled with structural violence.

In my first semester, I endured students making comments about my acne, which I was too poor to treat. Privileged students made comments about my unprofessional clothing, which was largely purchased from discount stores. I realized in that first semester that many students in the program saw me as nothing more than a former gang member who was likely a diversity admit. Those sentiments angered me because I had earned two college degrees in five years while maintaining a 3.87 GPA and working full-time. However, to the privileged students in the program, I was just the poor Puerto Rican from East New York who was rough around the edges and did not belong in their program. While dealing with privileged students was difficult, nothing could prepare me for the cruelty I would endure from faculty.

As I sat in class listening to faculty members and students discuss justice-involved persons, I was amazed at how out of touch academics were. The studies we read about gang members portrayed them as animalistic and predatory. I quickly realized that most scholars engaged in research that treated human beings like statistical cases to be analyzed from the safe confines of the Ivory Tower. In one class meeting, the professor showed us postcards from the Maricopa County Jail that depicted women arrested for prostitution working on chain gangs. The professor stated that Sheriff Joe Arpaio was "saving" these women by keeping them in jail. She further commented that even if they were innocent of their current charges, they likely committed other crimes that they were never charged with. I sat in stunned silence listening to this privileged professor explain why she believed jail was the right place for these women despite research to the contrary. Research indicates that prison causes psychological trauma (Anderson, Geier, & Cahill, 2016) while offering minimal rehabilitative programming (Ortiz & Jackey, 2021). Moreover, incarceration leads to long-term stigma and negative health consequences (Williams, Wilson, & Bergeson, 2020).

In another incident, a professor argued that crime was caused by moral failings in communities, not by the structural violence in those communities. When I expressed my disagreement with his statement, he told me, "Well, the statistics prove I'm right." During this class I became keenly aware of how out of touch with reality most professors are. Most professors conducted research that perpetuated oppression because positivist studies lead to grants and publications in high impact journals. Abstract empiricism had created the false belief amongst academics that objectivity, not justice, is the goal of research. "Thus, paradoxically, the less their contact with the subject matter the more knowledgeable [they] feel" (Young, 2011, p. 12). I knew I could never conform to this elitist approach to knowledge. I belonged in the trenches lifting people up as others had done for me. Because most professors focused on statistics, my doctoral education was largely devoid of critical thought. The doctoral program was more interested in transforming students into miniature replicas of the faculty than it was with actual justice. The only thing more problematic than the positivist nature of the doctoral program was the blatant racism and classism perpetuated by the faculty.

At the end of my first semester, a professor accidentally emailed me another student's final exam scores. When I notified the professor of their error, they justified their error by stating, "You both have first names that start with J, Hispanic surnames, and you look alike." I could not believe the blatant racism this professor exhibited. I discussed the incident with an administrator who told me to avoid drawing attention to the incident because I would likely need that professor's support later in my career. I could not believe what this professor was saying. He wanted to ignore the racism rather than address the issue to avoid tarnishing the program's reputation. Structural racism remains pervasive in academia because many academics deny its existence (Gray, Joseph, Glover, & Olayiwola, 2020) and institutions are reluctant to address the issue (Pilkington, 2012).

Although John Jay College's motto is educating for justice, their doctoral program perpetuated the oppression of marginalized scholars. Once a marginalized student was admitted, they faced numerous structural barriers, especially if they were vocal about creating change in the world. Most faculty members were focused on meaningless academic metrics of success like journal impact factors and large government research grants. Grants and publications meant nothing to me. I was battling for my doctoral degree so I could improve the lives of justice-involved people, not to earn meaningless academic accolades. After a few months in the program, I realized I did not belong there nor was my presence in the program appreciated. Sadly, my experiences are not unique. Other students of color have written publicly about their racialized experiences in the doctoral program (see Blount-Hill & St. John, 2017). The blatant racism in the program was compounded by the overt classism.

When my husband was laid off during my first semester in the doctoral program, I had to seek full-time employment. I began working forty hours per week while attending ten hours of classes and studying. It was exhausting but I finished the year with a high GPA. However, in my third year of the program, a new executive officer was appointed. By this point, the student body had elected me as president of the Criminal Justice Doctoral Students' Association. As president, I advocated for students' rights and represented student interests at program meetings. Being outspoken about students' rights would lead to a backlash from the new executive officer and other faculty in the program. I was called into meetings where faculty expressed "concern" about my progress in the program despite me having passed my four comprehensive exams while working full-time. The faculty wanted me to be docile and obedient like the privileged students were. However, I had a family depending on me for survival.

I explained to faculty that I was working three different jobs to keep a roof over my family's head. I sought advice from faculty members regarding how to proceed in the program while working. One professor suggested that I stop working and borrow money from my parents. Another professor told me to prioritize completing my degree over providing for my family. The comments were out of touch with the lived reality of working class students. Most faculty had never experienced poverty so they could never comprehend the struggles average people faced. It was in these meetings with the executive officer that I realized higher education, especially at the doctoral level, is riddled with classism. These meetings inspired me to help doctoral students of color and other marginalized groups overcome the structural violence in doctoral programs.

I publicly and unapologetically continued to advocate for students in the doctoral program. Subsequently, I struggled to find a committee who would work with me. Every topic I proposed was dismissed so I sought help from outside of my toxic department. I formed a committee comprised of two sociologists and three anthropologists rather than forming a committee of criminal justice professors. My committee was supportive of my work and I defended my dissertation proposal in my fourth year. However, during the summer between my fourth and fifth year, I experienced a mental health breakdown caused by the unrelenting discrimination. I could handle poverty and gang life. I could handle three jobs and writing my dissertation. What I could not handle was being treated different than my white counterparts were treated. The micro-aggressions, blatant racism, and overt classism made me want to drop out of the program. That summer I told Tomás of my intent to withdraw from the program. Tomás responded, "But if you quit now, who will speak for people like me?" He was right. The structural violence in the doctoral program made me lose sight of my larger goal: fighting injustice and creating a kinder world for marginalized people. I always believed John Jay College was the place to create that change. However, while John Jay College of Criminal Justice is a beacon for justice and equity in higher education, the doctoral program was an elitist institution determined to make life difficult for scholars of color and any student who dared to be vocal about the structural violence.

When I graduated from the doctoral program in 2015, I could hardly believe I had done it. Despite poverty, gang membership, physical and sexual violence, and the structural violence in my doctoral program, I became Dr. Ortiz. Sadly, little has changed in the doctoral program. Marginalized students continue to endure mistreatment. Since 2015, I have helped several students of color in the program who were threatened with expulsion for not making satisfactory progress. I will continue to help students in the doctoral program because I know many are suffering in silence out of fear of retribution from administrators. The structural violence in my doctoral program transformed me into a compassionate professor who seeks to uplift marginalized students. I reject academic elitism and I adhere to the scholarvist model (Green, 2018). I refuse to sit in the Ivory Tower and pillage communities for their knowledge just so I can publish in journals that no one will ever read. I belong in the trenches fighting for marginalized people and that is where I am today.

CRITICAL CRIMINOLOGY AND
SCHOLARVIST IDENTITY

During my time in the doctoral program, I was fortunate enough to take a class taught by the late critical criminologist Dr. Jock Young. Jock was an inspiration to me because he showed me that I could challenge the system.

I also took courses with Dr. David Brotherton, who would later become my dissertation committee chair. In Dave and Jock's classes I read articles and books that depicted the reality of gang life. These texts humanized gang members by focusing on the structural violence that leads to criminality. These courses were the only critical classes, and they were both taught out of the sociology doctoral program at the CUNY Graduate Center. As I read Jock's and Dave's work, I realized that I could be a critical criminologist *and* obtain a faculty position. I did not have to conform to the elitism that plagues academia. Dave and Jock inspired me to be more radical and vocal. I was determined to develop research that did not pathologize people from East New York and other marginalized communities. I was determined to be a critical criminologist who gave marginalized folk a platform to share their voices and experiences. I was determined to be like Dave and Jock.

Today, my research does not focus on individual or community-level moral failings like most of the works I read in my doctoral program. I am a critical criminologist who explores structural violence in the criminal injustice system. Being a critical criminologist means I critique and condemn the systems that create and perpetuate inequality, not the individuals who fall victim to inequality and discrimination. While I centered my experiences with racism and classism in academia, we must not ignore that the academy is also sexist (Savigny, 2014) and that women of color, particularly Black women, experience structural violence due to their intersectional identity (Patton, 2010). Women professors are less likely to be hired and promoted (Regner, Thinus-Blanc, Netter, Schmader, & Huguet, 2019), and they receive lower pay raises (Krefting, 2003) when compared to their male counterparts. Academia is problematic because it purports to be an institution that uplifts people but in reality it perpetuates marginalization through structural violence. Thus, nearly every piece I publish critiques academia's complicity in the oppression of marginalized people. Although one of my dissertation committee members cautioned against "biting the hand that feeds you," I believe my role in academia is to destroy the structural violence inherent in this elitist institution. Perhaps more importantly my allegiance is to the people living in the trenches, not to an academic career or prestige. Frankly, I will always feel more comfortable around gang members than academics.

I adopted the scholarvist model from Black feminist scholars. These powerful scholars focused on fixing communities and addressing violence in the trenches. Today, I spend the bulk of my time working to make the world a better place for marginalized persons. I serve as president of my town's Human Rights Commission, a position that allows me to mete out penalties for violations of human rights. I serve on the executive board of a reentry non-profit organization called Mission Behind Bars and Beyond (MB3). MB3 is a Kentucky-based organization that provides mentorship to individuals recently

88   *Jennifer Ortiz*

released from incarceration. Through MB3 I mentor formerly incarcerated women as they try to navigate the criminal injustice system's structural violence. In every woman I mentor, I see the same pain I saw in my husband's eyes when he came home. In every formerly incarcerated person I encounter, I am reminded of my uncle Apache. I have made it my life's work to help people like him combat structural violence. This work is why I fought for my doctoral degree. I believe I have a duty to use my privilege to lift others.

My approach to teaching also focuses on supporting and uplifting marginalized individuals. Inspired by Dr. Thompkins's radical compassion in the classroom, I developed classrooms that are inclusive of all students. I have adopted a radical compassion model in my classrooms that allows students to demonstrate their knowledge in ways that are appropriate for them. I eliminated exams from nearly all my courses, and I allow flexibility with assignments. In the end, I do not know how many of my students are enduring horrific life circumstances; I do know, however, that my class will never be a source of their trauma.

Although my early life was plagued by physical and structural violence, I managed to overcome structural barriers to become Dr. Ortiz. Education and gang membership took me from East New York to the Ivory Tower. Now that I know how toxic the Ivory Tower can be, I am determined to dismantle the Ivory Tower and develop a new structure that is welcoming of all people. Until my dying breath, I will fight on behalf of survivors of the criminal injustice system because no human being is beyond redemption. I am living proof of that fact.

REFERENCES

Anakwenze, U., & Zuberi, D. (2013). Mental health and poverty in the inner-city. *Health & Social Work*, 38(3): 147–157. https://doi.org/10.1093/hsw/hlt013

Anderson, E. (1999). *The code of the streets: Decency, violence, and the moral life of the inner-city.* New York: Norton W.W. & Company.

Anderson R. E., Geier T. J., & Cahill, S. P. (2016). Epidemiological associations between posttraumatic stress disorder and incarceration in the National Survey of American Life. *Criminal Behavioral Mental Health*, 26(2):110–23. doi: 10.1002/cbm.1951.

Berger, J. (1991). Dropout rate in New York shows decline. *New York Times.* Retrieved from https://www.nytimes.com/1991/06/13/nyregion/dropout-rate-in-new-york-shows-decline.html.

Blount-Hill, K.-L., & St. John, V. (2017). Manufactured "mismatch": Cultural incongruence and Black experience in the academy. *Race and Justice*, 7(2): 110–126. https://doi.org/10.1177/2153368716688741

Bolden, C. (2020). *Out of the red: My life of gangs, prison, and redemption.* New Brunswick, NJ: Rutgers University Press.

Brotherton, D. (2015). *Youth street gangs: A critical appraisal.* New York: Routledge.

Citizen, E. (2019). Inner city blues: Children raised in inner-cities face comparable PTSD causing conditions and consequences as military veterans and deserve our attention. Retrieved from http://dx.doi.org/10.2139/ssrn.3359012

Correia, D. & Wall, T. (2018). *Police: A field guide.* Brooklyn, NY: Verso Books.

Decker, S. H., & Lauritsen, J. L. (2002). Leaving the gangs, in C.R. Huff (ed.), *Gangs in America* (pp. 51–67). Thousand Oaks, CA: Sage.

Demir-Dagdas, T., Isik-Ercan, Z., Intepe-Tingir, S., & Cava-Tadik, Y. (2018). Parental divorce and children from diverse backgrounds: Multidisciplinary perspectives on mental health, parent–child relationships, and educational experiences. *Journal of Divorce & Remarriage,* 59(6): 469–485. https://doi.org/10.1080/10502556.2017.1403821

Dorahy, M. J. & Clearwater, K. (2012). Shame and guilt in men exposed to childhood sexual abuse: A qualitative investigation. *Journal of Child Sexual Abuse,* 21(2): 155–175.

Duany, J. (2012). *The Puerto Rican diaspora to the United States: A postcolonial migration?* Research paper presented at Center for Puerto Rican Studies at Hunter College. Retrieved from https://centropr.hunter.cuny.edu/sites/default/files/past_events/Jorge_Duany_Puerto_Rican_Diaspora.pdf

Edleson, J. L., Ellerton, A. L., Seagren, E. A., Kirchberg, S. L., Schmidt, S. O., & Ambrose, A. T. (2007). Assessing child exposure to adult violence. *Children and Youth Services Review,* 29(7): 961–971.

Fowler, S. K., Blackburn, A. G., Marquart, J. W., & Mullings, J. L. (2010). Would they officially report an in-prison sexual assault? An examination of inmate perceptions. *The Prison Journal,* 90(2): 220–243. https://doi.org/10.1177/0032885510363387

Gasper, J., DeLuca, S., & Estacion, A. (2012). Switching schools: Revisiting the relationship between school mobility and high school dropout. *American Educational Research Journal,* 49(3): 487–519. https://doi.org/10.3102/0002831211415250

Gray, D. M., Joseph, J. J., Glover, A. R., & Olayiwola, N. (2020). How academia should respond to racism. *Nature Reviews: Gastroenterology and Hepatology,* 17: 589–590. https://doi.org/10.1038/s41575-020-0349-x

Green, C. M. (2018). Against criminalization and pathology: The making of a Black achievement praxis. [Doctoral dissertation, CUNY Graduate Center]. CUNY Academic Works. Retrieved from https://academicworks.cuny.edu/cgi/viewcontent.cgi?article=3981&context=gc_etds

Holzman, E., Saidman, A., & Yellen, S. (Producers), & Russell, T. (Director). (2014). *The Seven Five* [Video File]. Retrieved from Netflix at www.netflix.com.

Human Rights Watch (2012). Decades of disparity: Drug arrests in and race in the United States. Retrieved from https://www.hrw.org/report/2009/03/02/decades-disparity/drug-arrests-and-race-united-states

Irwin, J. (1970). *The felon.* Los Angeles: University of California Press.

Irwin, K., Davidson, J., & Hall-Sanchez, A. (2013). The race to punish in American schools: Class and race predictors of punitive school-crime control. *Critical Criminology* 21: 47–71. https://doi.org/10.1007/s10612-012-9171-2

James, G. (1991). New York killings set a record, while other crimes fell in 1990. *New York Times*. Retrieved from https://www.nytimes.com/1991/04/23/nyregion/new-york-killings-set-a-record-while-other-crimes-fell-in-1990.html

James, G. (1993). East New York homicide breaks a deadly record. *New York Times*. Retrieved from https://www.nytimes.com/1993/12/20/nyregion/east-new-york-homicide-breaks-a-deadly-record.html

Johnson, K. R., & Johnson, J. (2012). Racial disadvantages and incarceration: Sources of wage inequality among African American, Latino, and White men. In J. J. Betancur & C. Herring (eds.), *Reinventing race, reinventing racism* (pp. 271–296). Leiden, The Netherlands: Brill.

Joldersma, C., & Perhamus, L. M. (2020). Stealing an education: On the precariousness of justice. *Teachers College Record*, 122(2): 1–24.

Kaiser, C. (1976, April 19). Blacks and Puerto Ricans a Bronx majority. *New York Times*. Retrieved from https://www.nytimes.com/1976/04/19/archives/blacks-and-puerto-ricans-a-bronx-majority-study-finds-blacks-and.html

Kohler-Hausmann, J. (2010). "The Attila the Hun law": New York's Rockefeller drug laws and the making of a punitive state. *Journal of Social History*, 44(1): 71–95. doi:10.2307/40802109

Krefting, L. A. (2003). Intertwined discourses of merit and gender: Evidence from academic employment in the USA. *Gender, Work, & Organization*, 10(2): 260–278.

Lee, B. X. (2019). *Violence: An interdisciplinary approach to causes, consequences, and cures*. New York: Wiley-Blackwell.

Mallett, C. A. (2016). The school-to-prison pipeline: A critical review of the punitive paradigm shift. *Child and Adolescent Social Work Journal*, 33: 15–24. https://doi.org/10.1007/s10560-015-0397-1

Mazza, J. J., & Reynolds, W. M. (1999). Exposure to violence in young inner-city adolescents: Relationships with suicidal ideation, depression, and PTSD symptomatology. *Journal of Abnormal Child Psychology*, 27: 203–213. https://doi.org/10.1023/A:1021900423004

Montalvo, T., & Ortiz, J. (2020) Perpetual punishment: One man's journey post-incarceration. In K. M. Middlemass & C. J. Smiley (eds.), *Prisoner reentry in the 21st century: Critical perspectives of returning home*. New York: Routledge.

Morris, E. W. & Perry, B. L. (2016). The punishment gap: School suspension and racial disparities in achievement. *Social Problems*, 63(1): 68–86. https://doi.org/10.1093/socpro/spv026

National Association of Criminal Defense Lawyers (2018). The trial penalty: the sixth amendment right to trial on the verge of extinction and how to save it. Retrieved from https://www.nacdl.org/Document/TrialPenaltySixthAmendmentRighttoTrialNearExtinct

NY CPL 720.35 Youthful Offender Confidential/Sealing.

Ortiz, J. (2017). Freddie Gray. In G. Robertiello (ed.), *The use and abuse of police power in America: Historical milestones and current controversies.* Santa Barbara, CA: ABC-CLIO.

Ortiz, J., & Jackey, H. (2019). The system is not broken, it is intentional: The prisoner reentry industry as deliberate structural violence. *The Prison Journal*, 99(4): 484–503. https://doi.org/10.1177/0032885519852090

Ortiz, J., & Jackey, H. (2021). Educational and skill-based prison programming. In J. Brent & L. Gould (eds), *Routledge handbook on American prisons.* New York: Routledge.

Pager, D. (2003). The mark of a criminal record. *American Journal of Sociology*, 108: 937–975.

Patton, T. O. (2010). Reflections of a Black woman professor: Racism and sexism in academia. *Howard Journal of Communications*, 15(3): 185–200.

Payne, A., & Welch, K. (2015). Restorative justice in schools: The influence of race on restorative discipline. *Youth & Society*, 47(4): 539–564.

Pearson, J. (2004). Building debt while doing time: Child support and incarceration. *Judge's Journal*, 43(1): 4–11.

Pilkington, A. (2012). The interacting dynamics of institutional racism in higher education. *Race, Ethnicity, and Education*, 16(2): 225–245.

Prison Policy Initiative. (2018). Out of prison and out of work: Unemployment among formerly incarcerated people. Retrieved from www.prisonpolicy.org/reports/outofwork.html

Régner, I., Thinus-Blanc, C., Netter, A. Schmader, T., & Huguet, P. (2019). Committees with implicit biases promote fewer women when they do not believe gender bias exists. *Nature Human Behavior*, 3: 1171–1179.

Roundtree v. *Brown*, 77 N.Y.2d 422, 427 (1991)

Savigny, H. (2014). Women, know your limits: Cultural sexism in academia. *Gender and Education*, 26(7): 794–809.

Schoneman, T. (2018). Overworked and underpaid: America's public defender crisis. *Fordham Political Review*. Retrieved from http://fordhampoliticalreview.org/overworked-and-underpaid-americas-public-defender-crisis/

Schwartz, A. E., Stiefel, L., & Cordes, S. A. (2016). Moving matters: The casual effect of moving schools on student performance. *Education, Finance, and Policy*, 12(1): 1–47. doi:10.1162/EDFP_a_00198

Stewart, R., & Uggen, C. (2020). Criminal records and college admissions: A modified experimental audit. *Criminology*, 58(1): 156–188.

Thacer, D. (2008). The rise of the criminal background screening in rental housing. *Law & Social Inquiry*, 33: 5–30.

Van Cleve, N. G. (2020). Radical compassion. *Contexts*, 19(4): 95–95. doi:10.1177/1536504220977952

Venkatesh, S. (2008). *Gang leader for a day: A rogue sociologist takes to the streets.* London: Penguin Books.

Weiss, D. C. (2019). This public defender was juggling 195 felony cases at once; "the workload can be overwhelming." *American Bar Association Journal*. Retrieved

from https://www.abajournal.com/news/article/this-public-defender-was-juggling
-195-felony-cases-at-once-the-workload-can-be-overwhelming

Weiss, K. G. (2010). Too ashamed to report: Deconstructing the shame of sexual victimization. *Feminist Criminology*, 5(3): 286–310. https://doi.org/10.1177
/1557085110376343

Whalen, C., & Vasquez, V. (2005). *Puerto Rican diaspora: Historical perspectives.*
Philadelphia: Temple University Press.

Williams, J. M., Wilson, S. K., & Bergeson, C. (2020). Health implications of incarceration and reentry on returning citizens: A qualitative examination of Black
men's experiences in a northeastern city. *American Journal of Men's Health*. https:
//doi.org/10.1177/1557988320937211

Wolff, N., & Shi, J. (2009). Contextualization of physical and sexual assault in male
prisons: Incidents and their aftermath. *Journal of Correctional Healthcare*, 15(1):
58–82. doi: 10.1177/1078345808326622.

Young, J. (1999). *The exclusive society.* New York: Sage Publications.

Young, J. (2011). *The criminological imagination.* Cambridge: Polity Books.

NOTES

1. The seventy-fifth precinct of the New York City Police Department has a
well-documented history of corruption. The precinct was the subject of many inves-
tigations that are highlighted in the documentary *The Seven Five*.

2. Chapters are local groupings of the larger gang.

Chapter 6

Navigating Survival

Contemplating Adversity and Resilience in Academia

Monishia Miller

My first semester teaching, I was nervous. It was only a few weeks back in the summer that I received a call asking me, no, telling me that I had what it takes to teach a research methods course at a university level. The confidence and certainty of the voice on the other line challenged my doubts at the time, and I distinctly remember freezing at this ask. My heart started to pound in my ears, and my brain kicked into gear. I recognized the feeling immediately: it was my warning system, an alert to be aware of the dangers that lie ahead. My immediate response was, "No, not me, there is no possible way that I am qualified enough to teach at a university." I began to run through my head all the reasons why I should not take this opportunity, and at that moment, a wonderful thing happened. The caller on the other line told me that I was full of shit and if I didn't have my ass up there to meet with the department chair before the start of the semester, I would regret it for the rest of my life. It was my mentor, a woman who I dared to be just like. She knew things that I didn't know. She could see for miles ahead because she was unafraid and had a map. Damn, why did she have to be right?! I took a deep breath, wiggled my shoulders, and said, "Yes, I'll be there. Thank you for thinking of me." It took everything in me to get to that interview because I was heading toward uncharted territory and it was scary! Not in a million years would I have thought that I would have an opportunity to become an instructor at a university. I harbored fear, uncertainty, and doubt, and I was sure that some-how, I was going to mess it up.

It was the first day of the semester, and I played over and over in my head all the questions, all the reasons why. Why did I skip breakfast? Why did I wear these shoes? Why did I say yes? I'm crazy, right? I must be crazy. Who in their right mind is going to believe that a previously homeless teenager, who's foster mother kept enough tabs on her to make sure that she not only graduated high school but became the first in her family to go to and graduate college, all while standing up against the monster that chased her in her dreams while she was awake, could do this?! Yes, it was the first day of the semester and I was feeling like a fugitive on the run, an intended, perfect pun as I made my way to my first class of the day. It was at the door that I noticed my heartbeat. It was racing but not in my ears or my brain. It was not trying to figure out an escape route. I paused. I had no time to define the feeling at that moment, so with my hand on the handle, right before I entered, I closed my eyes, took a deep breath, said, "Thank you, Lord," smiled to myself, and remembered exactly who I am.

My favorite superhero is Wonder Woman. She's strong and independent, and she fights for your rights in "tights and the old red, white, and blue." And let's not forget that she pretty much runs the Justice League. What I love most about her, and other superheroes, are their backstories. Mainly we see these stories emerge out of an experience that the superhero has had that changed their trajectory from obscure unknown, to right in the middle of a full-blown saga. Just like superheroes, we have our very own backstories.

My backstory starts on a cool dark night in my hometown, Oakland, California. I was born and raised there, and up until this night, had lived there my entire life. I was in the backseat of my foster mother's friend's car. It was eleven thirty at night, and my stomach churned with excitement and fear of the unknown. My foster mother sat in the front seat ahead of me, going through the checklist that we meticulously numbered and crossed off several times before. I could hear the pride in her voice; I was holding on to it for dear life. I could feel her support, which I needed to keep from passing out. And her love, oh her love for me was real, complete, whole, and now weaved into the tone of her voice. All the care and warmth that she had given me over the past few years had prepared me for this moment. My foster mother made sure that I wasn't leaving anything behind. We planned down to the minute details, right down to the clothes I was wearing, which were roomy and cozy. I needed to be comfortable for the trip; it was going to be an eight-hour bus ride. However, what she didn't know, but probably could have guessed, is that I had a plan of my own, one that was also meticulously put together. My plan did not focus on the trip. It focused on the idea that I would have the chance to reinvent the essence of who I am. I could stretch my brain power and be who I want to be. It was an ambitious plan. I would go to college, major in political science, run for student body, and begin my way to the governor's mansion.

Would my plan go smoothly, just the way I imagined it, or would it crumble? Only time and the bus ride would tell. Soon I would be able to leave behind the memories of heartache, disappointment, and discontent. I took a deep breath, smiled to myself, and wiggled my shoulders as I thought about my new life adventure in college. I had worked hard and overcome a lot of obstacles, and it was this moment, yes, this one, where I was off to create a new life. There was nothing and no one to stop me from living the life I wanted to live or from being who I wanted to be. Yes, this was it. I had planned the perfect midnight escape.

If you had asked me before I started college, I would have told you that I had a typical, normal childhood; except that I was born to an unwed, teenage mom, who was sixteen years old when she found out she was pregnant with me and had me when she was seventeen. I am an only child. I do not know who my father is. My mother and I lived with my grandparents, while we were growing up. My grandparents were hardworking, self-made people. They migrated to California from Texas in 1935. My grandmother was a strong, Christian woman who did not take any mess from anyone. My grandfather was a burly man whose voiced boomed when he spoke, which automatically commanded respect. He was a kind and gentle man, and for four years, they were our foundation. Then one day, the house swirled with confusion; everyone was upset. Various family members were in and out of the house crying and screaming. I was scared as I sat and watched the family trying to make meaning of what was going on. Their emotions moved from consoling each other, to fighting one another. I sat, watched, focused on the tight feeling in my stomach, noticing how alone I was, how not one family member looked my way. They did not tell me what was happening, but I had already figured it out. My grandfather was gone. At the funeral, I sat in the front row. I wore a blue ruffled dress, white tights, and a pair of black patent leather Mary Janes. Everyone commented on how cute and strong I was. I was not strong. I was four and I was scared. I had never done anything without my grandfather, and I wasn't sure what I was going to do now that he was gone.

After my grandfather's death my great uncle's voice began to cover me in ice. He lamented about how adorable I was and how we had nothing to worry about because he would be around. He would make sure that our grandmother, his sister, my mom, and I were taken care of. It was something in his voice that pressed against my chest, and gave me a weird, funny feeling. I was four when I learned what real, painful loss was, how family ties shift in ways that are unexpected and dangerous, and that I was the most adorable little girl my great uncle had ever seen. I look back now at this moment, and it is clear; at four years old my great uncle began grooming me for molestation.

It was some time after that my grandmother told my mom that she wasn't allowed to take me anywhere else and that she would have to leave me behind. I had started kindergarten and I needed to be home at night so I could get ready for school the next day. Shortly after school started my mom moved out. Her infrequent visits became no visits at all. I blamed starting kindergarten for my mom being absent from my life for a long time. Why would school, which I loved, prevent my mom from wanting to be with me? I was five years old when I first drank alcohol, started kindergarten, and found myself dealing with another profound loss. Looking at that moment now, I see how I entered a new stage of childhood. This stage set me up to be further at risk. The next few years of my young life would alter the course of any destiny that was predetermined.

My mother leaving left a huge hole that I filled with food. I was a chubby, loud, rambunctious kid and there was no question that my favorite treat was a McDonald's Happy Meal with an orange soda. My grandmother would buy Happy Meals for me as a reward for good grades, good behavior, being top helper at school, and following rules and directions. I loved school, it was a great way to get attention and recognition for doing well, and again, that Happy Meal was always the top prize. I was pretty good in all subjects except for reading. I had a hard time keeping my words from moving and changing positions on the page. It was awful. The kids at school would tease me endlessly and say that I would rather eat my books than read them. I was growing tired of the teasing, and weary of all the practice, until my grandmother gave me a Justice League coloring book. The coloring book was formatted like a comic book, and I could read without fail what the characters were saying. That's when it clicked! Spoken words are reading words. Yes, this was it! Now I could practice reading out loud. Conquering my main first-grade obstacle meant I could focus on drawing and coloring. Coloring helped me focus and soothe my thoughts after a long day at school. I would color and trace the characters in my coloring books over and over. Then I would draw them freehand on a separate sheet of paper. This practice made me good at drawing, so when my teacher read a story about a small town, she asked us to draw something she had read about for an art contest. I drew what I thought Main Street would look like in that town and I won the art contest. My teacher thought it was a good drawing and entered it into the school district art contest and I also won that contest. It was a big deal. I received the award at an assembly in front of the whole school. The feeling of having my named called and walking on that stage to receive my award gave me a much needed boost of confidence.

Later that same day, my great uncle stopped by for a visit with a Happy Meal. He had learned from my grandmother that I had won a big award and that this would be a good way to show how proud they were of me. I was delighted that she was talking about me and bringing it to his attention that I was a good student. My good grades and behavior were my shield at school.

They kept the physical bullies away. Now that my uncle was learning about how smart I was he too would stay away . . . or so I thought. Instead, he cornered me and showed me nude pictures of women, telling me how beautiful they were and that I was just like them. I had never seen a naked woman before he showed me, but I knew in my little mind that I looked nothing like the women in those pictures, it just made me feel strange and out of sorts, and I wasn't sure why he was showing them to me.

My great uncle started coming over more frequently and every time he would come, he would bring a McDonald's Happy Meal with an orange soda. He quickly became my favorite uncle because every time he showed up, he had a Happy Meal! He had also stopped cornering me and showing me pictures of the nude women. His language was the same about me being a beautiful girl, and about how pretty I was all dressed up, but that had become popular opinion. He and other members of our community would complement my grandmother on how lovely she'd dressed me, that I was such a lady.

One day when I was in third grade my uncle arrived, but he didn't have a Happy Meal! He asked my grandmother if it was okay for him to take me to McDonald's to get the Happy Meal and bring it back home. My grandmother said yes. I was excited! I did that annoying kid dance you do when you get something that your sibling doesn't . . . yeah, I was excited! I kicked back in the front seat listening to some oldies on the radio as we drove. When we arrived, I jumped out of the car like Batman in pursuit of Riddler. My uncle told me that I was a big girl now, and I could order a Big Mac, large fry, and a large orange soda. I was shocked! I couldn't believe he was going to spend all that money for a Big Mac, but he assured me that it was because I was a big girl and I deserved to get it. I agreed, ordered, and bounced happily back to the car. We pulled out of the parking lot and headed back home. The smell of the food teased me the whole car ride home. It smelled so good and I was hungry. My uncle asked about school and my friends. He praised me for being a smart, beautiful young lady, and reiterated several times that I was so grown up and that I carried myself well. I did not understand why he was saying all of this is. I thought to myself, "Well, yes, I'm a good girl who gets good grades. I do what I'm supposed to do because I have goals! I have to make it to the sixth grade." We arrived back at my grandmother's house and parked in front of the house. As I was gathering my things to get out of the car, my uncle grabbed my knee hard. I looked up because it startled me. Through his teeth, he said, "You need to understand how beautiful you are." *My heart started and my brain kicked into gear.*

"Okay, but you're hurting me," I said. He softened his grip of my knee and with the other hand, he reached and opened the glove compartment, pulling out a folded-up magazine. He opened it to a page that was worn and dogged eared, and there she was, in full color. Her legs were spread wide open, her face twisted into an expression that I did not comprehend. Her hands were touching forbidden places. Fear struck me, hitting me in the dead center of my chest. I thought I was going to die. I took a deep breath to catch air, to catch my fear. I was on the move.

He grabbed my arm hard and said, "You're going to understand how beautiful you are, you understand me." I was terrified; my brain would not let me comprehend what was happening. All I wanted to do was run but I could not move. Then he said, "You're going to appreciate how beautiful you are, because you are just like her." My body tightened. *What's wrong with my arm?* "Let me go. I need to run!" I screamed. It seemed a lifetime. He was not releasing me and I was terrified. I need to get away but how do I get away? *Is this real? Is that picture real or am I imaging it? Why can't I piece together what's happening?* I'm sitting there looking at this woman spread eagle and I'm now connecting the dots. Then fear turned to calm . . . Something clicked.

"Okay, but you know you need to let go because you're going to snap my arm," I said. And he let me go. I grabbed my things quickly and got out of the car. I rushed in the house and my grandmother was pleased that we were back safely. She noticed me but she didn't actually *see* me. I'm sure my eyes were screaming what my mouth could not put together. *She didn't see me.* She noticed that I was holding my food and told me to go to the table to eat. I was still struggling to figure out what happened. I sat there staring into space, trying madly to connect the dots, to figure out the pain in my arm. I could feel my heartbeat in my ears. *What did I do? How could I have let this happen?* I didn't have an appetite. I was eight years old when my great uncle first assaulted me.

After the incident in the car, automatically, whenever I heard his voice, my heart would start and my brain would kick into focus. I used this alert as my personal warning system. It was now my responsibility to stay safe. So I made sure to stay with my grandmother when he came around. By now, my mother was back and in and out of the picture. She would occasionally pick me up and I would spend some weekends with her. It was a relief to have some space where I was not worried about my surroundings. My mother had a steady group of friends that she hung around, and just like the old days, there was music, alcohol, drugs, and food. Minus the alcohol and drugs, I would dance, eat, and DJ the parties that my mom would have at her place when I stayed with her. I was nine years old when I partied with my mom and her friends. She was twenty-six. I would continue bouncing between her house and my grandmother's house until I was twelve years old.

Going between my two homes, I picked up a few habits and behaviors that my grandmother didn't like. One of those was wearing jeans. She was a very traditional woman and wearing pants was not ladylike, but my mom was okay with me wearing pants because I would climb, run, jump, and play in dirt. I would hang with the boys at school and in the neighborhood. We would challenge each other's strength, to see who could run the fastest or make it to the second bar on the monkey bars in one leap. Yes, I was building my strength like a boy because I was responsible for keeping myself safe. Then one day I got in trouble. I can't remember exactly what happened or what I did; I just remember that I was sent to my grandmother's room because that's where I slept most nights at her house, to take a nap. I was bent on not going to sleep. I was going to spite her. I must have been tired, because I fell asleep. The next thing I remember was waking up to being molested. I could not see him, but I knew it was him. I laid still, playing like I was asleep. I was devastated because I had failed at keeping myself safe. I remember trying to roll over in the bed, trying to get away from him, but he caught me by my ankles and pulled them apart. I couldn't get away. I just laid there, paralyzed. The next thing I remember is standing next to the bed. I was free, but I was standing next to the bed, watching as it happened. I just stood there, watching, as I broke into pieces. I was ten years old when my uncle sexually assaulted me.

I was eleven when I ran out of hiding spaces. I would get caught every time, and I would have to do more "tricks and treats" to get released. Some days, I wouldn't hide. I would just wait until my grandmother would leave and for the game to begin. That summer, everything changed. I turned twelve and my mother came, packed all my belongings and moved me in permanently with her. We lived in a two-bedroom above-garage apartment. We didn't have much furniture, but it was awesome because we were together. I was old enough to catch the bus alone, so I would still spend a lot of time in my old neighborhood. The freedom to run with my friends and explore the city became the theme of that summer. I loved watching boys stumble over my girlfriends, trying to get their digits—back then that's what we called a phone number. My mom still had her steady crew of friends and they still partied, but with a bus pass in hand, I was able to escape to my old neighborhood and spend time with my friends. The next few years of living with my mom would enlighten me to not only why she was never around, but why she thought the best place for me was my grandmother's house.

My eighth grade school year flew by fast. I would finally be at the high school with the homegirls and I was in a great place mentally, physically, and, dare I say, spiritually. My mom and I were living in the same home. Our apartment now had furniture and I had my own room. She still loved to party. Sometimes, the grocery money went to partying, but I didn't care; the end-of-the-month baloney and cheese sandwiches were good. Besides, my grandmother was still living in my old neighborhood, and if push came to shove, I would go there for a hot meal. On my last day of eighth grade, I went straight home to change and waited for the time to head out and meet my friends. As I walked up the driveway that led to our apartment, I looked up and noticed that our front door was slightly opened. My heart started and my brain focused. Time itself seemed to slow down. I slowly pushed the door open, and with a sigh of relief, I found my mother sitting on the edge of her bed, crying. She was holding a red bag in her hand. I walked slowly toward her and called to her. She looked up, with tears in her eyes, and said, "I must stop now. This is going to ruin my life." I looked down at her hands and recognized that the red bag I thought she was holding was blood, and that both of our lives were heading in a direction that I didn't want to go. My mother was holding a broken crack pipe. After finding out that my mother was doing drugs, life got complicated, but by this time I was equipped enough to dig in my heels and focus on surviving. That summer I spent most of my time between my best friend's and my grandmother's houses. At times I would go and check in on my mom to make sure she was alive. She had a new boyfriend that creeped me out. I was now a pro at picking out creepy men, and he and I never saw eye to eye.

Summer was over and it was time for high school. I got involved with the student body, clubs, JROTC, and other community programs. It was during this time that a good friend of mine introduced me to a program that helped underprivileged, low-income students gain the skills necessary to apply and go to college. The program sounded amazing and fun. It allowed high school students to stay over the summer in college dorms, while taking college courses. During the school year, students would take two college courses on Saturday. My first summer in the program was after my freshman year in high school, and I opted to stay in the program the whole summer, meaning I did not go home on the weekends.

The program was amazing. The resident assistants had movie nights, ice cream socials, and game nights in the dorm. The program counselors had all the resources you needed to succeed in high school and college. The professors were fun, encouraging, and resourceful, and our tutors were all about making sure that we had A's in all of our classes. On the last day of the program, we all packed up, said our goodbyes, and waited for our rides home. I waited and waited for my mom to pick me up, but she never came. I called her in advanced to remind her to pick me up, so when she didn't come, I thought she forgot. I was livid as I called all the numbers of her friends I could remember, trying to track her down. I had no luck, until I called one of her friends who announced to me that my mother had moved to Atlanta, Georgia, and she thought that my mom took me with her. What? This is crazy, she moved out of the state?! She didn't forget; this woman was ruthless. My mother had taken the opportunity while I was in my program to marry the creepy boyfriend, pack up her apartment, and move to another state. I was fifteen years old when I became homeless, and the reality of my survival was now all on me.

I called a friend who I knew had a car and asked if he could give me a ride to my mother's friend's house. I was aware that I would have to keep my cool because he liked me. That day he was an unaware lifesaver. I was able to spend a few weeks with my mom's friend, but I was not allowed to stay permanently because they were a military family. I told my mom's friend that I would stay in Oakland with my grandmother, so I could be closer to school, and that I would be okay. The truth about staying in Oakland was that I was couch surfing from friend's house to friend's house. My grandmother's house had fallen into disarray and there was no one there to take care of either her or the house. I was just too young to realize she needed a caretaker, so I kept moving. Eventually my friends' parents told them I had worn out my welcome. I went back to my grandmother's house and found out there was no electricity. I called my grandfather and told him that he needed to come and care for our grandmother and he told me that he would but first, I needed to get lost. I ended up staying the rest of that year with a good friend of mine. We had grown up together in the neighborhood and her parents knew my mom, so they invited me to stay with them. It was the end of my sophomore year when my foster mom heard that I was on the street, or at least I didn't have a permanent place to stay. She knew me because her family and my family knew each other. She was aware that my mom had moved and left me here. She'd reached out to me through a student who was at my high school. The message was for me to stop by and see her. That day was emotional. She got right to business and began caring for me on the spot. She had already talked to my mom and summoned her to California. She didn't need her to stay; she just needed guardianship. If it were not for her taking me in, I would have been lost forever. I was fifteen years old when my foster mother took me in, and she made sure that every day after that it was possible for me to dream.

***

One of the first classes I took in college was Introduction to American Government. I was super excited to take this class because I saw it as the start to a long political career that would begin with me as a lawyer. I'd run for office to become a senator and eventually governor. College was a challenge, but it wasn't the kind of challenge I was used too. I had been through a lot before I arrived on campus and I had built up a skill set that allowed me the flexibility to thrive even during hard times. However, this time, I couldn't quite figure out why my grades had slipped from excellent in high school to just average in college. I also didn't understand the culture of my campus, which was nice but not as welcoming as high school had been. I enjoyed my classes. I learned new theories and ideologies, and about how a lot of now dead guys formed our perfect union.

One day, I walked into class and noticed that I was the only Black student in the class. *Why had I not noticed before?* I sat down, took out my notebook, and made eye contact with my TA, and, at that moment, *my heart started, and my brain began to kick into gear. What? How could this be happening?* I felt pressure closing my throat, fear rising from my feet. I was trapped, but it made no sense. I was in class and had to get through the lecture. I fought to stay present, but I lost it. I grabbed my things and ran out of the class. The air hit my face, sweat trickled down my back, and I stumbled to the nearest tree for support to stay on my feet. *What the hell just happened?* I was eighteen years old, and I just had my first panic attack.

I returned to my government class for the next meeting. I decided beforehand that I was not going to make eye contact with my TA. I also decided that I would sit a few rows back to make sure that there was a buffer between him and me. I also wanted a better lay of the land, where I could catch any misunderstandings before they triggered another response. I had not figured out why I was triggered in the first place, but it was still fresh in my mind that it was only forty-eight hours beforehand that I had run out class like a mad woman. It was also clear that I had to figure out a way to keep it together to get through the quarter. I walked in and took my seat. The TA immediately called on me, but I was not ready. I was still recovering from the panic attack and I hadn't prepared for class. He repeated the question, and I answered honestly, "I don't know. I had an emergency and couldn't prepare for class." Then his face switched. I felt his look before he even spoke a word. *My heart started and my brain kicked into focus*, but this time, I was in familiar territory and something new happened. A hot streak rose from my core. My reaction was not to flee but to stand firm.

"I'm going to tell you now, so you don't have to waste your time. Black women have no place in political science," he said calmly. I lost it! I pushed the desk in front of me away. Then I pushed the next row aside and I got in his face. Immediately chaos ensued as my classmates pulled me away. I was yelling and screaming, and he was yelling and screaming back. Once I was outside, another student handed me my backpack and I stormed off. I needed air and a plan. I was sure after that scene I was going to get kicked out of college.

It turned out that I had someone in the class who thought I was treated unfairly. He took it upon himself to find me and convince me to get help. He said that I should go to the advising office and ask to take my final in there. When I met with the advisor, I told her what happened and about how I was now afraid that I would not be able to stay. She assured me not only that I was going to stay, but that I would also be able to go back to class if I wanted to. I did not want to go back to class, so she gathered all my assignments and my final to take in her office. She set a meeting for me to come back, and when I did, she had all the assignments and my final. To this day, I am grateful that

I was able to complete the course. I am also grateful that the confrontation with my instructor happened. Looking back, I can see now how that moment prepared me for a journey that I didn't know I was going to take.

At the beginning of the next quarter, I sat in my advisor's office deciding my next steps. I needed to figure out a different way to reach the governor's office. Despite the craziness at the beginning of the school year, it was still within reach. My advisor suggested that I step back and take a quarter to explore other classes. She convinced me that it was going to be good grades and my LSAT score that would get me to law school, not necessarily my major. I enrolled in an introduction to sociology class. Sociology quickly became my point of interest, and the next quarter I enrolled in a sociology class called Criminological Theory. My professor for this class was different than the professors I had previously. He had a lot of energy and it was obvious he was excited about what he was teaching, which made the class inviting and fun. Time flew by in that class. We always ran out of time. We used articles and books that were fun to read and he gave amazing examples. What stood out most was how much he cared for us as students. We were using a popular criminology textbook, but it was out of my budget, so I was using the copy that was on library reserves. One day during lecture, the professor sat the textbook, a notebook, a pen and pencil on my desk, and kept lecturing. I didn't mind. We needed the book for this lecture, so I was grateful for the loan. After class I walked to the front of the class to thank my professor and to return the book. Without a beat he said, "That's not my book." I was immediately confused, and said, "Yes, it is, you sat it on my desk during lecture." With a smile he said, "No, I didn't. That book was there all along." Then it clicked. I thanked him for the book and the supplies and left the class. I cried all the way to my dorm because for the first time in my life, I was seen. It altered my perception of people, life, college . . . everything. I wanted to be just like my professor, kind, caring, compassionate and confidential. He knew I needed the textbook and supplies. Did he also know that I was a former foster youth, first-generation college student, and survivor? I was thinking through all the possibilities as I stood in line at the advising office, applying to change my major from political science to sociology.

I worked hard in my new major. There was a lot to learn. I read everything I could pick up and piece together that gave me an understanding about sociology, criminology, and criminal justice. Just as I was learning all these new concepts and theories, I was learning that I was a good student. The exciting new life I planned had changed course, and it looked as if it were crumbling. What I thought was a crumbling was actually the beginning of my calling. Still, I had to focus on surviving, so I quickly switched into survivor mode. It was time to buckle down and get my degree. I needed to graduate. So I was focused on surviving when a friend asked me if I was looking for a job. She said the group home she was working for needed an overnight case worker. I didn't know anything about group homes, but I told her I was interested and agreed for her to bring me an application. Since I had no knowledge of group homes, I called my foster mom to see if she had ever heard of group homes. She said, "Yes, silly, you would have been in a group home if I didn't take you in!" Like a flash, I connected the dots. I told my foster mother about the opportunity to work at a group home. She was excited because I was going to help kids who were just like me. I was excited because I was looking at my senior year and I needed a job. My friend brought me the application and I filled it out on the spot. Within a week, I was interviewed and hired.

The group home I worked for was a network of homes across the county. The organization had six houses in total, three for girls and three for boys. The home I worked in was in a great neighborhood. What fascinated me the most about this group home was that the neighbors knew we were there, but if the girls weren't loud, obnoxious, or a nuisance, they left us alone. Group homes are set up to give minors a home-like environment to give them a stable placement during treatment. Our minors were diagnosed with serious emotional disability (SED). The programs we were administering were for sober living, life skills, and high school graduation. Another colleague and I added a community college component to the program. My first day on the job was busy, but I had found my calling. I was going to help and advocate for youth who were neglected, abused, and abandoned. Working in the group home was rewarding and reflective. It reminded me of the support my foster mother provided me. She made sure I had financial assistance, education, and occasional pep talks about how I was going to be okay. I could see and feel that she wanted me to succeed. What she poured into me is what I brought to my work every day in the group home. I understood each juvenile because they reminded me of myself. I wanted to be seen, heard, and loved—the exact same thing they wanted too. It was in this position that I learned how to connect with others like me, and learned to be open and observant to the needs of those who had experienced adversity and trauma in their lives.

I worked in that program for a total of two years before applying to the county probation department and graduate school. I was accepted into graduate school and was hired for the probation job simultaneously. This was very exciting, but I had some big decisions to make. I had decided to apply for graduate school because I knew it would give me more opportunities to serve in the community. Having a master's degree would open job opportunities that would eventually give me the ability to change policy and procedure. While working with minors in the group home, I learned about the laws, policies, and procedures that affected their daily lives. I wanted to be a part of changing policies that caused more harm than good. I decided to accept both the probation position and my spot in the graduate program in criminal justice administration at California State University, Los Angeles.

My first year of graduate school, I commuted between school and work. At school, I had found my groove, but on the job I had a lot to prove. It took six months for me to stop being a floater and find a permanent unit. I was placed on a unit where the minors had dual status, which meant that they had a case in both the child welfare and juvenile justice systems. The unit was minimum security, and we had a lot of opportunity to counsel them one-on-one or in groups. Working on the unit was much like my time in the group homes, but in juvenile hall, your skill set was tested. The minors were facing a different set of challenges that could take them away from their families, and the way they processed their experience with crime and trauma was different than the minors in the group homes. My team and I worked well together and the unit ran smoothly but more than often we were dealing with outbursts and defiant behavior. It was time to get creative. One of my team members decided to offer the incentive of a movie night if we could go a week without any incidents. I added, that if we were able to get the whole unit on board with the movie night, we should pick one minor we could build a rapport with. If we could get these kids on board, we could use them as leaders and have them model the behavior we wanted to see on the unit. The ideas worked and our unit turned around! We had the fewest behavioral issues compared to other units and I saw every action film created.

Juvenile hall was more policy and procedure and there was not much one could do for a minor outside of what the law and the courts ordered. Because of this, I simply learned how to listen and take note of the stories minors shared with me. It taught me a lot about how people process violence and trauma. I did not know at the time but this skill set would help me later.

It was not long after our unit turnaround that my team was split up. We were good, and if you were good, you got sent to a unit that's not so good. I was never again placed in a unit where I would bond with my team. I was now unit to unit and burnt out. Floating was wearing me down, and so was my commute. Something had to change. One night, I was working a double shift and I was bone tired; the only thing keeping me afloat was a comment that my graduate advisor made on my recent paper. He wrote, "You can write." That one comment focused me, acknowledged me, and destined me for something greater. That night in the hall, we were at all hands on deck because we were shorthanded. Officer Johnston was called in to assist in operations. He was a probation officer that worked with the gang unit. He commented on how well the unit ran and thought I made a great partner. He also commented that I should look into applying for the field. I would make a good probation officer. What happen next was deliberate, honest, and life altering. First, I told him I was in school working on my master's degree in criminal justice. Next, he commented that I would have made a good probation officer, but working on my master's degree in criminal justice would put a target on my back. The powers that be wouldn't let me near a promotion if they got wind that I had a master's degree. Being a woman was already working against me. Now add being Black and showing up smarter than everyone else in the room, he said, "Yeah, you're going to get blacklisted." *Deep breath, hold for four seconds, exhale.* He said what I already knew. Why else would I be floating from unit to unit, updating, organizing, implementing, and creating as I went?

This territory was familiar, and the only reaction I had was, "here we go again. I have had this conversation before." You see, being a Black woman in the criminal justice field is not easy. Most of the time when you show up, your presence, intelligence, qualifications, and humanity are questioned and challenged. Most of the time, you are not recognized for your hard work and contributions. However, this time was different because it would be the deciding factor. I needed to make a move. I would finish my master's degree and go back into the community. Working in group homes for juveniles who were on probation and/or neglected, abused, or foster youth was work that I enjoyed, and now, I was going to be able to look for opportunities where I would also be able to utilize my degree. It was a challenge getting a position in community corrections programs. You needed a lot more experience than the time I had in corrections, and if not, you needed more credentials. I count it lucky that I saw an ad for a research associate at the University of California, Riverside for a school-based program for youth smoking cessation, and even though this program was not criminal justice related, it was working with a risk factor for youth. This position would give me the opportunity to develop my skills in research and evaluation. I couldn't believe I got a call for an interview. I got the job with the condition that I would complete the certification to become a youth advocate.

I completed my youth advocate certification and started my position as a research associate. Part of my job was acting as a liaison between a nonprofit organization, a school district, and the lead researcher at a university. Since I had experience working in the field and in the community, I had a good understanding of what it takes to have a successful team. Everyone would have to work together to build a team that had good leadership, communication, and flexibility. This project was the first partnership between the university and a community-based nonprofit, and since the target audience was minors, the stakes were high. My job was to make sure the parties understood the details of the research grant and the procedures for implementing the grant. We were doing road shows at local high schools educating students about tobacco use. Working on the grant with the university and the school district, I learned just how flexible you need to be. The school superintendent and the principal investigator had a different approach on the topic, which made them bump heads on a lot of the program outcomes. It was up to me as the liaison to mediate conversations between the two and come to a compromise. We were thirty days into our first outcome, when it became obvious that the school nurses should have been at the table from the start. After that meeting, I made sure that if I were mediating between the two top stakeholders, the school nurse would be the third. Including the school nurses made our program outcomes reachable: they tied all the health variables with juvenile risk factors together and we were able to collect great data on youth and tobacco use.

I had found my niche working in community-based programs, and my skill set on how to prepare and organize research and program evaluations made the work rewarding and lucrative. I enjoyed having a great foundation in understanding nonprofits, community-based organizing, and program implementation. It was not until we started our next project that my childhood experiences would come into focus. The idea of the project was to explore teenage attitudes on sex education. This was an interesting topic because sex education had been removed from most public schools, but we were able to find a couple of high schools who still had sex education in their curriculum because they had a high rate of teenage parents.

In a preliminary survey of all the high schools, we found that students wanted sex education. They wanted to learn how to use protection against sexually transmitted diseases, prevent pregnancy, and if you really got hairy hands from masturbation. Yes, it was the early 2000s and that myth was still floating around. I was in the middle of scanning surveys when I flipped one over to scan the backside, and a question caught my eye. The question read, "Will sex education tell you how to deal with your boyfriend pressuring you to have sex?" I felt the pressure in my chest first, then my heart started to pound in my ears, and my brain kicked into gear. I was triggered by the question. Working in the field with youth who had childhood adversity as myself taught me coping mechanisms that helped me focus on adapting stressors and noticing spaces for healing. Yet in this moment I thought of me . . . the little girl who dealt with the pressures of being afraid, molested, and tossed to the side. Sitting with this image and feeling made me sad. I was determined to shake it off and get back to work, but the feelings needed space and time. I lowered my head and began to cry.

One of the challenges of our new program was getting parents to buy in. Parents did not want sex education taught in "their" schools, so they rallied and pressured the district to shut down the project. They were afraid that sex education would lead to their children having more sex and experimenting with drugs. I thought it was ludicrous and felt that if the students had the education about sex, they would be informed and able to protect themselves from pregnancy, sexually transmitted infections, and sexual harm. The parents were successful in getting the district to abandon the project. It was now time for me to stretch, expand knowledge, and deal with what these parents refused to face. Our youth needed and wanted sex education, but it was clear this would not happen through the district. I shifted gears again.

I applied to become a victim advocate with a community-based organization. I was on call for health education workshops and the sexual assault hotline. It was with this organization that I learned how to form support groups and facilitate trust circles. It was also where I would learn to deal with my past and the pain of sexual abuse, feel the weight of how that affected me, and build the foundation to move toward healing. I learned to not be afraid to move freely about the world with a different approach to what happened to me, and to dream of a world built for me. It was then, I decided through sleepless nights, doubts of worth, and tears, that I would take my adversity and build a secret lair, one complete with the tools and resources that would deter and incapacitate any obstacle that would not allow me to understand my experience and heal. I knew that in my healing, I would be helping others to do the same.

Years later, I was working in the field as a youth advocate for minors who were in foster care and as a school safety officer for a K-12 school district. It had been almost a decade since I left probation, but the skills I learned in juvenile hall, being a youth and victim advocate, were useful when working with students. It was in these two positions as a school security officer and a youth advocate that I would use my own childhood experiences to help the kids I was working with. Basically, my approach to all issues about kids in trouble was to make sure that I did not leave out that I was once in their shoes, and since I wore those shoes, their success was my success. It was in the transition of being on patrol to being stationed at one campus, that I got the call to come and teach at Cal State Fullerton. I couldn't believe it! The voice on the other end of the line was telling me that I was more than qualified and that she had confidence that I could do the job, and with that expressed, I said, "Yes." After I hung up, I immediately thought, "What did I just do?! What was I thinking?" I closed my eyes, took a deep breath, held it for a few seconds, and exhaled. Yes, I am sure, the call was for me.

I had no idea how I would make it through my first semester at California State University, Fullerton. My uncertainty was not rooted in my abilities. No, it was coming from my instincts—a vibe—that my very existence would be questioned. One of the things I have gained from my childhood, is the ability to read people. It's a safety check. I observe, you show me who you are, and I believe it, and adjust accordingly. In the field, I mastered this skill. I was, at times, the only woman or the only Black woman on a project. The university was a challenging space because faculty worked individually. The lack of collaboration was different than working in the field or the community. My department was mostly white and male; thus, I would have to learn to navigate this space with my safety check in place. I had to figure out a way to thrive and be successful in this environment, making sure that I had support and a mentor who could guide me through what it means to be a faculty member. I was able to build a good support system by joining faculty and professional associations, and I had an amazing mentor who guided me through the ins and outs of faculty life. I also tapped into the professional development resources on campus. I became successful at managing and teaching my classes and navigating faculty life. I believe that success lies in my resiliency and in being true to who I am.

Staying true to who I am is what helps me thrive professionally and personally. The truth is that I am a first-generation scholar. I have experienced homelessness and foster care. I am a survivor of sexual abuse and assault. All of this makes it sound like a negative and dismal past, but it is nevertheless my story, one that I share to connect and build relationships in the community and in the classroom. One of the lessons I learned in the field is that you can't help someone who doesn't trust you; you must build rapport and make a connection. Once you gain trust, you can plan, build, create, and succeed. I have embodied the lessons I have learned about building a connection with my students by sharing my story and had it lead to my success and theirs. Over the years, sharing my story has created a safe environment for learning and debate. It is embedded in how I show up in the classroom. My childhood and young adult life experiences prepared me with the tools to be an instructor who can see beyond the textbooks. I appreciate how my instincts and training work together to spot a student who is in distress and has given me the kindness and caring to ask the right questions. It has also prompted me to make sure that my classroom and office are safe spaces and that there are resources for students to connect to on campus.

It has been a long road in my journey toward healing, I have learned how to use my childhood experiences to navigate spaces that could challenge my stability and need to be safe. I tap into my own needs and wants, my insights, my faith, and my skill set in every interaction with my students. I would have never guessed that everything that I had experienced in my childhood and in my young adult life would apply to how I show up in the classroom. Remembering my first day and how nervous and unsure I was, I couldn't even imagine the kind of impact I would make. That little girl who scrapped and scraped to protect herself became brave. She took an eight-hour long bus ride, by herself, to pursue a dream. When she was told she wasn't worthy or couldn't make it, she decided to press on and create her own path, deciding for herself as a young corrections counselor, that she knew her calling was something bigger. She took a chance and branched out, reached out to victims, and shared her story—her whole story. And when the field, a new journey called for her, she took the call.

It's the first day of the semester, and I'm playing over and over in my head all the questions, all the reasons why. Why was that breakfast sandwich the bomb with my iced tea? Why are these shoes so cute? I'm crazy, right? I must be crazy to be enjoying this busy day. Who in their right mind is going to believe that a previously homeless teenager, whose foster mother kept enough tabs on her to make sure that she graduated high school, who became the first in her family to go to and graduate college, who stood up against the monster that chased her in her dreams while she was awake, could do this?! I paused. I had years to define the moment. Who in their right mind would believe? Hand on the handle, right before I enter, I closed my eyes, took a deep breath, smiled to myself, and remembered exactly who, ME.

Chapter 7

Survivor of Death by Incarceration
Life without Parole (LWOP)

Steven Green

I believe to inform you of what being a survivor of a sentence of life without parole means to me, I must first address a few things. Almost thirty years ago, I was involved in a murder/robbery in which a person tragically lost their life. The victim's family is forever changed because of my actions/inactions that night. I regret every decision leading up to their murder, and I am sincerely remorseful for the harm I have caused. In telling my story, I do not wish to revictimize those familiar with the details, so I have not included them here. My account is about how I was sentenced to LWOP at eighteen years old for my role in that night's events and my journey to surviving the past three decades as a lifer (people sentenced to life in prison).

My knowledge about trauma and recovery is primarily based on the experiences and collective wisdom of trial and error from thousands of Californian "lifers" trying to heal from their childhood trauma while still living in a trauma production center (i.e., prison). I am also learning as a student of criminology how the different criminologists' theories both apply and fail to align with my lived experience. Understanding your childhood trauma and its effects on your life is a requirement for the California Board of Parole Hearings. The effects of these events have different names—character defects, causative factors, and contributing factors. To have a shot at reentry, you need to have vital insight and understanding into these issues. I demonstrated at my parole hearing that I had adequate insight into my childhood trauma and the maladaptive coping skills I developed that allowed me to take part in a murder/robbery. The parole hearings used to be in person—now they are held over Zoom. There are two commissioners, one district attorney, one lawyer for the incarcerated person, the incarcerated person, and up to ten victims/survivors.

During my parole hearing, the commissioners asked about my childhood, the level of education I reached prior to my incarceration, any violent encounters, drug and alcohol use, involvement in gangs, and any prior criminal behavior. After all the static factors of pre-incarceration are fully explored, the commissioners went through and discussed my in-custody behavior. Their review started from the day I entered the California Department of Corrections and Rehabilitation and worked their way through twenty-eight years of incarceration. They asked about my parole plans, my relapse prevention plans, and my new prosocial coping skills that had replaced my prior maladaptive ones. They also wanted to discuss how much community support I had for this transition. I had a lot, over seventy-five letters from organizations, friends, family, and the most important support reference, my letter of commutation from Governor Brown. This strenuous process determined I did not pose a current danger to public safety and I was granted parole.

I recognize that my childhood traumatic events helped shape the way I saw and reacted to the world. People are complex and not one-dimensional. I am a survivor—of domestic violence, gun violence, and gang violence. I am a survivor of a system that thought I should spend the rest of my life behind bars. I am also a father, husband, brother, and college student. Informing someone of my traumatic experiences is not excusing my choice to act a certain way. It is saying that I felt my options were limited, which is why I chose that path. I believe a traumatic experience is like a car crash. It affects all the occupants of the car differently. This analogy is how siblings can grow up in the same house and experience the same traumatic experience, but cope differently with this trauma.

INSIGHT INTO MY CAUSATIVE FACTORS

My mom was pregnant with me at fourteen years old and had me when she was fifteen. Within a year of my birth, I was living with my grandparents. This was the beginning of the back-in-forth between my mother and grandparents. I spent kindergarten with my mom, first grade with grandma, and second grade was split between the two of them. The moving between their houses never got any better. My mom and grandma also moved between my bouncing around. This meant different schools and teachers and no friends. Due to the frequent moves in my life, I developed the feeling that nobody wanted me, even though they told me they loved me. My biological father wasn't a part of my life until I was in the fifth grade. I only knew him for about six months before he died in a traumatic accident. His sudden death left me with a deeper feeling that I was alone.

My mom was both a victim and a perpetrator of domestic violence. My mom's choice of men was horrible, to say the least. I watched my younger sister's dad take a carburetor and beat my mom with it, putting her in the hospital. He went to prison for that, but they got back together when he got out. In her subsequent relationships, I saw my mom being abused by the various men she dated. Watching my mom being victimized by the people around her, I developed an emotional numbness or callousness towards domestic violence. It is how I could cope with the pain. As I grew older, I became emotionally detached as I dealt with the violence I witnessed, heard about, and experienced. I also blamed myself for not being able to protect my mom from her abusers.

Given my mom's experience as a victim of abuse, I suppose it's not surprising that she was also physically and verbally abusive towards my sister and me. Research has documented that younger parents, parents suffering from substance abuse, single-parent mothers, and families where the father was not biologically related to all the children are common factors in cases of co-occurring domestic violence and child abuse (Hartley, 2002). All those factors would describe my household while growing up. My mom had two types of abusive behaviors. The first type of abuse was a triggering event, like me misbehaving or breaking something. For instance, when I stuck a quarter between an extension cord and a TV, it triggered an outburst. The result was a blown-out TV. She beat me so badly I was not allowed outside, and if someone came over, I was told to hide. Another example is when I threw a football while inside my cousin's house and broke a picture frame. I was punched repeatedly in the face by my mother and told to sit in the car until she was ready to leave. During the ride home, and once at home, my mom dished out a few more punches. These events sent the message that if I did something my mom did not like, she would beat me until she felt I had gotten enough. As I grew older, if I did something wrong, I would not go home, or I would leave home before she got there. When I ran away and then came back, I realized my mom was so happy to have me home that all was forgiven.

The second type of abusive behavior were outbursts, which were the hardest to deal with; they were random, sudden, and unpredictable. There were times my mom would just burst into my room and start hitting me with the belt and break whatever was within her reach. These incidents really struck fear in me. I could not make sense of what happened. I would often ask myself, "What did I do?" These incidents reinforced my feelings that nobody loved me or wanted me around, particularly my mother. It felt like I was just there for her to punch on or whip until both of her arms got tired. My mom usually broke things I cared about (e.g., Lego® toys, Nintendo®, the game cartridges, and trophies). That caused me to lose interest in things I liked to do as I thought she would just break the stuff anyways. A couple of months before my arrest, my mom was diagnosed with premenstrual dysphoric disorder (PMDD).

During the summer after fourth grade, my self-esteem and emotional health was struggling. I had moved back with my mom. My mom lived in one of the worst places in Long Beach: poverty-stricken, gang-infested, and drugs were sold right in front of our house. When I went outside to play, some kids were nice; others called me "White boy," even though I told them my name was Steven. The way the kids said "White boy," it felt like they were insulting me. It felt derogatory, even though I did not understand what I had done or why they were calling me that. Later, when I went home, I asked my mom, "What race am I?" She replied, "Mexican." The next day, everybody laughed at me when I told them I was Mexican. I was the only "White" Mexican anybody had ever seen. Shortly afterward I started getting into fights. One day after school, I came home from a fight. My mom asked me what happened, and I told her, "Everybody says I'm White." It was shortly after this incident that I met my biological father and his side of my family. My birth father looked White—like me; however, he spoke Spanish. He also told me, "We are Mexican, just lighter than most." My racial identity was no longer a question for me; now I *knew* I was Mexican. As I began to embrace my Mexican identity, I expected others to recognize it too, which led to some emotional outbursts. I continued to get upset when people called me "White boy" for years to come. I was angry because people didn't see me or believe me. As people met my sisters, the doubts would go away as they "looked" Mexican. But anytime my heritage was questioned, I would challenge them to a fight. Not surprisingly, getting into fights often got me into trouble.

Drugs were also a regular presence in my childhood. As far back as I can remember, my mom sold and used drugs. Her various boyfriends also engaged in those activities. I was told by my mom, "If the cops ever ask you if there are any drugs in the house, you say no." This created my distrust for authorities. I remember in the fifth grade, coming home from school helping my mom grind rock cocaine into powder cocaine. She would weigh it and then I would put it into paper envelopes. This continued for about two years until her drug connection was arrested. Even though I processed the drugs for sale, I was never directly involved with her selling drugs. My stepdad was also in the drug trade as a trafficker, but he never directly involved me in his activities. My mom told me she only sold drugs "to make ends meet." My stepdad said he did it "to make pocket change." As I grew older, I believed it was okay to break the law to make money by engaging in these behaviors.

My criminal history began by stealing quarters from my mom. I stole other things as I got older, for example, skateboards, bikes, and cars. When my stepdad caught me and my friends sanding and painting stolen bikes, he asked me, "Where did the bikes come from?" I replied, "We found them."

He told me to finish what we were doing and get the bikes out there because we could not bring the cops to the house. As my criminality grew, I would trade various stolen items for other stolen items or for drugs—which I would then sell. When my stepdad would see the stolen stuff, he had one of two reactions. He would take something for himself, or he would just take everything. My friends and I called it "the big homie tax." Nevertheless, I believed I was doing the right thing by making my "pocket change" as it was normal behavior. My mother or stepdad did not punish me for my criminal behavior.

While I didn't have very many positive influences while growing up, two men had a positive effect on my life: my stepdad and my grandfather. My grandfather was always good to me. Unfortunately, I never thought of him as a role model, even though he would help me with every sport my grandparents enrolled me in and helped me with my schoolwork. But the strongest male influence that I had was my stepdad. While I understand now that he did the best he could at the time, he had his own faults. He was the biggest male role model and the most influential person in my life, and he was also involved in gang life. He was the only man who never hit my mom. He also helped me deal with my mom's episodes of anger. He thought he was helping by making me "street smart." He also gave me advice about girls. He made me feel loved and cared for, unlike the guys my mom usually dated.

He brought me to a park where I could play basketball and hang out with Mexican kids my age. He also introduced me to his friends (older gang members) and to kids my age (young gang members) as his son. This introduction gave me instant acceptance among everybody at the park. He started taking me to the park about three times a week. I quickly noticed a couple of things. My stepdad Rick became "Chino." I became "Steven, Chino's son," and as a result, there were no longer any questions of me being Mexican or not. The guys Rick introduced me to all had similar tattoos, and the park was their gang turf. I started to realize that no matter where I lived or how many times I moved, this group of friends would always be there. As a kid who had bounced around between my mom and grandparents, this felt like stability. I finally belonged.

As the months went on, I noticed most of the guys at the park were hustlers. They either sold drugs on the corner or stole from cars. Some did burglaries and pretty much anything you could do to "make" money. Research in criminology has long documented the relationship between gang membership and criminal behavior (Thornberry et al. 2003). I witnessed some guys getting "jumped-in," and I thought it was not that bad—my mom had done worse to me. The day I had decided to get jumped was when two friends and I were at a fast-food place across the street from the park. Five members of a rival gang got out of a car and jumped us. Afterward, my friend told me that

I should get jumped-in because people are already treating me like you were from our gang.

LIVING WITH BEING SENTENCED TO LIFE WITHOUT PAROLE IN PRISON (A.K.A. THE WALKING DEAD)

I have read many attempts to explain what it means to serve life without parole. Every single one has missed the mark, and mine may fall short as well. As an eighteen-year-old, I didn't understand the sentence of life without the possibility of parole. I had no point of reference to judge just how long that meant. I knew it meant forever or until I died. At eighteen, what does that mean? It meant the beat goes on. My life was now about my new world within the California State Prison system, where people with LWOP make up about 4 percent of the total incarcerated population in the state (CDCR, 2019). I was sent to Calipatria State Prison, a level IV maximum-security prison. At the time, it was the newest prison that opened in California, and it felt like the wild west. Everyone was fighting to establish dominance, and this included staff. Needless to say, I fit right in. For about the first five years or so, I was still acting in the same way that led to my incarceration.

Then one day, I walked out onto the prison yard, and my focus went right to this older man who had a hunch in his back. He was walking back from his work assignment with some freshly pressed blues over his arm. At that moment, I thought that was going to be me. That little voice we all have, mine screamed, "Hell NOOOOOO!" Literally, from that moment on, I knew I *had* to change. I was unclear on *how* to change or *what* exactly to change. I even debated *why*, considering that an LWOP sentence does not care if a person changes. Nonetheless, I did change. I started with the things like personal growth and hoped that no one would see these changes. Some might ask why I hoped no one would see these changes. In a level 4 facility, the prison culture expects you always to be who you were when you first entered the unit. To risk appearing soft or weak could bring negative attention and threaten your safety. I refrained from stealing things that people had left unattended. I stopped talking about people behind their backs, which had only brought me negative consequences in the past. Over time, these behaviors became easier for me, but there was still one major decision left—how do I stop being a gang member? After all, I was housed in a facility that was specific for gang-affiliated individuals. How do I leave that identity behind when it is reinforced every day by the institution and those inside?

Ultimately, I was able to move to a different yard, which allowed me to move away from the gang identity and discover who I was outside of that lifestyle. Around 2000, I helped start a self-help group. The group was focused on team sports to help develop a sense of community. Participants were also required to enroll in anger and stress management courses. Being part of a team-based activity required us to put these conflict resolution tools to use. In 2009, Calipatria State Prison started allowing some community colleges to send in correspondence courses that allowed me to work towards an AA degree. At first, I only took one class, which quickly led to four classes every semester. By 2016, I had earned five AA degrees and one AS degree, all with honors from Coastline Community College. I completed every degree Coastline offered to us. Then I started the programs through Palo Verde College, where I enrolled in a speech class. That speech class changed my life. My instructor brought in photocopies of some topics that we were supposed to design a speech around. The packet I grabbed was purely random, and I had no idea how much it would ultimately change my life. The packet was about Project Rebound at California State University, Fullerton.

Project Rebound is a program that began in 1967 at San Francisco State University and provides support to formerly incarcerated individuals. Project Rebound was created by Dr. John Irwin, who had served a five-year sentence for his role in a gas station robbery during the 1950s. During his time in prison, he earned college credits through correspondence courses. After his release, he completed his bachelor's and doctorate degrees at University of California, Los Angeles and University of California, Berkeley. Today, the program is offered at fourteen of the twenty-three campuses within the California State University system. Students who participate in the Project Rebound programs have a higher retention rate following their first year of college than the general university population. Eighty-seven percent of participants have either secured full-time employment or have been accepted into graduate programs following the completion of their undergraduate degree. Between 2016–2020, Project Rebound scholars had a 0 percent recidivism rate (Project Rebound, n.d.). The articles in the packet that I grabbed from my speech instructor highlighted the work of the director of the CSUF program, Romarilyn Ralston. She was formerly incarcerated and had earned her master's degree. The articles shared how she was now helping returning community members navigate the higher education experience at Fullerton. I kept the articles after the class was over for inspiration, not knowing the impact it would have for me later.

I continued taking courses in psychology and addiction studies. I was very fortunate to enroll in Adams State University in Colorado through a correspondence course. I traded my standard monthly canteen money and my quarterly packages from my family to enroll in courses that were quite expensive ($600 per course). The first class I enrolled in was victim advocacy. Like my speech class, this course had a significant impact on me. This is where I learned that my childhood traumatic experiences equated to me being a victim/survivor. Research consistently highlights that exposure to high rates of trauma increases the likelihood of arrest, spending time in jail, and being sentenced to prison (Jaggi, Mezuk, Watkins & Jackson, 2016; Wolff & Shi, 2012). For me, it created a duality of opposing labels. The state labels me as a convicted violent offender for the harm I caused, yet I was abused and victimized way before anything "criminal" occurred in my life. The first label is the hardest to peel off because few look beyond the moment when the harm was caused. The second label is quickly dismissed because of the harm I caused. This brings me back to my point that people are complex. On my new discovery of being a victim/survivor, I started asking my friends inside about their childhood. As it turns out, every one of them went through traumatic experiences growing up, or they were victims in one way or another. Yet none of my peers saw themselves as a victim or identified with this label. If I asked them, "Would you consider yourself a victim?" the reply almost always was no, and the more people who were around during these conversations would increase the odds of a "no" response. To imply that you are a victim would be to display weakness in an environment that thrives off exploiting such vulnerabilities. After taking the victim advocacy course, a program called Healing Action and Dialogue came to the prison yard in which I was assigned. Healing Action and Dialogue is a non-profit organization that does restorative dialogue circles, and the facilitators would bring a survivor into the prison to share their experience. My first time sitting there, I heard from a woman named Nora, whose son was murdered in a drive-by. That was the first time I had ever come face to face with the harm I had caused. I pictured Nora as the mom of the harm I had caused. Up until that point, remorse was an abstract concept. I had already made significant changes to my life and way of thinking by the time I met Nora, but she brought home the reality of the effects that I never saw but only imagined. Our justice system is adversarial from the beginning. There are separate sides of the court room. The victims/survivors cannot talk to me, and I cannot look at them. The two sides are separated and remain that way throughout the process; this includes incarceration. I was sentenced to life without parole. When am I able to see and hear the pain and harm I caused from the victims/survivors? How am I able to make amends for the harm I caused? Not to mention from the point of my arrest till my last day in prison I was surrounded by people who have been convicted of causing harm and are masking their pain and harm done to them. As my friends and I worked through our trauma, we learned how to forgive ourselves for the harm we did to others. We learned to forgive people who victimized us. There is never a time when we can offer healing to those we impacted the most, our victims/survivors.

I have been in a lot of these restorative circles now, and one of the most prominent sayings I have learned is, "Hurt people hurt people, and healed people heal people." Walking out of a powerful session and onto the yard, I only saw people who had unresolved trauma to work through. Today, I still see our prison population the same way. I believe working through unresolved trauma is very difficult in a trauma-producing center (i.e., prison). Since coming home, I have been working through the trauma of being incarcerated for twenty-eight years where there was no hope for me to come home for a long time. If you recall, I described that at eighteen, LWOP means that the beat goes on. At thirty-eight, LWOP felt like I was a zombie just staggering through life with no purpose. No matter how much I changed, there was no going home ever. Some people could earn time off their sentence for good behavior, working, attending self-help classes, earning a GED, taking college courses, and earning a vocational trade. None of this applied to me as someone with a sentence of LWOP.

In California, there has been a lot of criminal justice reform in the past ten plus years. Yet each of these efforts largely ignored the issues of LWOP sentences. No politician wanted to admit that LWOP was worth addressing. They would be perceived as being soft on crime, much like how Michael Dukakis was portrayed during the 1988 presidential election. As a result of the U.S. Supreme Court decision in *Miller v. Alabama* (2012), which held that mandatory LWOP sentences for juveniles were unconstitutional, California introduced and ultimately passed two pieces of legislation on juvenile LWOP. Senate Bill 9 (SB9) allowed anyone under the age of eighteen at the time of their crime and sentenced to LWOP to petition and be resentenced to twenty-five-to-life. This resentencing would allow those cases that had previously been denied the opportunity for parole the ability to appear before the parole board (California Senate Bill 9, 2012). In 2017, Senate Bill 394 further revised SB9 to effectively end juvenile life without parole (California Senate Bill 394, 2017).

While these bills focused on juvenile LWOP, they did not impact my case as I was eighteen years old at the time of my offense. Cases like mine were excluded from consideration under these juvenile LWOP reform policies, even though research shows no significant difference in cognitive capacity and brain functioning between an eighteen-year-old and someone just a few months younger (Johnson, 2019). Such studies also may not acknowledge the role of trauma in this process. In recent years, California's laws started to change, which shifted people's hope towards being able to go home. In 2018, I applied to Governor Brown for commutation based on all the work I had done and the changes I had made over the past twenty-six years. My petition was approved, and my sentence was reduced to twenty-six years to life. This meant that I was now eligible for parole, which I was ultimately granted. I was released from custody on September 21, 2019.

SURVIVING LIFE AFTER LWOP

When I was enrolled in that speech class, I never realized how that speech on Project Rebound would ever impact my life. On my first day out, I went straight to the John Irwin House to meet everyone part of Project Rebound. The John Irwin House is the first transitional residence for formerly incarcerated individuals navigating higher education in the United States. I missed a peer-to-peer meeting with all the Project Rebound members that day by an hour. I returned on Monday and my eight-month stay living at the house began. While the semester had already begun at California State University Fullerton (CSUF), I was encouraged to enroll in some computer courses to help me catch up with the rest of the world. My first semester at CSUF was in spring 2020. I had enrolled in several classes and was doing well. Then with about two months left in the semester, COVID-19 came and changed our lives. The campus was shut down and everyone was trying to adjust. While adjusting to the online learning curve, I was admitted to the hospital for a medical emergency that stemmed from an issue that was largely ignored for over ten years while I was in custody. As a result, I had to withdraw from my classes. That first semester felt like a complete waste of time, even for circumstances beyond my control. The following year was a bit of a yo-yo for me academically. In some courses, I thrived. In others, I struggled because of these health challenges. I felt I was treading water and making no progress academically. This was hard as I wanted to graduate with my bachelor's degree and apply for Ph.D. programs to be a college professor. Meanwhile, my internal clock was ticking as I just wanted to move forward. I am constantly wondering when my health will take a turn for the worse in the back of my mind.

Despite my anxieties, one of the lessons I learned from serving LWOP is perseverance. In addition to pursuing my educational goals, which include working towards my bachelor's degree with majors in criminal justice and public administration, I am heavily involved in criminal justice reform in California. I volunteer with the Anti-Recidivism Coalition's policy team (a group of formerly incarcerated individuals) to help transform the language around criminal justice legislation. I am a state-wide organizer for Families United to End LWOP (FUEL), which supports families who have loved ones serving LWOP and other extreme sentences. I am a part of the National LWOP Leadership Council through Human Rights Watch. I also keep in contact with many men up and down California who are currently incarcerated, and I have gone back into prisons trying to deliver the message of hope and provide much needed information on the commutation process and the Board of Parole Hearings process.

During the twenty-eight years I spent in prison, I learned a lot about the challenges I faced growing up and how they impacted me. As a teen, I thought I found stability from joining a gang. I was very wrong. I first learned about stability at Calipatria State Prison. It took me two decades to understand what it meant to be a pillar in the community. I was involved in helping younger men, who were incarcerated with me, not to make the same mistakes I had and encouraging people to stop using drugs and participating in violent acts. I overcame my abandonment and low self-esteem issues by learning that self-worth and confidence come from within, not from others. As I grew older, I reflected on my parents with empathy and understanding of how immature my parents were mentally, dealing with their own trauma, addictions, criminality, and being young parents. They did what worked for them, which clearly was not always the best decision. When I was young, I was forced to deal with the effects of domestic violence any way I could. Leaving the house meant not being in an abusive environment, so I stayed away a lot. I was seeking control of my life, trying to gain a sense of autonomy. I have forgiven my mom for her abusive behavior. I now know that violence is never the answer to solving a problem. Over my twenty-eight years of incarceration, I have learned to use my words to iron out disagreements. I have seen how violence affects victims, and I will not put anyone through that again. I regret ever being violent to anyone for any reason. My regret and shame for my role in a murder, coupled with my unwillingness to harm anybody, forced me to learn how to use my words.

The biggest challenge to my reentry was learning who I was outside of prison. I had to be a father, husband, and brother. All the examples that I had to date were far from the best. I also had to figure out who forty-six-year-old Steven is. All my points of reference were from eighteen-year-old Steven's viewpoint. Being a husband and a father for six hours during visitation made me the perfect husband and father. My wife came to see me every other weekend for about seventeen years. During those six hours, I gave my undivided attention to my wife and kids. Everyone was on their best behavior. It was naive of me to think that this is how they act all the time. I came home to two teenage girls and a wife full of expectations. I quickly realized that I had the chance to work on myself and resolve my childhood traumatic experiences while incarcerated. Meanwhile, my wife and girls did not. My wife had a lifetime of trauma to work through, from her involvement in the foster care system, and the incarceration of her stepfather, brother, and husband. The longer I am away from prison, the more I realize that my prison experience was traumatic, and now I need to heal myself. Over the course of my twenty-eight years in prison I have witnessed multiple stabbings, seen my friends get shot with a mini-14, and other violent acts. I lock every door in the house whether it's day or night. It brings me the sense of security of my cell door being locked and no one being able launch a surprise attack. I still need to see as much of my surroundings as possible, to determine where the threat may come from and have an exit plan just in case something bad happens. The harder things to adjust to are the inhumane treatment for over two decades. Being thought of and treated less than a human, animal, and anything else that should be treated with compassion and dignity. That is just the tip of the iceberg. My wife and girls are discovering ways to heal from their traumatic experiences. My girls' trauma is directly related to my incarceration. In their earlier childhood they believed all the daddies were in a special place that was far from home and wore blue uniforms. As they grew older, they had to keep my incarceration a secret. They felt ashamed that their dad was in prison, even though they did not do anything. My girls were paying for the sins of the father. This makes parenting and being a husband a little more complicated, especially since I am the root cause of some of their trauma. When arguments arise, these traumas come to the surface. It's been two years since my release and the relationships with my wife and girls are strengthening every day due to a lot of work and commitment by all of us.

Life without the possibility of parole is just the death penalty by another name—death by incarceration. It is designed to crush your soul. I am not sure if I have survived LWOP yet. While I am free, my fight continues.

REFERENCES

California Department of Corrections and Rehabilitation (CDCR) (2019). Offender data points for the 24-month period ending in June 2018. Retrieved at https://www .cdcr.ca.gov/research/wp-content/uploads/sites/174/2021/06/201906_DataPoints .pdf?label=Offender%20Data%20Points%20Report%20June%202019&from =https://www.cdcr.ca.gov/research/offender-outcomes-characteristics/offender -data-points/

California Senate Bill 9 (2012). https://leginfo.legislature.ca.gov/faces/billNavClient .xhtml?bill_id=201120120SB9

California Senate Bill 394 (2017). Retrieved from https://leginfo.legislature.ca.gov/ faces/billNavClient.xhtml?bill_id=201120120SB9

Hartley, C. C. (2002). The co-occurrence of child maltreatment and domestic violence: Examining both neglect and child physical abuse. *Child Maltreatment* 7(4): 349–258.

Jaggi, L. J., Mezuk, B., Watkins, D. C., & Jackson, J. S. (2016). The relationship between trauma, arrest, and incarceration history among Black Americans:

Findings from the National Survey of American Life. *Society and Mental Health* 6(3): 187–206

Johnson, S. (2019, March 20). Why is 18 the age of adulthood if the brain can take 30 years to mature. Retrieved at https://bigthink.com/mind-brain/adult-brain

Project Rebound (n.d.) Retrieved at https://www2.calstate.edu/impact-of-the-csu/student-success/project-rebound

Thornberry, T. P., Krohn, M. D., Lizotte, A. J., Smith, C. A., & Tobin, K. (2003). *Gangs and Delinquency in Developmental Perspective.* Cambridge University Press, Cambridge, UK.

Wolff, N., & Shi, J. (2012). Childhood and adult trauma experiences of incarcerated persons and their relationship to adult behavioral health problems and treatment. *International journal of environmental research and public health,* 9(5), 1908–1926. https://doi.org/10.3390/ijerph9051908

Chapter 8

Growing as an Intersectional Scholar Means Rejecting Misogynoir

Unlearning as an Act of Survival

Toniqua C. Mikell

Those of us who stand outside the circle of this society's definition of acceptable women; those of us who have been forged in the crucibles of difference—those of us who are poor, who are lesbians, who are Black, who are older—know that survival is not an academic skill. It is learning how to take our differences and make them strengths. For the master's tools will never dismantle the master's house. They may allow us temporarily to beat him at his own game, but they will never enable us to bring about genuine change. And this fact is only threatening to those women who still define the master's house as their only source of support.

—Audre Lorde (2007, p. 112)

Every Black feminist, including those who have colonized and appropriated the work of Black women scholars while simultaneously oppressing Black women, knows Audre Lorde's quote "The master's tools will never dismantle the master's house" (Lorde, 2007, p. 112). Most of us have interpreted this to mean, generally, that the tools used for our oppression cannot be used to liberate us from the oppressor. I extend that narrative here by framing *the tools* as patriarchal white supremacy, which maintains *the house* of criminology. I interrogate the assumption that success in criminology is attached to submitting to the master's tools. Experiencing, learning, and internalizing the biases of the discipline is trauma (Winters, 2020), and healing from that trauma includes a process of unlearning. In this way, I engage survivor criminology as a trauma-informed approach to the study of crime and justice and as a trauma-informed pedagogy that is necessary to undo and offset the misogynoir that is embedded in the discipline itself.

This edited volume understands survivors as people "who have had close personal encounters with institutionalized oppressions based on racism, heterosexism, and poverty" who heal through "translating their close encounters with trauma into a platform for advocacy" as stated in the introduction. Those of us *forged in the crucibles of difference* are subject to control by those who wield power. Scholars who are products of that fire situate our work—our teaching and research—in service to freeing ourselves and others like us. There is an element of surviving the academy that is enmeshed with surviving misogynoir. Even while I write this chapter as a survivor of criminology, I write from my position as a survivor of sexual assault and intimate partner violence. I suspect that sadly my experiences are not unique. It is through these parallel experiences as Black women across class, gender, and sexuality spectrums that we have survived the world and thus survive criminology.

SURVIVAL IS NOT AN ACADEMIC SKILL

The first criminology undergraduate program was founded in 1916 at the University of California at Berkeley as a bachelor's degree granting program for police officers (Oliver, 2016). The evolved anti-carceral abolitionist I am now often considers how I came to identify so deeply as a criminologist. A discipline that studies institutionalized power structures that control, criminalize, and kill people like myself is no place for me. How did I get here?

My life plan was law school, early on, but after flopping on the LSAT I decided to shift gears. That test was miserable, and I absolutely could not sit through it again. A master's degree and a state job with the Department of Probation, Parole and Pardon Services was my backup. I wanted to be part of the justice system and affect change from the inside. I was unsure of what kind of change I would be creating as a probation officer surveilling and waiting for people to break the law. Looking back on it, probation officers are cops and I absolutely did not want to be a cop. Perhaps, I thought that being a good cop would matter. Amid that identity crisis, my brother was arrested and incarcerated. Everything I thought I knew or felt about the legal system was shaken and confused. Around that same time, my mentor and advisor during my master's degree suggested that I consider a doctoral program. Being a probation officer felt wrong by this point and I had no other plans. I was closing in on finishing my thesis and had not yet figured out the next thing. A doctoral program seemed like a good idea. I really had no clue what kind of misogynistic position I was setting up for myself by staying in graduate school.

Some of my most unpleasant graduate school memories took place in my criminology theory courses. White male professors. Self-appointed gatekeepers to advanced degrees in *their* field. Obviously, most sectors in a capitalist society demand competition and, for some, the only way to win is to convince others that they have no business in that space. I especially acknowledge the notorious power of imposter syndrome in every corner of the academy, which seems to be most potent among graduate students. But for me, in those classrooms with those professors it was suffocating. The sort of white male gaze that minimized everything it touched was different. It was painful. It was cold. It was invisible violence that reminded me that I did not belong in that space. In hindsight, the joke is on me, though, because these same professors praised the "genius" of *The Bell Curve*. Clearly a missed red flag on my part. Back then I dismissed the discomfort as my own sensitivity to the exposure of being the token Black person. As I have grown, unlearning misogynoir, for me, has meant unlearning impostor syndrome. It means silencing the voice telling me that my white male peers are better than me, despite every proof of their mediocrity.

Fast forward to the first semester of doctoral school when my car is stolen for the second of multiple times. According to Murphy's Law anything that can go wrong, will go wrong. This means that my car was stolen the night before my final theory paper was due. I emailed my professor explaining that while walking my dog, I had discovered a strange man in my car rewiring the ignition to steal it. Between being shaken from that surprise, interacting with the police—which is traumatic for Black people anyway—and dealing with the car insurance company, I really could not focus on finishing that paper. I asked for an extension from 5pm that evening to the universal academic standard of midnight. I was told no because it would be unfair to my peers if I had more time. Notwithstanding, my peers did not have their cars stolen that evening, but the professor was sticking to rules. I submitted what I had and accepted whatever came of it. I would later find out that one of my classmates, a white male, had plagiarized much of his paper and was allowed to "revise and resubmit with proper citations and resources." Yet I could not receive extra time in light of my incident. The legitimate trauma that I experienced as the victim of a crime and the subsequent interactions with police was insignificant to the larger goals of preserving the white patriarchal supremacy of the discipline.

In addition to surviving straight white men who gatekeep the discipline, as a Black woman scholar, I have had to survive the very curriculum of criminology. For sure, my survival has meant a begrudging acceptance of the racist, heteronormative, elitist, sexist explanations of crime that have been taught to me by agents of whiteness who also judge my work through their white-informed lenses. For example, many of us learn about Cesare Lombroso and his scientific approach to identifying the criminal man by observing physical and biological markers of difference (Lombroso, 1876/2006). This is the white-washed version of early positivist criminology that myself and others have learned, and, by virtue of our credentials, are expected to teach to those who aspire to learn criminology. What we do not learn about—at least I didn't—are the racist motivations for this work. I was teaching criminology theory as a faculty member by the time I learned that Lombroso's science was adopted in the United States as a direct critique of slavery abolition.[1] It both caused and sustained fear of emancipated Black people. Lombroso's theory of the criminal man provided scientific proof that dark-skinned people in Italy, and by extrapolation, Black people in the United States, were inferior humans and prone to criminality. This connection was never presented during my time as a student. Thus, I have had to accept the knowledges of the field that center *white*ness, further marginalize minoritized people, and dismiss the reach of institutionalized racism, sexism, classism, and xenophobia. However, there is peace in unlearning. Unlearning for my survival has meant compartmentalizing the facts of foundational criminology literature as pieces of information presented by *white* men for *white* men, those who historically and presently police access to education and information and use science as justification for oppression (Lynch, 2000).

Unlearning misogynoir means rejecting the essentialist "facts" of the field. It is possible to teach the history and foundations of criminological scholarship and acknowledge the reality that those foundations are racist, sexist, and elitist. They are the foundations built on the criminalization of status quo disruption, thereby criminalizing the rebellions of my ancestors and revolutions of the Black women before me. I wholeheartedly reject those propositions! As a queer Black woman, my survival in the world demands that I reject the idea that my existence and demand for equity is criminal. As an intersectional criminologist I position my work to explore and disrupt the social structures that criminalize and victimize Black women (Potter, 2015). Therefore, I cannot survive within *the house* of criminology by utilizing *the master's tools*—unchallenged acceptance of foundational criminology—because *they will never enable us to bring about genuine change*. Thus, my survival in the in the academy and in all social spaces, requires that I reject the notion that my presence is deviant.

During graduate school I always carried a certain level of discomfort where I regularly doubted my presence in most spaces. Despite knowing then what I know now—that Black women are the most educated bloc in America—I still felt like I had no business in a doctoral program (Katz, 2020). I was in a doctoral program when most people in my family were done with school after their high school graduation. Furthermore, I was *the* Black girl in my program. The only one. If I made it, we all made it. But if I didn't, then Black women everywhere were unfit for criminology Ph.D.s and I was the empirical evidence of that. Obviously, no one ever said those words to me, but individual Black people have always been perceived as the representative of the entire race (Jackson et al., 1995). One of us cannot fail because that would mean that all of us are failures. I was qualified to be in this space. Why did I feel otherwise?

The stress of tokenism has physical and mental health ramifications (Winters, 2020). On top of that, graduate students' mental health is already a documented mental health crisis (Barreira et al., 2018; Evans et al., 2018). The pressure that I had assumed upon myself is rooted in misogynoir. In this instance, an internalized misogynoir. The culture of grad school coupled with the institutionalized misogynoir of the academy plunged me into the darkest depths of physical and mental health chaos, never mind the anti-Black sexism that was part of my everyday existence in the Bible Belt of the United States. Nonetheless, I made it. I survived and my continued survival informs the way that I operate in the classroom and other academic spaces.

UNLEARNING MISOGYNOIR MEANS REJECTING THE ESSENTIALIST "FACTS" OF THE FIELD

If we accept one of the larger goals of criminology to be understanding what causes crime so that we can prevent it, it is incumbent upon me to situate my research and pedagogical approaches towards the liberation of Black women across all socioeconomic backgrounds and gender and sexuality spectrums. Therefore, I cannot present mainstream criminology as the definitive answers to solving crime because mainstream—white-male, heterocentric—criminology does not present a full understanding of power structures or identity politics (Delgado & Stefancic, 2017; Potter, 2015; Unnever & Gabbidon, 2011).

Within criminology we often deal with theories developed by white men in the course of studying white men and boys. Then, at some point in our engagement with the theory we talk about weaknesses and strengths. The weaknesses tend to address something along the lines of the theory not having the strongest explanatory power for some population or instance that it was truly never designed to explain. For example, the field's dominant general theories—strain (Agnew, 1992), control (Gottfredson & Hirschi, 1990), and learning (Akers, 1998)—were developed and tested based on the lives and deviance of white men (Isom Scott & Mikell, 2019). For women's criminality the assumption is that one could just add women, run the same models, and the results would have the same explanatory power. Of course, feminist criminologists have rejected this approach by highlighting the social position of women in a patriarchal society and the vastly different socialization processes for boys/men and girls/women (Belknap, 2001; Broidy & Agnew, 1997; Daly & Chesney-Lind, 1988; Isom Scott & Mikell, 2019). Furthermore, Black feminists, critical criminologists, and intersectionality scholars know that this difference in social positions extends far beyond the experiences of men versus women (Crenshaw, 1989; Potter, 2015; Russell-Brown, 2009; Williams & Battle, 2017). To engage with the study of crime "scientifically" while ignoring the historically and contemporarily ingrained power structures of who and what is deemed criminal is an affront to reality.

Mainstream theories of crime, at least in the early stages, observed the actions of white boys and men to explain why individuals within the power majority engage in deviant behaviors. With privilege stacked in their favor how and why do these young white men come to a life of crime? Meanwhile, Black people are perceived to be inherently criminal by virtue of just being Black. White people within a settler-colonial-driven society have attributed Black folks' deviant behavior to a natural trait of Blackness (Isom Scott, 2020). Therefore, historically, Black people's criminality did not necessitate theorizing because crime was considered just part of who we are. Those of us who are observant know better. It almost seems laughable that this same approach—one rooted in misused privilege—would be applied to Black folks, especially Black women, who in many ways live far outside the power majority with minimal innate privilege.

Misogynoir is a building block for mainstream approaches to crime. On the one hand we have anti-Black racism embedded in the development of criminological theory. On the other hand, we have sexism etched into our patriarchal social structure and the criminalization of women who do not conform to acceptable expressions of femininity. Therefore, Black women *who stand outside the circle of this society's definition of acceptable women* are simultaneously lumped into the label of criminal and excluded from explanations of crime. These frameworks cannot be used to understand us nor can they be used to free us from the oppression of a patriarchal carceral state. Growing as an intersectional criminologist means centering that reality because *the master's tools will never dismantle the master's house.*

My survival in the world demands that I reject the idea that my existence and demand for equity are criminal. In that same spirit, I must reject the "empirical data" or "evidence-based findings" that there is something inherently criminogenic about being a Black person or expressing Black culture. Criminology is not the end-all-be-all to understanding what "causes" crime. Those explanations are colored by the theorists and scientists who provided them. For me, within the general discipline of criminology, a straight white man's analysis of crime, justice, and socialization cannot be the loudest voice discussing Black women's criminality, victimization, and criminal legal system processes, mainly when white men's work seldom includes actual Black women. The way mainstream theories of crime understand culture is rooted in white, middle-class, hetero-patriarchal norms. Those norms do not apply to those of us who live at the intersections of otherness, oppression, and stigma.

Black people have endured generations of trauma that continues to impact our existence today (Degruy-Leary, 2017). In my scholarship and pedagogy, crime, victimization, and carceral state violence against oppressed people are personal, and those who live in the margins know that *the personal is political.* Therefore, while I respect the groundwork of mainstream criminological research and theory, as a Black woman, these works do not speak for me nor do they represent the sociopolitical navigation of Black women. As an intersectional criminologist, I utilize "a perspective that incorporates the intersectional or intersectionality concept into criminological research and theory and into the evaluation of crime or crime-related policies and laws and the governmental administration of *justice*" (Potter, 2015, p. 3). Thus, studying crime in a way that centers the experiences of privileged people within a system that feeds on the underprivileged is counterproductive. The study of the legal system must be informed by the lives of those who are most egregiously victimized by it—the survivors of that system.

CONCLUSION: THE MASTER'S HOUSE IS NOT THE ONLY SOURCE OF SUPPORT

When I was a graduate student instructor, an undergraduate student I had in class mentioned tying in an assignment for my class with another project for another class. One day she asks me how she can present her work in her other class without coming across as the crazy, angry Black lady because that class was not as "woke" as our class. I looked her in the eyes and told her that a Black woman armed with facts will always be the angry Black lady.

It is an otherworldly experience when one gives advice that they struggle to incorporate in their own life. How could I mentor a young Black woman intent on changing the world when I regularly minimized myself to be acceptable to my peers? How do I encourage her to speak her truth despite its reception, when I had consumed the proverbial Kool-Aid of criminological "truth" and was building a career feeding that same Kool-Aid to others? Hearing my own words of affirmation come out of my mouth to that student was a significant turning point for me as an emerging insurgent scholar. That was one of many ah-ha moments where I began to understand that I can exist within criminology without contributing to the white male supremacy of discipline.

Learning how to do that has been a process. Each day is a test in rejecting respectability and unpacking my own internalized misogynoir.

As a middle-class tenure-track university faculty member there are layers and levels to my privilege. As a pansexual untenured Black woman educator who does critical work there is a substantial amount of marginalization that comes with where I fit into the academy. I recently saw something on Twitter that said, "I am no longer shrinking myself to be digestible for others—you can choke." There is power in that declaration. I am a survivor of many injustices: intimate partner violence, sexual assault, systemic sexism, institutionalized racism, and generations of trauma as a Black woman. Not shrinking myself to be digestible to others and standing in the truth of my own survival are how I disrupt criminology. For me, being a survivor is akin to the way we understand overcoming addiction. There is no "used to be" for addiction; it is a continuous process of maintaining sobriety. Survivorship is similar. Survival is an ongoing process. Therefore, incorporating this active work of surviving into criminology is not only natural for many of us; it is necessary for the continued growth and evolution of criminology. Just as it is necessary for our growth and evolution as people.

REFERENCES

Agnew, R. (1992). Foundation for a general strain theory of crime and delinquency. *Criminology, 30* (1), 47–87.

Agozino, B. (2012). Editorial: Race-class-gender articulation and crime in the US. *African Journal of Criminology and Justice Studies 6* (1–2), i–xxii.

Akers, R. (1998). *Social learning and social structure: A general theory of crime and deviance*. Boston: Northeastern University Press.

Barreira, P., Basilico, M., & Bolotnyy, V. (2018). *Graduate student mental health: Lessons from American economics departments*. Cambridge, MA: Harvard University.

Belknap, J. (2001). *The invisible woman: Gender, crime, and criminal justice*. 2nd ed. Cincinnati, OH: Wadsworth.

Broidy, L., & Agnew, R. (1997). Gender and crime: A general strain theory perspective. *Journal of Research in Crime and Delinquency, 34* (3), 275–306.

Crenshaw, K. (1989). Demarginalizing the intersection of race and sex: A Black feminist critique of antidiscrimination doctrine, feminist theory and antiracist politics. *University of Chicago Legal Forum*, Issue 1. http://chicagounbound.uchago.edu/uclf/vol1989/iss1/8

Daly, K., & Chesney-Lind, M. (1988). Feminism and criminology. *Justice Quarterly, 5* (4), 497–538.

Degruy-Leary, J. (2017). *Post-traumatic slave syndrome: America's legacy of enduring injury*. Portland, OR: Joy DeGruy Publications.

Delgado, R., & Stefancic, J. (2017). *Critical race theory*. New York: New York University Press.

Evans, T. M., Bira, L., Gastelum, J. B., Weiss, L. T., & Vanderford, N. L. (2018). Evidence for a mental health crisis in graduate education. *Nature Biotechnology, 36*, 282–284.

Gottfredson, M., & Hirschi, T. (1990). *A general theory of crime*. Stanford, CA: Stanford University Press.

Isom Scott, D. A. (2020). Status, socialization, and identities: Central factors to understand disparities in crime. *Sociology Compass 14* (9). https://doi.org/10.1111/soc4.12825

Isom Scott, D. A., & Mikell, T. (2019). "Gender" and general strain theory: Investigating the impact of gender socialization on young women's criminal outcomes. *Journal of Crime and Justice, 42* (4), 393–413.

Jackson, P. B., Thoits, P. A., & Taylor, H. F. (1995). Composition of the workplace and psychological well-being: The effects of tokenism on America's Black elite. *Social Forces, 74* (2), 543–557.

Katz, Nikki. (2020). *Black women are the most educated group in the U.S.* Thought Co. https://www.thoughtco.com/black-women-most-educated-group-us-4048763

Lombroso, C. (1876/2006). *Criminal man*. Durham, NC: Duke University Press.

Lorde, A. (2007). *Sister outsider: Essays and speeches*. Berkeley, CA: Crossing Press.

Lynch, M. J. (2000). The power of oppression: Understanding the history of criminology as a science of oppression. *Critical Criminology, 9* (1–2), 144–152.

Oliver, W. M. (2016). Celebrating 100 years of criminal justice education, 1916–2016. *Journal of Criminal Justice Education, 27* (4), 455–472.

Potter, H. (2015). *Intersectionality and criminology: Disrupting and revolutionizing studies of crime*. New York: Routledge.

Russell-Brown, K. (2009). *The color of crime* (Vol. 45). New York: NYU Press.

Unnever, J., & Gabbidon, S. L. (2011). *A theory of African American offending: Race, racism, and crime*. New York: Routledge.

Williams, J. M., & Battle, N. T. (2017). African Americans and punishment for crime: A critique of mainstream and neoliberal discourses. *Journal of Offender Rehabilitation, 56* (8), 552–566.

Winters, M. (2020). *Black fatigue: How racism erodes the mind, body, and spirit*. Oakland, CA: Berrett-Koehler Publishers.

NOTE

1. Lombroso's physical markers of criminality—atavistic stigmata—originated from racist stereotypes about dark-skinned Sicilians during the Italian Unification of 1861, during which Lombroso was a military doctor (Agozino, 2012). This falls within the timeline leading up to the American Civil War in 1861 to 1865 and the Emancipation Proclamation in 1863.

Chapter 9

When Did Black Lives Ever Matter

Babette J. Boyd

Several years ago, one of my students approached me after class; he appeared puzzled. He asked if I had any thoughts how to respond when someone said, "All lives matter," in response to the statement that "Black Lives Matter." It was incomprehensible there was so much negative sentiment in response to what was really a very simple and completely matter-of-fact statement, especially coming from his vantage point. It is a simple statement, a reminder, (that should not be necessary), that Black people are part of the human race, the only race, not socially constructed. Just because we have not been treated as such doesn't diminish the humanity of Black lives. Harm inflicted upon any part of humanity should be understood to diminish every part.

At our core, both my student and I understood the message that Black Lives Matter means to convey. What was difficult to understand was how there could be people who did not understand it? This was the real question he was posing. The phrase "all lives matter" is disingenuous and meaningless, but how do you put into words what the lived experience of Black folks makes self-evident? That all lives did not and have not ever included Black lives? At that moment, I couldn't come up with a reply.

Then I decided to just craft an argument, designed to explore, question, and respond to the statement that "all lives matter." I set it to rhyme as a vehicle to express this argument. I wanted the argument to be succinct but as complete as it could be, to try to capture the magnitude of over four hundred years of oppression and exploitation and how the lives of Black people embody not only their own subjugation but are a surrogate, in many respects, for the horrors that people all around the globe experience every day at the hands of other people. Giving breath to the words "Black Lives Matter" is pivotal for us to not only understand but to live out its meaning.

Several references may need further explanation. The reference to former President Trump getting deferments was meant to question the idea that it is an act of disloyalty to question or criticize the actions of the United States. About three years after the protest about Black Lives was first launched, in 2013, Colin Kaepernick decided to kneel at a football game as a protest against the loss of Black lives to police violence. At the time he took a knee, he didn't say anything; he just kneeled. The blowback was fierce. Then president of the United States, Trump, weighed in calling it an act of disloyalty, saying that Kaepernick shouldn't be playing if he didn't want to stand up during the National Anthem (BBC News, 2018). It was this statement by the president that evoked the phrase about the draft.

Standing or kneeling based on a principle takes a great deal of courage, and statements about how we protest are an act of silencing the voices of those who would speak out. I was reminded of innumerable efforts Black people have made for justice, such as the march on Bloody Sunday in Selma, Rosa Parks refusing to give up her seat on the bus in Montgomery, the Little Rock Five trying to attend high school in 1957, and the raised fists at the 1968 Olympic games in Mexico City of Tommie Smith and John Carlos. The act that most resonated with me as representing the multi-faceted and interlocking injustices to Black people that included the silencing, the racism, the constant threat of violence, the inequality, the effects beyond social status, the claim of disloyalty to country, and the ultimate hypocrisy of the reaction to these acts of bravery and protest, was most effectively brought into relief by contrasting Donald Trump's five deferments (four for college and one for heel spurs) to avoid serving in the military of the United States, with Muhammad Ali, risking his freedom, his title, and the loss of millions of dollars by conscientiously objecting to the draft.

In the more than four-hundred-year battle to achieve the equality and justice necessary to continuation and development of the human species on this planet, the institutions created in the United States have sometimes been leaders in achieving this and at other times have been reactionary and extraordinarily harmful: it's like "taking two steps forward, and three steps back." As an attorney, I have been acutely attuned to the use of the law and legal tools that have been used to advance equality and justice and those used to instantiate and perpetuate the obverse. I sought to call out these efforts and how the Supreme Court has sought to rationalize and legitimize their part in undermining any progress that has been made to move the two steps forward and how these two cases have been at the forefront of moving us three steps back. I picked three cases all from the last thirty-five years, *McCleskey v. Kemp* (1987), *Citizens United v. FEC* (2011), and *Shelby County v. Holder* (2013).

The first case, *McCleskey v. Kemp* (1987), represented the vast extent to which racial prejudice has infected the criminal justice system and the fact that the criminal law has likely never been implemented fairly, in the service of repressing crime or fostering justice, but more as a tool to repress the weakest in society.

Briefly, the *McCleskey* case involved the constitutionality of the death penalty in Georgia. He showed, using an exhaustive, empirical study that's become known as the Baldus Study, that Blacks who killed whites had a statistically significant higher percentage of being sentenced to death than whites who killed. The significance of this decision is that the existence and proof of racial bias in death penalty cases meant that there was a very high likelihood (almost a certainty) that this bias was not limited to just death penalty cases but infected the entire criminal justice system. Had the Supreme Court overturned the death sentence in McCleskey's case, it would have upended the entire system, and they chose not to step into the abyss. Accordingly, McCleskey was executed on September 25, 1991 (Neklason, 2019).

The two most recent cases, *Citizens United v. Federal Elections Com'n* (2010) and *Shelby County v. Holder* (2013), decided in the last fifteen years have had a particularly deleterious effect on democracy and all lives not represented in the top 10 percent of this country. These two cases also show how hostility to Black lives can be used as a fulcrum to bring about a hostile takeover whereby all lives will be devastated.

Citizens United v. FEC was decided by the U.S. Supreme Court in 2010. For more than a hundred or so years, Congress has made attempts to regulate financing of federal elections. They have enacted various laws requiring such things such as identification of donors, limits on contributions, and restrictions relative to advertisements during particular periods during the election cycle. (See generally *Citizens United v. FEC*, 558 U.S. 310, 394 (2010) (Stevens J., dissenting)). There has also been a number of occasions where the Supreme Court has weighed in, interpreting, defining, and delineating the contours of permitting corporate contributions and expenditures on behalf of candidates for federal office (Stevens). Both Congress and the Court have recognized the differences between a corporation and an individual, when it comes to the guarantee of free speech, and recognized that these differences justified treating a corporation different from an individual. In the case of *Citizen's United*, the Supreme Court determined that corporations had the same free speech rights as individuals and could donate, from their general treasury, without limit to political campaigns. This decision essentially destroyed any possibility of controlling corporate influence in elections. The individual voices of living breathing people who make up the *polis* will be overwhelmed and silenced by an anonymous group of individuals who can hide behind the corporate veil, influence politicians, and protect their private fortunes. In the process of glossing over the reality that noone really knows who the owners (or speakers) are in a corporation and the fact that, to the extent the speakers are individuals they already have a right to speak, the Supreme Court has allowed an endless supply of dark money to invade politics. Corporations do not have a conscience. As it has often been said, citing Lord Thurlow Edward, an English jurist: "Corporations have neither bodies to be punished, nor souls to be condemned, they therefore do as they like" (Edward, 1731–1806).

The Supreme Court declared §4(b) of the Voting Rights Act of 1965 "VRA" unconstitutional in *Shelby County v. Holder* 570 U.S. 529 (2013). Section 4(b) required that several states, known as the "covered states," and certain jurisdictional units within those and other states to seek permission or "preclearance" from the U.S. Attorney's Office prior to enacting new laws that had the effect on either diluting or diminishing the ability of minorities to vote or select a candidate of their choice. Jurisdictions selected for preclearance were chosen based on "a 'coverage formula' defining the covered jurisdictions as States or political subdivisions that maintained test or devices as prerequisites to voting, and had low voter registration or turnout, in the 1960s and 1970s" (*Shelby County*, at 529).

The VRA contained a bailout provision but, in order to bailout, a covered jurisdiction has to, "among other prerequisites for bailout, these jurisdictions and their subdivisions must not have used a forbidden test or device, failed to receive preclearance, or lost a §2, suit, in the ten years prior to seeking bailout" (*Shelby County*, 570 U.S. 529, 539). Shelby County couldn't bail out because the attorney general had recently objected to proposed voting changes (*Shelby County*, at 540).

> The Voting Rights Act was designed by Congress to banish the blight of racial discrimination in voting, which has infected the electoral process in parts of our country for nearly a century. (*South Carolina v. Katzenbach*, 383 U.S. 301, 308, 86 S. Ct. 803, 808, 15 L. Ed. 2d 769 (1966))

Further, the Court explained:

> Two points emerge vividly from the voluminous legislative history of the Act contained in the committee hearings and floor debates. First: Congress felt itself confronted by an insidious and pervasive evil which had been perpetuated in certain parts of our country through unremitting and ingenious defiance of the Constitution. (*South Carolina v. Katzenbach*, 383 U.S. 301, 309, 86 S. Ct. 803, 808, 15 L. Ed. 2d 769 (1966))

Congress reauthorized the VRA in 1970, 1975, 1982 (for twenty-five years), and in 2006 (for another twenty-five years) (*Shelby County v. Holder* (570 U.S. 529, 559) (2013) (Ginsburg, J. Dissenting)). Each time the VRA was extended, Congress conducted extensive hearings and took thousands of pages of testimony from interested persons. As Justice Ginsburg noted:

> Although the VRA wrought dramatic changes in the realization of minority voting rights, the Act, to date surely has not eliminated all vestiges of discrimination against the exercise of the franchise by minority citizens. Jurisdictions covered by the preclearance requirement continued to submit, in large numbers, proposed changes to voting laws that the Attorney General declined to approve, auguring that barriers to minority voting would quickly resurface were the preclearance remedy eliminated. (Ginsburg, at 563)

As a result, of the decision in *Shelby County*, the covered jurisdictions will not need to seek preclearance, rather they will be able to enact laws and have them in effect for years before the Supreme Court can rule on them, and then they can just enact a new law that is slightly different and delay a determination of the constitutionality of that law for another number of years. This was the very problem that preclearance was designed to prevent. Litigation is an extraordinarily expensive, lengthy, and cumbersome process. Justice Ginsburg noted in her dissent just one example from Texas. The particular use of the primary to prevent Blacks from voting was found unconstitutional in Texas in 1927. However, Texas then reenacted a slightly altered version of the same law and that was declared unconstitutional, seventeen years later in 1944. Not, to be deterred, Texas yet again slightly altered the same law, which then remained in force for another nine years before it too was declared unconstitutional in 1953. Thus, it took twenty-six years and three Supreme Court decisions to resist only one unconstitutional device. In the interim, other devices were constantly being devised. Thus, voting laws can be created more easily than variants of a dreaded disease.

These cases serve a warning alike to that given by Martin Niemöller, during WWII:

First, they came for the Socialists, and I did not speak out—

because I was not a socialist.

Then they came for the Trade Unionists, and I did not speak out—

because I Was not a Trade Unionist.

Then they came for the Jews, and I did not speak out—

because I was not a Jew

Then they came for me—and there was no one left to speak for me.

Thus, I offer this remonstrance, as a reminder of the history of this country that illuminates the meaning of BLACK LIVES MATTER.

WHEN DID BLACK LIVES EVER MATTER?

Each time Black folks raise their voice in protest,
There are always some who suggest,
That they have had it tough too,
And there is no need to pay special attention to you.
If "All lives matter" should be the refrain,
And "Black Lives Matter," are one and the same.
Then, let's take time to think it through.
To see if "all lives matter" to you.
Did all lives matter when Blacks were brought against their will,
From their Ancient Homeland, bound, chained, raped, and killed?
Did all lives matter when you changed the English common law of descent,
So, the children of your crimes,
Would be a commodity to be bought, sold, and spent?
Did all lives matter when you changed their African names,
Blinding them to the great People and Nations,
whose blood runs through their veins?
Did Black Lives Matter when you sold away their kin
Knowing they would never see them again?
Did all lives matter as you drove Blacks southward to the cotton gin
And Natives westward, while devouring the land belonging to them?
Did all lives matter when the Constitution was conceived,
Not unless Blacks were three-fifths of a person was what you believed?
Did all lives matter when Black people were hunted down by dogs,
Shot and maimed trying to escape your laws?
Did all lives matter as thousands were lynched;
while smiling, picnicking, white people gleefully pinched
Black body parts as trophies and souvenirs?
Ignoring the cries of our spirits throughout these many years?
I think we've established that all lives didn't matter then,
Two-hundred and forty-six years of bondage established a trend.
That would lead to Jim Crow and continue for a hundred years more,
As new ways of oppression and cruelty came to the fore.
Did all lives matter in the case of *McCleskey vs. Kemp*?[1]

To his execution Warren was sent.
It confirmed what we all knew in our head,
That Blacks who kill whites will wind up dead.
Killed by a system that values white lives many times more,
And of the Black lives lost, no one keeps score.
Even at war there is disparity.
Black veterans have been killed with impunity.
Conscientiously objecting Muhammad Ali went to jail,
While Trump got five deferments in the mail.
All lives don't matter when Blacks are mired in hopeless inequity,
Trapped and cornered and unable to flee,
Not only Jim Crow but avarice, ignorance, lies, and apathy?
What a strange and perverted democracy!
Do all lives matter when it comes to the vote?
You keep changing the rules and widening the moat.
Poll taxes, literacy tests, Grandfather Clauses,
Redistricting, Gerrymandering and Corrupt Registrars,
Disappearing polling places, inconsistent times,
stuffed ballot boxes, felon disfranchisement, and long waiting lines.
Fanciful new laws, spun in rapid succession,
All designed for voter suppression.
In fact, the only people that will be left to vote,
are those with no souls to be damned or bones to be broke.
I ponder parenthetically:
How can lives of corporations matter more than we?
They will vote into perpetuity.
Maybe you say, that was a time far and away,
But if that were true, there wouldn't be so many George Floyds,
Trayvon Martins, Tamir Rices, Breonna Taylors, and Sandra Blands
today.
Black women still only make sixty percent of white men's wages,
And too many black people spend their lives in cages.
Black mothers, fathers, and children too
Are taken at too great a rate
by drugs, violence, fear, and hate.
Oh, and there's one more thing to understand,
This is not just about the Black man.
It's Black women and children too,
It's Black with white and Black LGBTQ,
It's Black with Native American, Black and Trans;
Black mixed with anything all suffer at your hands
Violence and hate are the wages of Evil
And not the dominion of any one people.
When we say Black lives matter what we really mean to say,
Is that it's time to realize that it has never been that way.

This is just a short list but as I read the history
All I see is that this nation has caused untold misery
To folks of color and I am hard-pressed to cite
A time when Black lives mattered as much as white.
It's clear that "all lives matter" lacks legitimacy,
There's *Citizen's United v. the FEC*,[2]
Telling us Corporations are people just like you and me.
And just when we try to lift up our shoulders,
You hurl upon us yet another boulder,
Dear Lord, what are we to do with *Shelby County v. Holder?*[3]
So, as you look upon massive inequality,
COVID, Climate Change, Endless wars, and the Reality
That Black Lives really represent the many lives you have been content,
To destroy on each Continent.
You have pushed all other humanity aside,
And crushed it beneath the weight of your greed, gluttony, envy, and pride.
Maybe it is time to contemplate our ultimate fate.
Consider, where this world going with all the hate?
What will you tell the Maker, when your time comes due,
About how you treated people different than you?

REFERENCES

BBC News. (2018, May 24). Trump: NFL kneelers "maybe shouldn't be in country." Retrieved at https://www.bbc.com/news/world-us-canada-44232979

Citizens United v. Federal Elections Commission, 558 U.S. 310 (2010).

Edward, T. (1731–1806). English jurist. Retrieved at https://www.oxfordreference .com/view/10.1093/acref/9780191826719.001.0001/q-oro-ed4-00010943

Neklason, A. (2019, June 14). The "death penalty's *Dred Scott*" lives on. *The Atlantic.* Retrieved from https://www.theatlantic.com/politics/archive/2019/06/legacy-mccleskey-v-kemp/591424/

NOTES

1. 481 U.S. 279 (1987)
2. 558 U.S. 310 (2010)
3. 570 U.S. 529 (2013)

Chapter 10

Survivor Methodology for Healing and Transformation

A Love Letter to Survivors of Childhood Sexual Abuse

Lauren J. Silver

We've been asked by the visionary editors to write as our survivor selves in integration with our scholarly and educator selves. This is a call that motivates me and ignites my fear of vulnerability. It is with fits and starts that I continue and ask you to accompany me on this journey. While deciding how to best structure this chapter, I envisioned a wheel with multiple spokes to the center. This nonlinear structure is compelling and I circle through four spokes, or literacies as I call them: *creative literacy*, *relational literacy*, *emotional literacy*, and *analytical literacy*. Each of these literacies emphasize different entry points—ways of knowing—that together map out a survivor methodology. I begin with a preface to the multiple entrances I'll take to the core of this chapter, like the spokes on a wheel that are all needed and held together through the center node and the outer rim to make movement. None of the wheel's parts work alone and all parts are needed in synchrony for the wheel to function. This chapter names a *survivor methodology*, which extends from feminist methodology. Feminist methodology (1) centers the analysis of gender in intersection with other forms of oppression (Cohen, 1997; Combahee River Collective, 1983; Crenshaw, 1994; Pillow & Mayo, 2012), (2) makes visible the researcher's identities and roles in knowledge construction (Davis & Craven, 2016; Silver, 2020), and (3) creates knowledge to inform social justice movements and practices (Davis & Craven, 2016). Survivor methodology builds on and expands feminist methodology to center survivor identities and embodiments in both research methods and educational approaches, as I demonstrate below.

I'm a feminist ethnographer of critical child and youth studies and I'm a survivor of repeated childhood sexual abuse. I am white, queer, cisgendered, a member of a transracial family, and an antiracist accomplice. I'm not trained in the discipline of criminology; my interdisciplinary training is in anthropology, sociology, and education. But I speak to criminologists as my work centers transformative justice[1] and the abolition[2] of harm and trauma in children's intimate and social worlds. I focus on co-constructing and co-theorizing with those young people who are most marginalized, criminalized, and violated through the intersections of white supremacy, racism, heteronormativity, transphobia, misogyny, ableism, ageism, and capitalism. My voice and perspective at the intersection of my identities matter and I choose to speak. I am writing to you—a student, an educator, a scholar, and an activist—because for some reason you've been drawn to or asked to read this book and chapter. I'm assuming you care about survivor perspectives and the value and contributions our stories make to the world we cocreate through scholarship, education, and activism. Nanette, a stand-up comedian engages her audience while identifying as a survivor and offers: "All I can ask is just please help me take care of my story" (quoted in Gilmore & Marshall, 2019, p. 61). I too ask you to hold our stories lovingly as we imagine together a world of safety, well-being, and joy for all beings.

Dear reader, I draw upon a number of concepts from abolitionist social movements and scholarship, each with rich foundational histories, herstories, and their stories. Elaborations on these perspectives appear in footnotes, as the concepts come up in the chapter. I hope you will take the time to explore many of the foundational Black, Latinx, feminist, Indigenous, and queer readings, which have shaped me and my approach to what I'm calling a survivor methodology. Survivor methodology works through contact among diverse survivors to transform intersectional and interlocking oppressions. While I center the eradication of childhood sexual abuse, racism, misogyny, ableism, and other forms of domination must be abolished as codetermining systems of violence.

Some contributors to this volume have posed the question, what is trauma-informed research? I offer a response through raising other related questions: What would the abolition of childhood sexual abuse look like? How would it feel? And how would education and scholarship matter in creating this imagined future? How would we experience liberation through our families, communities, institutions, and societies? What does survivor methodology show us about ourselves and each other and what forms of care would be necessary? While I cannot answer these questions definitively, I draw upon the visionary imagination at stake in these questions, while following the lead of Mariame Kaba, a survivor and abolitionist. Mariame asks us to live our visions for collectivist futures through a million loving experiments in the now (Kaba, 2021). These questions create space for healing and validation where children and adult survivors alike would no longer experience the harm, denial, and shame that come from childhood sexual abuse (Simmons, 2019).

IN FOUR ENTRANCES

Entrance One: Poetry—Creative Literacy
The glow.
I keep the shades open when I sleep during snowstorm.
In the brief moments during night of lucid wakefulness
I am reminded by the glow from window.
Ahh.
Ahh.
I love snow-covered space outside my home.
Majestic beauty
As if nature has come to us.
And breath taken
Becomes breath returned.
Breath taken
Becomes breath returned.
As if the landscape gets my blood moving
In spirals
In twirls
My blood is dancing.
I am awake.
I am awake. Do you know the meaning?
It is power.
It is powerful to be awake after Childhood Hidden.
It is powerful to speak. To write. To connect. To be.
I was the little girl who looked down.
I was the little girl whose steps were unsteady.
I was the little girl who was terrified of making a mistake.
I was the little girl who shuddered in shadows.
I was the little girl who hid in closets.
I was little Girl Afraid.
My breath never came easy—jagged, catching breath.
To be that little girl.
Healing. I am that little girl. That little girl is me.
I get to hold her hand.
I want to write a love story.

I want to write a love story to the traumatized child who rises like the phoenix
To the traumatized child who was undone.
To the child who survived to thrive.
I was Child Hurt.
That child lives here.
I speak here because so many of us did not make it.
To the traumatized child who is the living dead.
To the traumatized child who was murdered.
To the traumatized child who was made ill.
I speak here because I can.

ENTRANCE TWO: RELATIONAL LITERACY

I've only met Kim Cook once in person—the co-editor on this volume who invited me to contribute my chapter to this gallery of voices. It was an unlikely gathering that led to healing and connections I could never have predicted. My dear friend, Stacia Gilliard-Mathews, organized the gathering—an "Author Meets Critics" event at the Annual American Society for Criminology meeting in November 2015 in Washington, DC. This was my first, and so far, only visit to this professional meeting but it left lasting imprints and spurred beautiful relationships. My book, *System Kids: Adolescent Mothers and the Politics of Regulation* (Silver, 2015), had just been published and my "critics," a fabulous dream team of feminist criminologists, included Kim Cook, Jill McCorkel, Jody Miller, and Jamie Fader. I remember posing for a picture with the group and a message, "We love you, Stacia." We texted the photo to Stacia, who wasn't able to join us because she was in the throes of trying to heal from cancer, an illness that ultimately extinguished her life. I dedicate this chapter to Stacia—my friend whose absence is mourned by so many of us. She was brave. She was powerful. She was light. She believed in me and my voice. She was the one who brought Kim and me together.

We had only three audience members at the gathering, two of whom I brought, and the third, Vera Lopez, an equally fantastic feminist criminologist who would also become a friend. I think it was Kim who suggested we move our chairs in a circle, and this shift helped mediate the intimacy and healing space of the gathering. I shed many tears during this conversation in which I was gifted with the insights and emotionally poignant connections made by these beautiful humans. Kim gave me language for something that I had not yet had a language for—she engaged with my work through survivor criminology (Cook, 2016) or what I'm calling here survivor methodology.

As brief context, *System Kids* is a feminist ethnography in which I share my memories of being a social worker and researcher advocate with young Black mothers and their children as we navigated a large, urban child welfare system (Silver, 2015). The youth participants were adjudicated delinquent or dependent and they all lived together in a supervised independent living program, run by a private nonprofit agency contracted by the state. The book reveals the ongoing intricacies of state violence and surveillance and showed how systematic harms restricted young moms' identities, family well-being, and the capacity of the social workers to care for them. I didn't reveal my status as a survivor until the book's "afterward," in which I engaged reflexivity about how my identity shaped the emotional and embodied landscape of the project (Silver, 2015). Kim compared reading my book to a beef stew—she sensed an aroma while reading the book. It wasn't until she came to the afterward that she realized the special flavor she had picked up on was my survivor-infused lens and approach. She too outed herself as a survivor of domestic violence and we have periodically stayed in touch ever since. I find this beef stew analogy really beautiful and it is one that I will always remember. The flavor connects us as survivors in ways that infuse our passions and commitments. This flavor need not always be made explicit in order to be powerful. When our survivor identities are vocalized in academic and educational encounters, there is a form of relief and release that happens (at least for me) from being seen and from seeing.

After meeting Kim, I've written reflexively in more direct ways about how my identity as a survivor shaped and continues to shape my ethnographic scholarship (Silver, 2020). Kim has worked tirelessly to articulate a multifaceted approach to survivor criminology (Cook, 2016) and has in partnership supported this volume to fruition. Even through brief encounters across survivors, such as the one I've just described, we meaningfully co-construct each other's realities and pathways. In particular, being "out" in our survivor identities is a radical feminist act in any academic or professional context that has historically and continues to silence and minimize our forms of expression and knowledge-building. Connecting as survivors is memorable and is much needed in our scholarly and educational spaces. Kim changed me and I believe I have changed her. As survivors, we bridge power divides and communities to cocreate knowledge while caring for one another, and working toward greater justice for all of us. This is the core of the wheel, radical love.[3] And, now, we move to the third entrance or spoke for this piece: emotional literacy.

ENTRANCE THREE: EMOTIONAL LITERACY

When collaborating, it is important to respect the emotional landscapes we inhabit, as we approach knowledge construction, education, and scholarship. Emotionality works hand-in-hand with intellectual analysis in ways that can be destructive or reparative. If feelings and thoughts remain unconscious, these can collectively gel into intergenerational forms of violence, social panics, or social shaming. For the purpose of analysis and discussion, I include separate entrances on emotional literacy and analytical literacy, even as these survivor methodologies are never actually separate. My decision to include the emotional entrance first is intentional and a feminist act. Too often in the academy and more widely across global patriarchal societies, we are taught to suppress our feelings, while rational thought is always considered superior (Harney & Moten, 2013; Spooner & McNinch, 2018). However, recognition of rationality is not equally available to everyone. Women, children, and people of color continue to be perceived as irrational, childlike, and without the capacity to reason. People who are enslaved, women, and children in different ways and at different historical and contemporary moments continue to be recognized as the property of men and heteronormative families (Armah, 2019; Bernstein, 2011; Patton, 2011). Physical control of bodies translates into forced emotional regulation—in which those who are oppressed perform particular kinds of emotional masks sanctioned by their oppressors (Armah, 2019; Du Bois, 1903).

We see the mask in the contemporary United States when parents teach their Black children to use survival tactics when confronted by police officers, all the while hoping and praying that their children will survive these inevitable encounters. Having to wear this mask is a form of trauma that may cover the accumulated and complex trauma of Black people's encounters with police (Ryan, 2020). The emotional futility is painful, as we know from the murder of Breonna Taylor and many others; Black women, Black children, and Black people are killed with impunity by officials of the carceral state, simply for existing (Lindsey, 2020). As white parents of a Black child, my wife and I give "the talk," even as we feel the sting of shame and pain that we are not required to wear the same mask that we teach our daughter to put on. Our daughter, who is five at the time of this writing, has been with us from her birth. Our racial identities are forever contingent on one another and our family story is one that we write against and through the violent grain of white supremacy and homophobia (Mariner, 2019). From the murky muddy water, the lotus flower blooms. Can the "afterlife of slavery" (Hartman, 2007) that in part formed our family be transformed (at least in specific moments) through radical love? We are responsible for our daughter's racial literacy and for her protection, even when she enters Black-centered spaces that do not include us. We talk and will continue to give "the talk" in different ways as she grows. Black survivorship in racist America is not a form of survivorship that I will ever experience but it is one that I must be intimately familiar with as I raise my daughter. Black Lives Matter (BLM) coalesced as a movement largely through the leadership of several Black queer women in the wake of the police killing of unarmed eighteen-year-old Michael Brown in August 2015. BLM pushes for social and material change, and the movement connects these shifts with affect and a fight over whose feelings matter. (Wanzo, 2015). While BLM movement building is personal for our family, survivor methodology must be intersectional and extend beyond any specific social identity.

Feminist scholars suggest more work is needed to understand how affect provides a way to move between public feelings (collective experience) and private individual narratives of trauma (Cvetkovich, 2007). Affect is managed in the public sphere through official rules and policies of recognition (Cvetkovich, 2007). Public feelings (collective expressions of dread, shame, anger, or even affection) shape the social policies, practices, and institutions of the family, schools, social welfare, economy, criminal justice, and so much more (Cvetkovich, 2007; Lesko & Talburt, 2012). For example, U.S. media campaigns have since the 1980s focused on "stranger danger," and child abduction rather than addressing incest and family violence in the home where most child abuse and sexual abuse occur (Whittier, 2015). Racial terror, discussed above, and the terrorizing of children through sexual abuse, which I address next, are interconnected and work across intimate and structural levels.

An inability to deal with uncomfortable or scary feelings results in the normalization of white supremacy, patriarchy, homophobia, sexual abuse, and other forms of oppression and trauma. Even for scholars, like myself, who do not study emotion outright, survivor methodology shows us how essential it is to integrate affect into how we construct knowledge. The emotional life of a sexual abuse survivor can oscillate through fear, guilt, shame, grief, anxiety, rage, relief, joy, and love. I've noticed that shame, guilt, fear, and anxiety often cover deeper emotions of grief and rage. Rage in my process of healing has been particularly scary but also particularly cathartic as an aesthetic that often ties to grief. Rage and grief support the unburdening and dislocation of shame from my personhood and from our social body. *Shame*, not rage, is the killer. Internally, shame is what eats me and keeps my voice silent; externally my face is fixed in a plastic smile and my body is rigid. As rage and grief have gradually and unexpectedly found expression across the landscape of my personal healing process, the shame in my muscles and psyche gradually distills in ways that I can only see from the present. For instance, my voice, confidence, and joy have taken shape through dancing, poetry, art, storytelling, and teaching—and these dynamics are present in my life's work as a mother, a wife, and as a scholar educator. This life that I now have access to has come through a sort of emotional cleansing and creative expressive healing process; as you can see emotional literacy connects in poignant ways to creative literacy. When I allow myself to grieve, feel sad, and experience anger and rage (in the privacy of my home, journal, and through artistic expression), this creates room for me to experience joy, love, and thriving.

How much healthier would all of our children be if adults provided safe places and outlets to express their feelings such as rage and sorrow, rather than criminalizing them, stifling their pain, and discounting their suffering? In particular, how could we extend this kind of grace and support to Black, Brown, queer, and disabled children who are adultified, denied innocence, and criminalized at much higher rates than white children? (See, for example, Cox, 2015; Ferguson, 2001; Meiners, 2016; Morris, 2016; Rios, 2011.) How much healthier would our world be if we provided the same kinds of spaces for adults to safely express their feelings of rage and grief, rather than locking them up and throwing them away? (Meiners, 2016)

I want to clarify that my conscious healing and capacity for emotional literacy did not develop until adulthood because as a child, I didn't have the freedom and power to sever my relationship with my abuser. I recognize that my survival has been shaped by the social identity privileges I received and continue to receive through my whiteness, material benefits from my middle-class family, access to the intergenerational transfer of wealth, and the critical consciousness I gained through my education. I had the resources to afford mental health services, as an adult. I had my white girlhood, which led teachers and other adults to see me as "innocent" and treat me as someone capable of learning, even when I felt blameworthy. My white girl privilege allowed me access to the educational tools that would eventually help me to find a language for what was happening to me. Not only did my white girl privilege inspire educators and other officials to see me as a worthy human, but white girlhood allowed me to avoid criminalization and state surveillance. No one identified me as the abused child, the at-risk child, or the risky child, and this lack of identification with maligned categories saved me—I continued to suffer in my home but external signifiers, or social stigma, didn't stick to my identity.

The suffering I experienced in private did not result in my being tossed aside, abandoned, or locked up, like so many Black and Brown children who are sexually abused, criminalized across contexts in schools, child welfare, juvenile justice, neighborhoods, hospitals, and other settings, and then retraumatized (Morris, 2016; Rios, 2011). For instance, compare my trajectory to the pathways Michelle Storrod (2021) identifies for Black and Brown girls who experience sexual abuse, poverty, and the stereotype of "being from" a harshly stigmatized northeastern city. In *Digital Justice, Girls, Phones, and the Juvenile Justice System,* Michelle found that many of the girls who participated in her study had experienced sexual trauma, sex trafficking by adults, had been pushed out of school, criminalized, court-ordered into locked facilities and group homes, and caged away from their everyday communities. The girls' survival strategies, including running away from abuse, were criminalized and instead of targeting the traffickers and circumstances that victimized the girls, officials locked the girls up for their "own safety" and "protection." Therefore, survivor methodology requires an intersectional approach (see for example, Cohen, 1997; Combahee River Collective, 1983; Crenshaw, 1994). In abolishing sexual abuse, we must acknowledge interlocking oppressions that have sustained rape culture so that we do not homogenize or mischaracterize the survivor as white or as girl. Prioritizing interlocking oppressions of racism, transphobia, poverty, and others, I recognize that I'm able to speak now in part because of the privileges that have guided my trajectory.

As a child, my imagination and ability to dissociate saved me. These tools provided a place where I could go inside myself because my home was not safe. As an adult, widening emotional literacy led to my freedom. Being able to experience rage led to my *no*—no more relationship with my abuser and no more relationship with the family members who would harbor him, stifle my voice, and ignore my pain. I didn't have the agency or the freedom to express this *no* as a child. While my emotional experience of moving from victimization to a survivor identity is personal to me, I believe there are particular aspects of my journey that signal avenues for social healing. First, all children (and adults) require safety, care, and dignity in order to express a wide range of emotional literacy. Because of the carceral state, children and particularly children of color, queer children, and disabled children do not tend to have access to these kinds of liberating spaces across everyday settings (Meiners, 2016). Second, as more humans collectively build and experience these conditions of care and radical love, isolation will diminish and people will be able to heal (Kaba, 2021). These kinds of safe spaces foster emotional literacy, which can be used to abolish the violence we live with and have lived with for centuries—childhood sexual abuse, racism, misogyny, poverty, and others.

That is, if we survive (and again, I want to emphasize that many of us do not), some of us remain trapped in victimization, incarcerated without hope, and some of us are lost to suicide or homicide. If we survive, many of us gain the liberatory consciousness to perceive our trauma and our healing as bigger than our individual selves. As we gain the emotionality and language to name intergenerational trauma and abuse, we begin to feel and know that none of us is wholly responsible for our suffering. When our intimate and social emotions are brought to critical consciousness along with language that recognizes harm and healing, we create new ways of caring for one another (for example, mutual aid projects[4] and abolitionist projects that result in "no throwaway" humans).

ENTRANCE 4: ANALYTICAL LITERACY

Scholars of childhood studies seek to understand how children and youth experience everyday life, as complex and intentional beings. Scholars theorize children's participation and subjugation in the history of and ongoing formation of global societies (Bernstein, 2011; Bluebond-Langner & Korbin, 2007; Oswell, 2012; Rios, 2011; Stephens, 1995). I didn't know this consciously, but I believe I became a childhood studies scholar because I wanted access to my inner child's story. As a child, I didn't have language to explain what was happening to me and I felt confused and disoriented by the nonreality of my experience. Life became nightmare. I was trapped literally and analytically because one cannot know the horrors one must endure in situations of incest; therefore, one starts to question whether one knows anything. I questioned everything I knew or thought I might know. My identity was compromised and shaky because I couldn't know myself. Fast forward to the present: I am an educator. Year after year, I teach a course in youth identities to my students. This journey from not knowing my identity to teaching is pure joy, empowerment, and freedom; it's what I call here analytical literacy.

I wanted to give my inner child language so that she could speak, name and analyze her oppression, and find connection with others. As she sought an intellectual life, she came to know terms and language for different kinds of oppression and intersectionality; she came to analyze her world. She came to believe and gradually is coming to feel that she was not to blame for her captivity and the puppet roles she played without thinking. She was not to blame for the plastic smile and mask that covered immeasurable suffering and annihilation. Yes, she wore a mask too. Her insatiable drive for perfection and the "perfect family" covered horrible secrets. I didn't want her to feel so abandoned and freakish. I wanted to give her a metaphoric bath through language, through naming, through claiming. My story is still not fully accessible, even to me, and perhaps, this is why I devote my life to feminist ethnography with children and young people. I love stories, but even more, I love freedom and the feeling that comes from being an educator and an inspiration on someone else's freedom journey. To be an educator and to be influential in shaping consciousness and critical analysis—to help others find their stories and their place in the stories of others—is generative beyond words.

And it is here where I engage critically with my field of childhood studies, which calls attention to children's voices and stories while centering young people's everyday lives and participation in their social worlds. Childhood studies as a field has been largely silent in the face of the #MeToo movement, and the realities of ongoing childhood sexual abuse and trauma (Whittier, 2015). Scholars of children's agency must reckon with the child who has experienced or is experiencing sexual trauma. The intimate act of child sexual abuse and the social denial of its reality are reflections of interpersonal, inter-generational, and colonial relations of exploitation, denial, and shame. In their study of girlhood, trauma, and life-writing, Leigh Gilmore and Elizabeth Marshall (2019) show us why the myth of "childhood innocence" has never garnered child protection. Institutions, families, and intergenerational struc-tures of violence substantiate a rape culture that obstructs and harms children, and children of color and queer children, in particular (see Armah, 2019 for a Nigerian perspective). The U.S. legal system forces children and those who are victimized to testify in court in order to substantiate and prove the reality of their trauma and their trustworthiness (Powell et al., 2017). Instead of put-ting the weight of confinement on the shoulders of the child or the adult vic-tim, it is time to confront the ubiquity of violence and sexual violation in our midst. It's not only in the court of law where children are forced to substanti-ate their assaults; many children who tell their stories to family members and community members are not believed or are discounted. When children tell their trauma stories, their narratives are too often told back to them in ways that mark the child as culpable, shameful, and untrustworthy.

It is an ethical imperative that the child's voice not be relied on to shatter the matrix of confinement, dispossession, and trauma endured by children and all of us. We must find different ways to center children. Self-determination is largely imagined or aspirational for the child who is captive in the night-mare and trapped behind the mask of upholding family and societal secrets. We cannot romanticize a notion of freedom for this child. And it is from this positionality that I circle back to the first entrance: poetry as creative literacy. I use poetry as an entrance to signify the survivor-centered tools that go beyond linear ways of telling. As survivors, many of us have drawn upon forms of art, imagination, and other creative literacies in order to access elements of our stories. Analytical and emotional literacies are shaped by a wide range of creative tools for making sense through writing, speaking, poetry, making art, music, dance and others. Autobiographics, as method, encourages self-representation through spanning multiple genres, as well as narrative, visual, and embodied ways of disclosing knowledge. More broadly, autobiographics encourages the centering of children's ways of knowing without forcing a particular normative mode of storytelling (Gilmore & Marshall, 2019).

Why do we collectively shield the rape, the rapists, and the systems of oppression that maintain the rape? The volume, *Love with Accountability*, is a collection of reflections by Black survivors of childhood sexual abuse (Simmons, 2019). The authors write about accountability across Black communities and families, considering what safety might look and feel like when community members support one another and reduce harm without relying on the police or prisons. In the collection, Kai Green (2019) writes about intergenerational forgetting, suggesting "I can't remember" is taught and learned in families. Green speaks into the void around the Black girl, the conditions of care and knowing that are absent across both intimate and social spaces that could dignify the child, and in particular the Black child, who has been sexually assaulted. Green (2019, p. 46) explains: "When Black girl told Black mother what was happening, there was nothing done to remove her from the situation, so she learned to live with it." Green explains that they cannot speak about accountability because the conditions that would be required for accountability do not yet exist. Green (2019, p. 47) asks:

> What does accountability look like when you are the only one who remembers what happened? What does accountability look like when you remind your loved ones of that thing that happened, that was not love, and they say, "I don't know what you're talking about" and walk away? How does silence fill your mouth after that? Your body remembers. Your Black girl spirit remembers. You know what happened, and you want to heal, but there are no apologies to be had. You are forced to swallow an inherited silence that your Black family has built as a wall of protection.

This passage hits the heart of why analytical literacy is an essential condition for healing and accountability outside the carceral state. "Inherited silence" and "forgetfulness" continue without words, without knowledge, and without a space of reckoning. I agree with Kai Green (2019, p. 48), who claims, "You must remember and affirm your truth in spite of forgetfulness." And this is where I draw inspiration, from other survivors, who continue to speak and dream in spite of an absence of care and dignity from our intimate and wider social worlds. We must be love for one another and for the children, the radical love that is needed for healing and transformative justice. This chapter is my love story, which I write for myself and for all of us. I join Kai Green and many others to write this love story into the void. I yell, raise my fists, and cry forth to all who will read this: it is time to abolish child sexual abuse! As a community of survivors engaged in healing and abolition, we can lovingly craft the creative, relational, emotional, and analytical literacies needed to dignify our children and the children who live within us.

THE CORE AND THE RIM: RADICAL LOVE
AND ABOLITIONIST ACCOUNTABILITY

Each entrance centers literacy—creative, relational, emotional, and analytical—and, when included as an ensemble, connect us to both the core and the rim of the wheel. The wheel of survivor methodology is reminiscent of the medicine wheel, drawn from Indigenous practices and commonly used in restorative justice circles (Generation Red Road, n.d.). With radical love at the center and the spokes (or entrances) held together at the rim through abolitionist accountability, we can create new ways of being in the now. Radical love is the core of my wheel analogy. Kelley (2016, p. 15) draws upon James Baldwin's understanding of "love-as-agency" as Black communities have long drawn upon love as the "motivation for making revolution." Love and inquiry are the necessary ingredients for resistance and making the world anew—it is through a loving vision that communities can move beyond the trauma caused from state-sanctioned racism, poverty, and gender violence to "radical healing" and transformation (Ginwright, 2015; Kelley, 2016). Doing scholarship and educating through radical love does not mean that we are innocent of all mistakes or that we cease being responsible or reflexive about what it means to love in the context of state and interpersonal violence (hooks 1989; Tuck 2018). Many victims are also victimizers and vice versa. These statuses often coexist within the same person. If we cannot isolate and criminalize the victimizers as separate from the victims, then how do we engage in transformative justice and stop the intergenerational transmission of trauma? I believe abolition provides a way forward.

Abolitionists build intentional communities and practice naming harm, reducing harm, creating safety, and holding each other accountable when we mess up without relying on the police and other forms of carceral confinements. Mariame Kaba (2021) and others (see for example, Spade, 2020) model how to intentionally resist carceral logic and open up new kinds of realities and futures through community-building. Imagination—something many of us survivors are well versed in—is key because currently, there is no outside of the carceral—punishment is everywhere, in our institutions (policing, criminal justice, schools, child welfare, others) and in our hearts and minds. We live a carceral reality. I imagine a future where there are no throwaway children and no throwaway humans. What happens when we embrace the principle and action that no one, even humans who have committed heinous acts, deserves to be thrown away? What happens when we believe systems and humans can change and transform in ways that support collective well-being? What happens when we start practicing these beliefs in all the ways that we can?

I don't want my perpetrator to be harmed or locked up. I did not use the criminal justice system and my abuse was never identified by the state. I also want to recognize that I do not speak for all survivors and my abolitionist perspective is just one among many others. I want my perpetrator to stop harming others and I wish we lived in a world where his capacity to accept responsibility could be facilitated through creative, relational, emotional, and analytical literacies. I wish he would accept accountability for the harm he has caused me, apologize, and heal. Recently, in a book talk supported by Haymarket Books, Mariame Kaba addressed an audience of over one thousand participants and expressed frustration at the naysayers who claim abolitionists want murderers and criminals to be free to continue to hurt people. She exclaimed: "Who are they talking to? Most of us are survivors of harm and violence ourselves. . . . I find it ridiculous." (Haymarket Books, 2021). Kaba explains that abolitionists want a society where we hold one another accountable for harm but we know that locking people up doesn't do anything to prevent cycles of trauma from continuing (Kaba, 2021).

As a survivor, I realize that there are no parts of myself that I want to throw away, no matter how scary and unclean some of these parts seem to me. Many survivors (but again, not all) don't want to harm the people who harmed them or their communities—even the worst, most damaged parts deserve the opportunity to heal. As survivors, we model and enact the courage it takes to transform our societies.

CONCLUSION

When I read excerpts of this chapter to my wife, she beautifully shared her key takeaways, offering:

> Respect survivors.
> Center survivors.
> Listen to survivors.
> "Yes, that's it!" I responded.

As scholars, we offer this volume in respect of our various experiences with trauma and harm and our abilities to thrive despite all attacks on our humanity. We do not speak with one voice and survivor scholar perspectives are as diverse as our embodiments. Yet collectively acknowledging the ways that we have survived intersectional harm, violence, and oppression to our bodies, spirits, and intellects is indeed a feminist act. I offer this chapter lovingly, as a radical act in the academy. Voicing our personal experiences openly and collectively as a coalition of scholar survivors, we imagine and forge visionary paths in the academy.

In creating new space for ourselves, we intentionally create space for future coalitions of diverse bodies where an extensive range of experiences and emotions set the tone—the center for the academy (Cohen, 1997; Spooner & McNinch, 2018). How do we center experiences of the marginalized in ways that abolish institutions of harm and create new ways of relating, educating, and creating knowledge? And I end here, as I began. I am a white, cisgender, female professor of childhood studies. I am a mom. I am married to a white cisgender woman and we are raising a Black daughter. I am queer and a survivor of repeated childhood sexual abuse. My wounds are not physically visible. I can pass as someone near the center. As someone with privilege in the academy, my hope is that one day, I will no longer be in the position to nurture and welcome diverse bodies to the table of the university. In fact, many of us seek to abolish the table entirely. Instead, let's build a gallery, where there is no center and no periphery (hooks, 1989)—a space for co-creation and multiple forms of expression and knowledge sharing. If we abolish the exclusionary table where many cannot fit, we can disrupt the power of the overseer and the enslaved—in all of its iterations. My love story is for all survivors of childhood sexual abuse and for those who did not make it—I offer this survivor methodology as a map for transformation and healing, among a gallery of others. May we love one another so that one day we will see reflections of care shining back at us from all angles. Together we create the conditions for the abolition of childhood sexual abuse.

RESOURCES FOR THE ABOLITION OF CHILDHOOD SEXUAL ABUSE

- generationFive: http://www.generationfive.org
- Love WITH Accountability: https://www.lovewithaccountability.com/about-lovewithaccountability
- The Heal Project: https://www.igrivera.com/the-heal-project.html
- Just Beginnings Collaborative: https://justbeginnings.org
- Survivors' Agenda: https://survivorsagenda.org
- Survived & Punished: End the Criminalization of Survival: https://survivedandpunished.org/

REFERENCES

Armah, E. A. (2019). Colliding Traumas. In Simmons, A. S. (Ed.), *Love with Accountability: Digging Up the Roots of Child Sexual Abuse* (pp. 45–49). AK Press.

Bernstein, R. (2011). *Racial Innocence: Performing American Childhood from Slavery to Civil Rights.* New York University Press.

Bluebond-Langner, M. & Korbin, J. E. (2007). Challenges and Opportunities in the Anthropology of Childhoods: An Introduction to "Children, Childhoods and Childhood Studies." *American Anthropologist, 109*(2), 241–246.

Cervantes-Soon, C. G. (2017). *Juarez Girls Rising: Transformative Education in Times of Dystopia.* University of Minnesota Press.

Cohen, C. (1997). Punks, Bulldaggers, and Welfare Queens: The Radical Potential of Queer Politics? *GLQ: A Journal of Lesbian and Studies 3*(4), 437–465.

Combahee River Collective (1983). In Smith, B. (Ed.), *Home Girls: A Black Feminist Anthology* (pp.197–208). Kitchen Table Press.

Cook, K. J. (2016). Has Criminology Awakened from Its "Androcentric Slumber"? *Feminist Criminology 11*(4), 334–353.

Cox, A. M. (2015). *Shapeshifters: Black Girls and the Choreography of Citizenship.* Duke University Press.

Crenshaw, K. W. (1994). Mapping the Margins: Intersectionality, Identity Politics, and Violence against Women of Color. In Fineman, M., & Mykitiuk, R. (Eds.), *The Public Nature of Private Violence: The Discovery of Domestic Abuse* (pp. 93–118). Routledge.

Cvetkovich, A. (2007). Public Feelings. *South Atlantic Quarterly 106*(3), 459–468.

Davis, D., & Craven, C. (2016). *Feminist Ethnography: Thinking through Methodologies, Challenges, and Possibility.* Rowan & Littlefield.

Du Bois, W. E. B. (1903). *The Souls of Black Folk: Essays and Sketches.* A.C. McClurg.

Ferguson, A. A. (2001). *Bad Boys: Public Schools in the Making of Black Masculinity.* University of Michigan Press.

generationFIVE (2017). Ending Child Sexual Abuse: Transformative Justice Handbook. http://www.generationfive.org/wp-content/uploads/2017/06/Transformative-Justice-Handbook.pdf

Generation Red Road (n.d.). Revitalizing and Promoting Generational Healing. https://www.genredroad.org

Gilmore, L. & Marshall, E. (2019). *Witnessing Girlhood: Toward an Intersectional Tradition of Life Writing.* Fordham University Press.

Ginwright, S. (2015). Radically Healing Black Lives: A Love Note to Justice. *New Directions for Student Leadership*, 33–44.

Green, K. M. (2019). Fast. In Simmons, A. S. (Ed.), *Love with Accountability: Digging Up the Roots of Child Sexual Abuse* (pp. 45–49). AK Press.

Harney, S., & Moten, F. (2013). *The Undercommons: Fugitive Planning and Black Study.* Minor Compositions.

Hartman, S. (2007). *Lose Your Mother: A Journey along the Atlantic Slave Route.* Farrar, Straus and Giroux.

Haymarket Books (2021, February 23). We Do This 'Til We Free Us: Abolitionist Organizing and Transforming Justice. [Video] YouTube. https://www.youtube.com/watch?v=xWL9a1f9uW0

hooks, b. (1989). Choosing the Margin as a Space of Radical Openness. *Framework: The Journal of Cinema and Media 36,* 15–23.

Kaba, M. (2021). *We Do This 'Til We Free Us: Abolitionist Organizing and Transforming Justice.* Haymarket Books.

Kelley, R. D. G. (2016). Black Study, Black Struggle. New Democracy Forum. *Boston Review,* March/April, 10–17.

Lesko, N., & Talburt, S. (2012). Enchantment. In Lesko, N., & Talburt, S. (Eds.), *Keywords in Youth Studies: Tracing Affects, Movements, Knowledges* (pp. 279–289). Routledge.

Lindsey, T. (2020). "The Lack of Mobilized Outrage for Police Killing Black Women Is an Injurious Erasure." *Bustle* website, June 3, 2020. Accessed June 5, 2020. https://www.bustle.com/p/the-lack-of-mobilized-outrage-for-police-killing- black-women- is- injurious- erasure- 22953764

Love, B. (2019). *We Want to Do More Than Survive: Abolitionist Teaching and the Pursuit of Educational Freedom.* Beacon Press.

Malatino, H. (2020). *Trans Care.* University of Minnesota Press.

Mariner, K. A. (2019). *Contingent Kinship: The Flows and Futures of Adoption in the United States.* University of California Press.

Meiners, E. (2016). *For the Children? Protecting Innocence in a Carceral State.* University of Minnesota Press.

Morris, M. (2016). *Pushout: The Criminalization of Black Girls in School.* The New Press.

Nash, J. C. (2013). Practicing Love: Black Feminism, Love-Politics, and Post Intersectionality. *Meridians: Feminism, Race, Transnationalism 11*(2), 1–24.

Oswell, D. (2012). *The Agency of Children: From Family to Global Human Rights.* Cambridge University Press.

Patton, S. P. (2011). Why Black Children Can't Grow Up: The Construction of Racial Childhood in American Life, 1880–1954. Dissertation, May.

Pillow, W., & Mayo, C. (2012). Feminist Ethnography: Histories, Challenges, and Possibilities. In Hesse-Biber, S. N. (Ed.), *Handbook of Feminist Research: Theory and Praxis* (pp. 187–205). Sage.

Powell, A. J, Hlvaka, H. R., & Mulla, S. (2017). Intersectionality and Credibility in Child Sexual Assault Trials. *Gender & Society 31*(4), 457–480.

Rios, V. (2011). *Punished: Policing the Lives of Black and Latino Boys.* New York University Press.

Roberts, D. E. (2002). *Shattered Bonds: The Color of Child Welfare.* Basic Civitas Books.

Roberts, D. E. (2020). "Abolition Is the Only Answer: A Conversation with Dorothy Roberts." *Rise Magazine,* October 20, 2020. Accessed October 20, 2020. https://www.risemagazine.org/2020/10/conversation-with-dorothy-roberts/

0160 Lauren J. Silver

Russo, A. (2019). *Feminist Accountability: Disrupting Violence and Transforming Power*. New York University Press.

Ryan, J. (2020). The Weight of Words: Framing the Muted Voice of Traumatized, Black, Urban Childhood. Unpublished manuscript, December 10.

Santos, B. S. (2005). The Future of the World Social Forum: The Work of Translation. *Development 48*(2), 15–22.

Shange, S. (2019). *Progressive Dystopia: Abolition, Antiblackness, and Schooling in San Francisco*. Duke University Press.

Silver, L. J. (2015). *System Kids: Adolescent Mothers and the Politics of Regulation*. The University of North Carolina Press.

Silver, L. J. (2019). Transformative Childhood Studies: A Remix in Inquiry, Justice, and Love. *Children's Geographies 18*(2), 176–190.

Silver, L. J. (2020). Queering Reproductive Justice: Memories, Mistakes, and Motivations to Transform Kinship. *Feminist Anthropology 1*, 217–230.

Simmons, A. S. (Ed.) (2019). *Love with Accountability: Digging Up the Roots of Child Sexual Abuse*. AK Press.

Spade, D. (2020). Mutual Aid: Building Solidarity during This Crisis (and the Next). Verso.

Spooner, M., & McNinch, J. (2018). "Introduction." In Spooner, M., & McNinch, J. (Eds.), *Dissident Knowledge in Higher Education* (xxiii–xxxii). University of Regina Press.

Stephens, S. (1995). Children and the Politics of Culture in "Late Capitalism." In Stevens, S. (Ed.), *Children and the Politics of Culture* (pp. 3–48). Princeton University Press.

Storrod, M. L. (2021). Digital Justice, Girls, Phones, and the Juvenile Justice System. Unpublished manuscript, March 13.

Tuck, E. (2018). Biting the University That Feeds Us. In Spooner, M., & McNinch, J. (Eds.), *Dissident Knowledge in Higher Education* (pp. 149–167). University of Regina Press.

Wanzo, R. (2015). The Deadly Fight over Feelings. *Feminist Studies 41*(1), 226–231.

Whittier, N. (2015). Where Are the Children? Theorizing the Missing Piece in Gendered Sexual Violence. *Gender & Society 30*(1), 95–108.

NOTES

1. *Transformative justice (TJ)* works outside carceral punishment and is an approach to holding one another accountable for the harm we cause while taking steps *within community* to amend and heal—this approach is similar to and commonly referred to as restorative justice. TJ rectifies the structural conditions that make harm possible and calls attention to state violence, which must be healed, not restored, so that society can be actively transformed (generationFIVE, 2017; Kaba, 2021; Meiners, 2016; Russo, 2019; Silver 2019).

2. *Abolitionist praxis* is rooted in the "afterlife of slavery" (Hartman, 2007) and signals historical and contemporary approaches to eliminate the carceral state and

its institutions that surveil, punish, and contain Black, Brown, Indigenous and queer bodies (Meiners, 2016). In contemporary times, "abolitionist schooling" (Love, 2019; Shange, 2019), the abolition of the "family policing system" (Roberts, 2002, 2020), and the abolition of child sexual abuse (Simmons, 2019) extend from this foundation and ethic. Abolition is a "two-step" (Shange, 2019) and with the elimination of carceral institutions must come reimagining, experiments in liberation, new ways of relating, and infrastructures of care and radical love (Kaba, 2021). My work is grounded in this ethic and I explore *abolitionist childhood* as a way of enacting a world where the relationships, institutions, and environments that harm children could be undone and built anew to promote healing, freedom, and well-being.

3. *Radical love* refers to a process of mutual humanization and dignity that extends across boundaries of power and works toward social justice (Cervantes-Soon, 2017). In other words, radical love is active—it moves through and beyond affect to bring together communities in service to transformation.

4. *Mutual aid* "is collective coordination to meet each other's needs, usually from an awareness that the systems we have in place are not going to meet them. Those systems, in fact, have often created the crisis, or are making things worse. We see examples of mutual aid in every single social movement" (Spade, 2020, p. 7). Also, see https://millionexperiments.com for examples community mutual aid projects from across the globe.

Chapter 11

Survivor Criminology as a Scholar/Activist in the Me Too Movement and #MeToo Activism

Meredith G. F. Worthen

schol·ar/ac·tiv·ist
　　those who are both specialists in a particular academic field as well as advocates in community-based efforts, movements, and campaigns dedicated to political and/or social change

Creating a space for conversations about issues that most would rather leave silenced/hidden is in many ways the "bread and butter" of both activism and activist scholarship. Digital activism has been an especially attractive location for scholar/activists across many disciplines and community-based efforts because it is free, widely accessible, and requires little more than an email address and internet access. In recent years, scholar/activists in the fields of criminology and criminal justice who are interested in lifting up the voices of survivors of sexual violence have flocked to The Me Too Movement and the digital space of #MeToo. Together, the bridges between survivor criminology, digital activism, and #MeToo have carved out an exciting path for scholar/ activists dedicated to confronting sexual violence. In this chapter, I first offer a working definition of a scholar/activist. Next, I discuss the importance of self in survivor criminology. Then, I provide an illustrative example of my own work with #MeTooMeredith and more about #MeToo digital activism. Finally, I consider future directions for scholar/activists.

WHAT IS A SCHOLAR/ACTIVIST?

A scholar/activist is someone who engages in both academic and community efforts to bring support and awareness to a particular group and/or issue. Being a scholar/activist means that one's academic life is necessarily embedded in one's activist work in ways that are nearly impossible to disentangle. This can manifest in a variety of formats from publishing scholarly work about activism in academic spaces, to giving public/community talks, to boots-on-the-ground community efforts such as nonprofit work, volunteerism, and participation in demonstrations and protests.

Scholars, especially professors at academic institutions, have worked toward developing narratives about the importance of scholar activism across numerous disciplines such as criminology, critical race studies, education, feminist studies, human geography, and religious studies, among others (Apple, 2016; Daniels, 2018; D'Arcangelis, 2018; Murji, 2020; Quaye, Shaw, & Hill, 2017; Reynolds et al., 2020; Zine, 2004). While each will have their own personal interpretation of what it means to be a scholar/activist, the through line is this: academic work + public engagement = scholar activism.

SURVIVOR CRIMINOLOGY AND ME TOO: THE IMPORTANCE OF SELF

Due to its focus on centering the importance of survivors' voices in conversations about crime and the criminal justice system, survivor criminology is an especially attractive location for scholar/activists. By critically investigating crimes/criminal justice while also supporting survivors of crime, survivor criminology can also be a good fit for those who are survivors themselves. In particular, the personal narrative of having been through a crime can inform the work of scholar/activists who engage in survivor criminology.

When The Me Too Movement first came to my attention, I was struck by the tremendous work Tarana Burke (the founder of The Me Too Movement) has been doing for decades to support survivors of sexual violence. After pitching her life story to Bio.com, I had the opportunity to write her biography in early 2018 (Worthen, 2018). In doing so, I became further intrigued as to how I, a white, cisgender woman of privilege working as a professor in academia, could perhaps be a part of The Me Too Movement. My teaching commitments in the course/text I developed many years ago, *Sexual Deviance and Society* (Worthen, 2016), already placed me in a good position to discuss these issues with my students; however, the grassroots activism of The Me Too Movement is about more than just discussion—it is about making changes that fight against rape culture and support survivors. Even so, the ways to be a scholar/activist in this area were not entirely clear to me and I remained unsure how I could best fit into this world.

On September 27, 2018, that all changed when I watched Dr. Christine Blasey Ford testify to the world about her experience of sexual assault by (now) Supreme Court Justice Brett Kavanaugh. Just like many other survivors, I was triggered into not only reliving my past experiences, but also, feeling (quite viscerally) the far-reaching effects of rape culture including the cycle of denial, dismissal, belittlement, shame, and excuses I have personally endured over and over for many years. I thought about the hundreds of students who have disclosed their sexual assaults to me over the years and the millions more who are seeking out a safe place to tell someone what happened to them. While hearing Dr. Ford speak on national television with millions of viewers hearing her story, I specifically thought about how important it is to have a platform where people can hear their own story but how troubling and scary it can be to expose your face and your identity when doing so. This also reminded me of how Alyssa Milano's October 15, 2017, tweet, "If you've been sexually harassed or assaulted write 'me too' as a reply to this tweet," went viral so quickly in the year just prior with thousands of replies, comments, and retweets, with some even sharing their own personal stories in her tweet's thread. In that moment it all came together, I decided to push through the barriers of rape culture and work toward cultivating a grassroots effort to provide a digital platform where *all* survivors of sexual violence could share their stories anonymously—and #MeTooMeredith was born.

#METOOMEREDITH, THE INSTAGRAM ACCOUNT

#MeTooMeredith is a simple idea: survivors of sexual violence and harassment send a direct private message to @MeTooMeredith on Instagram and then I request permission to post their story without identifying information. After that, I post their story on the Instagram page. I had no idea if this was something that would take off but empowered by the many survivors coming forward through The Me Too Movement and #MeToo, I wanted to try. It worked. In the few days following the one-year anniversary of Alyssa Milano's first #MeToo tweet, @MeTooMeredith received about one hundred stories and more than one thousand followers (Worthen, 2019). To date, #MeTooMeredith has more than five thousand followers, more than one thousand published anonymous stories, and the inbox remains overloaded with #MeToo stories waiting to be published on the Instagram page.

Using social media to give a voice to survivors of sexual violence, #MeTooMeredith is doing digital activism *and* survivor criminology. What is more, scholarly research focusing on #MeTooMeredith has produced important findings. A content analysis of stories (N = 202) posted on #MeTooMeredith dated from October 14, 2018, to October 14, 2019, found consistent evidence of rape culture, including minimizing harm (e.g., boys will be boys), victim blaming, and perceived barriers to disclosure including fear of repercussions, feelings of personal shame, not believing that their assault "counts" as rape or a crime of any sort, and fear of disbelief (Brown, Moser, & Cook, 2021). Clearly #MeTooMeredith exposes how survivors of sexual abuse, violence, and harassment are belittled and ignored. Together, the collective work of publishing academic pieces about #MeTooMeredith and running the #MeTooMeredith Instagram page is just one example of the academic work + public engagement combination of what it means to be a scholar/activist engaged in survivor criminology.

#METOO AND DIGITAL ACTIVISM

As researchers have noted, the use of #MeToo is "perhaps one of the most high-profile examples of digital feminist activism we have yet encountered," but it is certainly not the only form (Mendes, Ringrose, & Keller, 2018, p. 236). Other exemplars of hashtag activism such as #BeenRapedNeverReported (which largely trended in 2014) and #WhyIDidntReport (which started trending in 2018) have also been successful in bringing attention to survivors of sexual violence and the systemic problems in rape culture and the criminal justice system (Keller, Mendes, & Ringrose, 2018; Schneider, George, Marvin, & Carpenter, 2020). What is more, it is important to remember that #MeToo digital activism is building from various decades-old movements including Take Back the Night, which started in the 1970s (Kretschmer & Barber, 2016; Take Back the Night, n.d.), as well as rape reform legislation changes (Spohn & Horney, 1993; Williams, Singh, & Mezey, 2019), and the introduction of community-based rape crisis centers and sexual assault nurse examiner (SANE) programs in the 1990s (Ahrens et al., 2000; Baumer, Felson, & Messner, 2003; Campbell & Wasco, 2005; Spohn & Horney, 1993). Scholars starting in the 1980s also provided firmly grounded evidence that one in four women have experienced rape (Campbell & Wasco, 2005; Koss, Gidycz, & Wisniewski, 1987; Russell, 1982) and exposed false claims surrounding rape and sexual assault (i.e., rape myths), especially those involving the stranger rape myth (Burt, 1980; Koss et al., 1987). Today, #MeToo digital activism provides an exciting way to continue to fight for survivors of sexual violence and an important vehicle for scholar/activists engaging in survivor criminology.

In fact, recent research demonstrates notable changes post-#MeToo. Along with the massive influx of #MeToo social media posts (with nearly one-third of #MeToo tweets written in a language other than English according to one study, Anderson & Toor, 2018), internet searches for the #MeToo-associated terms have increased exponentially (Caputi, Nobles, & Ayers, 2019; Williams et al., 2019). Specifically, an analysis of U.S. internet search volume comparison data found that keyword searches for "sexual harassment" and "sexual assault" were 86 percent higher than expected from October 15, 2017, to June 15, 2018 (Caputi et al., 2019, p. 258). More generally, both men and women report being significantly less likely to view sexual assault reports as "false complaints" post-#MeToo (Szekeres, Shuman, & Saguy, 2020). Furthermore, research suggests that many of the hashtags that frequently co-occur with #MeToo are centered around activism (i.e., #TimesUp, #WithYou, #Resist) (Williams et al., 2019). Thus, it is clear that there has been an increase in global conversations about sexual violence in the post-#MeToo era, with much of it focusing on the need for social and political changes in the areas of rape legislation reform, sexual harassment laws, and movement toward gender equity.

Seeking to make such changes, many are answering the call of The Me Too Movement with their own versions of grassroots digital activism. Beyond the official Instagram page of The Me Too Movement (@TheMeTooMvmt), there are many other activists doing amazing work including @EndRapeOnCampus, @JDoeJustice, @MeTooManyVoices, @NoMoreOrg, @RAINN, @SurvivorsofColor, @TheJHF, @GOTU_app, @UnapologeticallySurviving, and @WhyIKeptQuiet (to name just a few).[1] Their work is briefly described in Table 11.1.

Table 11.1: A Very Short List of #MeToo Activists on Instagram

Name	Instagram Handle	Brief Description
GoTu the App	@GOTU_app	First anonymous app network for sexual assault survivors, survivor supporters & advocates
End Rape on Campus	@EndRapeOnCampus	We work to end sexual violence through direct support for survivors & their communities; prevention through education; & policy reform at all levels.
J Doe Justice	@JDoeJustice	Anonymous reporting for survivors of sexual misconduct to stop repeat offenders.

Me Too Many Voices	@MeTooManyVoices	MTMV Community Support Network Let's Support Survivors & Supporters of Survivors Trauma Educator & Victim Advocate Survivor Led Peer Support | Resources Survivor Shop
Me Too Meredith	@MeTooMeredith	Activist and voice for survivors. If you want to be heard, send your #metoo story and I will share it anonymously. YOUR VOICE MATTERS.
The Me Too Movement	@TheMeTooMvmt	From a viral hashtag to a global organization, we are working towards eradicating sexual violence by shifting culture, policies, and institutions.
No More Organization	@NoMoreOrg	NO MORE's mission is to unite and strengthen a diverse, global community to help end domestic violence, sexual assault and abuse.
RAINN: Rape, Abuse & Incest National Network	@RAINN	We run the National Sexual Assault Hotline & educate about sexual violence. Call 800.656.4673 or visit online. rainn.org to get help 24/7.
Survivors of Color	@SurvivorsofColor	Just another survivor supporting & empowering BIPOC, who've experienced sexual violence.
The Joyful Heart Organization	@TheJHF	Transforming society's response to sexual assault, domestic violence, and child abuse.
Unapologetically Surviving	@UnapologeticallySurviving	Welcome to our community of trauma survivors, supporters, & allies. We promote survivor empowerment, resiliency, & healing.
Why I Kept Quiet	@WhyIKeptQuiet	"Because one story is one story too many." A movement for sexual assault victims.

All descriptions listed here are taken from their respective Instagram pages.

While all in The Me Too Movement are attacking the systemic problems embedded in rape culture and working toward a world with less sexual violence, each of us is doing so in different ways that utilize our individual skill sets. Lawyers, social workers, licensed counselors, and others who want to get involved are joining #MeToo digital activism every day. For many scholar/activists, access to publications in academic journals, professional conferences, and university positions/resources provides a unique space for engaging with the academic work + public engagement combination. #MeToo activists are working to fight for survivors and to make changes at both micro and macro levels. This includes working with the criminal justice system to improve support for survivors, changing rape/sexual assault legislation, and most generally, creating a culture where survivors are believed through one-on-one interactions, on the street, in classrooms, in the workplace—anywhere and everywhere. Together, we can continue to make a difference.

#METOO SCHOLAR/ACTIVISTS LOOKING TO THE FUTURE

The success of #MeToo digital activism should be recognized as embedded in Tarana Burke's activist work surrounding sexual violence that was thrust into the public eye when Alyssa Milano tweeted the "Me Too" phrase (which also brought attention to the #TimesUp movement focusing more squarely on sexual harassment). Indeed, some have even hailed it to be a "watershed moment" in the acknowledgment of sexual violence (Hindes & Fileborn, 2020, p. 1). However, others have aptly critiqued "The Me Too Movement's" lack of inclusivity of people of color and Black women especially (Onwuachi-Willig, 2018), as well as men and LGBTQ people (Gill & Orgad, 2018; Hindes & Fileborn, 2020; Kunst, Bailey, Prendergast, & Gundersen, 2019).

As #MeToo digital activism moves forward, there are many things scholar/activists should consider. In particular, we should continue to use intersectional perspectives in our work (Collins, 2002; Crenshaw, 1991; Davis, 2008). We must bring to the forefront the knowledge that BIPOC, LGBTQ people, and men are survivors of sexual violence. The ways digital technologies have changed how we engage in protest should not go unrecognized or underutilized (Daniels, 2018). In the process, however, we need to be careful to recognize our own social locations and axes of privilege/oppression to best understand how they inform our work as scholar/activists. If we practice radical reflexivity (D'Arcangelis, 2018), we can grapple with being in spaces of privilege (e.g., academic institutions) as well as spaces that have been historically underrecognized, ignored, and silenced (e.g., nonprofits, volunteer efforts, protests).

In closing, it is important to recognize the complexities of the current sociopolitical climate: the extreme strains of the COVID-19 pandemic, the tensions exposed during the Black Lives Matter Movement, the frightening vulnerabilities experienced during (and after) the January 6, 2021, assault on the U.S. nation's capital, and the relief that has come from the U.S. election of President Joe Biden and Vice President Kamala Harris as part of a major step away from the extreme struggles with gender oppression and open mockery of violence against women that were happening regularly in public discourse until very recently (e.g., Donald Trump's comment "Grab 'em by the pussy," Victor, 2017; see also Rothe & Collins, 2019). Amidst this turmoil, #MeToo activism has thrived and those engaged in survivor criminology have found a space to be scholar/activists. This success is a testament to the importance of continued conversations about sexual violence and symbol of a new world where survivors will no longer be silenced.

REFERENCES

Ahrens, C., Campbell, R., Wasco, S. M., Aponte, G., Grubstein, L., & Davidson, W. S. (2000). Sexual assault nurse examiner (SANE) programs: Alternative systems for service delivery for sexual assault victims. *Journal of Interpersonal Violence*, 15(9), 921–943. doi: 10.1177/088626000015009002

Anderson, M., & Toor, S. (2018). *How social media users have discussed sexual harassment since #MeToo went viral.* Retrieved November 16, 2020, from Pew Research Center website: https://www.pewresearch.org/fact-tank/2018/10/11/how-social-media-users-have-discussed-sexual-harassment-since-metoo-went-viral/

Apple, M. W. (2016). Challenging the epistemological fog: The roles of the scholar/activist in education. *European Educational Research Journal*, 15(5), 505–515. doi: 10.1177/1474904116647732

Baumer, E. P., Felson, R. B., & Messner, S. F. (2003). Changes in police notification for rape, 1973–2000. *Criminology*, 41(3), 841–870. doi: https://doi.org/10.1111/j.1745-9125.2003.tb01006.x

Brown, R., Moser, S., & Cook, K. (2021). An analysis of @metoomeredith disclosures of sexual violence/abuse and the cycle of rape culture. In *Sexual Deviance and Society, Second Edition* (Box 12.8). London: Routledge.

Burt, M. R. (1980). Cultural myths and supports for rape. *Journal of Personality and Social Psychology*, 38(2), 217–230.

Campbell, R., & Wasco, S. M. (2005). Understanding rape and sexual assault: 20 years of progress and future directions. *Journal of Interpersonal Violence*, 20(1), 127–131. doi: 10.1177/0886260504268604

Caputi, T. L., Nobles, A. L., & Ayers, J. W. (2019). Internet searches for sexual harassment and assault, reporting, and training since the #metoo movement. *JAMA Internal Medicine*, 179(2), 258–259. doi: 10.1001/jamainternmed.2018.5094

Collins, P. H. (2002). *Black feminist thought: Knowledge, consciousness, and the politics of empowerment.* New York: Routledge.

Crenshaw, K. (1991). Mapping the margins: Identity politics, intersectionality, and violence against women. *Stanford Law Review*, 43(6), 1241–1299.

Daniels, J. (2018). W. E. B. DuBois for the twenty-first century: On being a scholar-activist in the digital era. *Sociological Forum*, 33(4), 1072–1085. doi: https://doi.org/10.1111/socf.12464

D'Arcangelis, C. L. (2018). Revelations of a white settler woman scholar-activist: The fraught promise of self-reflexivity. *Cultural Studies ↔ Critical Methodologies,* 18(5), 339–353. doi: 10.1177/1532708617750675

Davis, K. (2008). Intersectionality as buzzword: A sociology of science perspective on what makes a feminist theory successful. *Feminist Theory,* 9(1), 67–85.

Gill, R., & Orgad, S. (2018). The shifting terrain of sex and power: From the "sexualization of culture" to #MeToo. *Sexualities,* 21(8), 1313–1324. doi: 10.1177/1363460718794647

Hindes, S., & Fileborn, B. (2020). Reporting on sexual violence "inside the closet": Masculinity, homosexuality and #MeToo. *Crime, Media, Culture,* 1741659020909872. doi: 10.1177/1741659020909872

Keller, J., Mendes, K., & Ringrose, J. (2018). Speaking "unspeakable things": Documenting digital feminist responses to rape culture. *Journal of Gender Studies,* 27(1), 22–36. doi: 10.1080/09589236.2016.1211511

Koss, M., Gidycz, C., & Wisniewski, N. (1987). The scope of rape: Incidence and prevalence of sexual aggression and victimization in a national sample of higher education students. *Journal of Consulting and Clinical Psychology,* 55(2), 162–170.

Kretschmer, K., & Barber, K. (2016). Men at the march: Feminist movement boundaries and men's participation in take back the night and slutwalk. *Mobilization: An International Quarterly,* 21(3), 283–300. doi: 10.17813/1086-671X-20-3-283

Kunst, J. R., Bailey, A., Prendergast, C., & Gundersen, A. (2019). Sexism, rape myths and feminist identification explain gender differences in attitudes toward the #metoo social media campaign in two countries. *Media Psychology,* 22(5), 818–843. doi: 10.1080/15213269.2018.1532300

Mendes, K., Ringrose, J., & Keller, J. (2018). #MeToo and the promise and pitfalls of challenging rape culture through digital feminist activism. *European Journal of Women's Studies,* 25(2), 236–246. doi: 10.1177/1350506818765318

Murji, K. (2020). Stuart Hall as a criminological theorist-activist. *Theoretical Criminology,* 24(3), 447–460. doi: 10.1177/1362480619889106

Onwuachi-Willig, A. (2018). What about #ustoo: The invisibility of race in the #metoo movement. *Yale Law Journal Forum,* 128, 105.

Quaye, S. J., Shaw, M. D., & Hill, D. C. (2017). Blending scholar and activist identities: Establishing the need for scholar activism. *Journal of Diversity in Higher Education,* 10(4), 381–399. doi: http://dx.doi.org.ezproxy.lib.ou.edu/10.1037/dhe0000060

Reynolds, K., Block, D., Hammelman, C., Jones, B., Gilbert, J., & Herrera, H. (2020). Envisioning radical food geographies: Shared learning and praxis through the food justice scholar-activist/activist-scholar community of practice. Human Geography, *Online First.* doi: 10.1177/1942778620951934

Rothe, D. L., & Collins, V. E. (2019). Turning back the clock? Violence against women and the Trump administration. *Victims & Offenders,* 14(8), 965–978. doi: 10.1080/15564886.2019.1671284

Russell, D. E. (1982). The prevalence and incidence of forcible rape and attempted rape of females. *Victimology,* 7(1–4), 81–93.

Schneider, K. T., George, A. R., Marvin, L., & Carpenter, N. J. (2020). Sexual objectification in #MeToo and #WhyIDidntReport tweets: Links to sentiment and emotions. *Self and Identity*, 1–8. doi: 10.1080/15298868.2020.1831587

Spohn, C., & Horney, J. (1993). Rape law reform and the effect of victim characteristics on case processing. *Journal of Quantitative Criminology*, 9(4), 383–409. doi: 10.1007/BF01064110

Szekeres, H., Shuman, E., & Saguy, T. (2020). Views of sexual assault following #MeToo: The role of gender and individual differences. *Personality and Individual Differences*, 166(10203), 1–6.

Take Back the Night. (n.d.). History |Take Back the Night| Action Against Sexual Assault. Retrieved November 13, 2020, from Take Back the Night | End Sexual & Domestic Violence | Get Help! Website: https://takebackthenight.org/history/

Victor, D. (2017, November 28). "Access Hollywood" reminds Trump: "The tape is very real." *New York Times*. Retrieved from https://www.nytimes.com/2017/11/28/us/politics/donald-trump-tape.html

Williams, J. B., Singh, L., & Mezey, N. (2019). #MeToo as catalyst: A glimpse into 21st century activism. *University of Chicago Legal Forum*, 2019, 371.

Worthen, M. G. (2016). *Sexual deviance and society: A sociological examination.* New York: Routledge.

Worthen, M. G. F. (2018). *Tarana Burke*. Retrieved January 26, 2021, from Biography website: https://www.biography.com/activist/tarana-burke

Worthen, M. G. F. (2019, January 16). *@MeTooMeredith: An instagram platform for survivors of sexual violence & harassment.* Retrieved January 27, 2021, from Profmagazine website: https://www.profmagazine.com/single-post/2019/01/16/metoomeredith-an-instagram-platform-for-survivors-of-sexual-violence-harassment

Zine, J. (2004). Creating a critical faith-centered space for antiracist feminism: Reflections of a Muslim scholar-activist. *Journal of Feminist Studies in Religion*, 20(2), 167–187.

NOTE

1. Other than @TheMeTooMvmt, none of these groups are officially associated with The Me Too Movement. Tarana Burke does not endorse @MeTooMeredith. To my knowledge, Burke has not endorsed any of these grassroots efforts that build from #MeToo.

Chapter 12

Intersectional Biases in the Rural Courtroom

Stacy Parks Miller

In quoting Sarah Moore Grimké during her first oral argument before the U.S. Supreme Court, Justice Ruth Ginsberg stated, "I ask no favor for my sex. All I ask of our brethren is that they take their feet off our necks" (*Frontiero v. Richardson*, 1973). During my twenty-year span as a prosecutor of domestic violence, sexual assault, and homicide in rural areas, I witnessed the legal profession prove to be a stagnant dinosaur; so far seemingly unaffected by the shift in public sentiment about sexual bias, discrimination, and abuse, the players appear virtually immune from accountability. Growing up female in a small rural town in Pennsylvania, the message was clear to me: Men were the decision-makers, the earners, and the leaders. Women were in varying support roles with seemingly little choice, power, or protection. So ingrained were these themes that I concluded the only way to avoid being cast in that servant role was to flee at the first chance.

I first escaped to attend college, then law school where my suspicions were confirmed. Women lived limitless lives in more urban areas. When I graduated from law school in 1994, it did not escape me that almost 50 percent of my class was female. This thought went through my mind with immense satisfaction. I believed these statistics were a statement, a proclamation if you will, that women and men were equals in the legal profession. I believed that if a person dared to victimize women in any way, the courts were the safe place to vindicate swiftly and safely that wrong.

How wrong I would turn out to be. I would be quickly and steadily indoctrinated into every nuance of gender inequality in the legal profession: workplace sexual harassment, law enforcement/government gender bias, juror gender bias, workplace gender stereotyping, and gender bias in courtrooms run almost exclusively by the Old Boys Club. However, in the legal field, the divide between the sexes was not just about disparate earning power or stunted career advancement. In the legal field, the vast disparity between the treatment of men and women jeopardized liberty and cost innocent lives.

SURVIVING BIAS

Workplace Sexual Harassment: At my first job at a small firm in the late 1990s, my joy from being a practicing courtroom lawyer quickly faded. The language between the two men was routinely full of disparaging and sexual remarks. The obscene remarks worked their way into even the most innocuous conversations. Talking about a judge's secretary could easily include the modifier "bitch." The lawyer's longtime secretary, in her fifties, listened but never seemingly flinched. Law school turned me into a legal authority on sexual harassment, civil rights, and gender equality. I believed in those things, but it seemed this news had not yet reached this town. When I summoned the courage to talk to the owner about it, the attorney responded with silence and then apologized with a grim look on his face. He briskly assured me that they would "be more careful around me." From that point forward, both men barely spoke to me. I received my assignments by memo and was no longer included in important meetings. I had been "canceled" before the phenomenon had a name.

Law Enforcement/Government Gender Bias: I quickly landed a new job as a prosecutor. I assumed this unpleasant business was an anomaly—this small town, this lawyer, this firm. Immediately, the almost exclusively male State Police Troopers delegitimized my predecessor as a "weak woman." They described her as overly sensitive. This was my warning: take it if you want to be one of us. Locker room vulgarities, sexual remarks, and negative gender stereotypes abounded, regularly making their way into casual conversations. I went along without complaint to avoid being cast as a "troublemaker." On my first day, a sympathetic court reporter glanced at my pantsuit and worriedly whispered, "You can't wear those here; the judge does not allow it." She pointed to my pants. I only owned two pantsuits and no skirt. I was reeling. Is this allowed? Is it ethical? I stuffed my concerns and bought a cheap skirt that I wore dutifully for weeks. The day after I won my very first trial in front of this judge, I marched into court the next day wearing pants. He paused, looked down at me over his glasses, and then resumed dictating his order. The courthouse women started wearing pants but even these little victories would be few and far between.

Juror Gender Bias: I prosecuted a brutal rape case in this county. The young victim had been in a relationship with an abusive man who one night graduated from beating her to raping her. After an overnight period of beating, raping, and restraining her in the home, she escaped. She had significant bruises and the house was destroyed. After a grueling trial that almost broke the victim's resolve, the jury came back unable to render an unanimous verdict. The reason? An older farmer from this rural community hung the jury, telling the other jurors, "You cannot rape your wife. It is in the Bible." He hid this bias during the jury selection process but seemed proud to voice his position in the jury room. He suggested to the jury I was making "too big of a fuss" out of private marital problems. I quickly learned this ingrained rape culture was a minefield that all female victims had to navigate.

Gender Stereotyping: After serving as a criminal prosecutor for six years, I joined a private law firm closer to my family. It was 2001. Although the area still boasted a broad rural outskirt, the center of the county was anchored by a major university. I thought I was transitioning to a slightly larger community with an educated, professional, and intellectual population. I wrongly assumed this demographic would hold more expansive views on gender roles. I was the second woman to be hired in a prominent seven-person firm. While the language was much cleaner, not much else was new. After becoming a shareholder and part owner, I was in a meeting about providing disability insurance as a benefit. An older male attorney looked directly at me and said, "We view disability insurance as a need for men with kids." I paused and then asked him if people with vaginas were exempted from paying their mortgage if hurt or disabled as I had missed that exception to debt obligations in law school. I was met with humorless stares and caught some looks being exchanged that signaled I was going to be a topic of discussion later.

Courtroom Gender Bias by the Old Boys Club: All hell broke loose when I accepted a client who happened to be the ex-wife of a local attorney to enforce a condition of their divorce agreement. When my firm found out, they ushered me into a meeting and grimly explained, "We don't represent wives of other lawyers in domestic situations." In other words, the male lawyers in this community made a pact to disadvantage their wives in the event of divorce. I refused their request to invent a "conflict" requiring me to bow out.

Since the local judges knew the attorney personally, a neighboring county judge was appointed to preside over the wife's case. One of the lawyers at my firm quickly warned me that this judge was a primetime bully—old, sexist, and rude. He got a kick out of publicly humiliating people, especially women. He advised me to "flirt with him, go along—with your looks, you could easily become one of his favorites." At the hearing, the sixty-ish white male judge ushered me into his chambers where opposing counsel, a sixty-ish white male, was already seated. The judge opened with sexual innuendo. I sat stone-faced as they ribbed me to lighten up. They exchanged knowing glances and "the conference" was over. I sensed I had failed their test. Mid-hearing, when I was about to expose her ex-husband's misuse of the son's trust money, the judge stopped the hearing, ordering us back into chambers. The judge, exasperated, asked, "What is wrong with your client? She is a good-looking woman. Why can't she find a new man and move on? Do you realize this evidence could get him arrested or at least in trouble with the IRS?" The judge ordered the other lawyer to settle. The case settled in our favor, but my eyes were widely opened to precisely how much male lawyers and judges protected each other behind the scenes. I once again was reminded I could have a special role as an "insider" if I would simply "go along." As we stepped out of chambers, the lawyer and the judge were walking ahead of me, leaning into each other. I heard the word "bitch" exchanged between them. I had no idea if it was meant for me or my client, or more likely, both of us. The "old boys" network not only excluded female lawyers from full and equal participation in the profession, but undermined women litigants as well. Women litigants were largely unaware of these forces silently shaping the outcome of their cases.

Months later, this judge would attend our bar association's annual picnic. The host of the annual picnic? The lawyer for the local attorney. The picnic was on the lawyer's farm and there was plenty of alcohol, guns, and shooting. Unsurprisingly, I learned the two had attended private school together. They began ribbing each other and the judge referenced the lawyer's "faggoty tractor." Slurs about ex-wives abounded. The response from the other judges and lawyers in attendance? Uproarious laughter.

ADDRESSING BIAS

As I was stepping into courtrooms in the 2000s in rural communities in the center of Pennsylvania, staring back at me were older white male judges surrounded by a fleet of women serving "gender traditional" roles including court reporter, secretary, and office employees. Looking at the firms across town, I noticed only a handful of women partners in 2001. "Male-dominated" was an understatement. The bench was all men, top-down. Elected officials were almost all men. Where were all the capable women who graduated law school with me? I checked and many were associate attorneys in firms across the state. Men from my class were already landing partner roles. Women were conspicuously absent from the higher echelons of the legal system. In 2002 in Pennsylvania, women held only one of seven seats on the Supreme Court, five of fifteen seats on Superior Court, and five of nine seats on Commonwealth Court (The Pennsylvania Bar Association, Commission on Women in the Profession, 2002 Report Card, p. 14). Excluding Philadelphia, at the local county level, only 14 percent of Pennsylvania judges were female (Pennsylvania Supreme Court Committee, 2001, p. 340). Predictably, the few women who ascended to the bench also suffered sexual bias and discrimination.

In 1999, the Pennsylvania Supreme Court appointed a committee to determine whether racial or gender bias plays a role in the justice system. The committee's 2001 final report confirmed statewide sexism in all aspects of the court system (Pennsylvania Supreme Court Committee, 2001). The 2001 final report detailed that female judges sitting in only twenty-six of sixty-seven counties expressed a sense of not being "heard" by male colleagues and having their opinions invalidated or outright ignored (Pennsylvania Supreme Court Committee, 2001, p. 350). The report confirmed that suggestions in meetings were ignored until a male colleague made the same suggestion. If these trailblazing beacons of power with law degrees and the power of electability behind them felt marginalized, how could a female litigant or witness be free from the forces of gender discrimination?

Lawyers in my county testified publicly to the difficulties rural women and women lawyers endured in the male-dominated courts, confirming everything I had been witnessing. Lawyers across the state established that outrageous incidents were routinely occurring to women by sexist male judges with zero oversight. Universally, women lawyers commonly heard derogatory and sexual language and had to endure remarks about their bodies. Judges felt free to call them by their first names or some patronizing phrase like "dear" or "honey," depriving women of the respect automatically accorded to male attorneys (Pennsylvania Supreme Court Committee, 2001, p. 349). The women were often excluded from the all-important conversations and fraternizing between the male attorneys and judges (Pennsylvania Supreme Court Committee, 2001, p. 337). Women lawyers were scrutinized more harshly than men. If a woman made a mistake, it was usually attributed to her gender. These women were loath to report misconduct because it would result in serious unintended consequences for them and their career (Pennsylvania Supreme Court Committee, 2001, p. 334). Female attorneys carried an extra fear their clients would suffer retaliation if they reported (Pennsylvania Supreme Court Committee, 2001, p. 336). They were not wrong on any count.

The 2001 final report concluded that the "old boys' network" denied women full and equal participation in the system (Pennsylvania Supreme Court Committee, 2001, p. 343). Bias was evidenced in words, demeanor, and application of different standards to women and had a significant effect on a litigant's courtroom experience and outcome of their case (Pennsylvania Supreme Court Committee, 2001, p. 335–336). The report contained sweeping recommendations for change, including requiring judges seek to include a more diverse group of attorneys in appointed roles "to demonstrate that fairness is a reality in the justice system, not just a lofty ideal" (Pennsylvania Supreme Court Committee, 2001, p. 285).

With the grim realities exposed, women lawyers believed those responsible for policing judges' behavior, the Judicial Conduct Board, could no longer turn a blind eye. Hoping women would be treated equally and could freely report sexual bias without the fear of reprisal rose. Although the progress might be slow, we expected it to be steady. We would be sorely disappointed. Judges are held to precise standards. Their canons demand they be impartial and govern without bias or prejudice. They must refrain from manifesting through "words or conduct" any bias or prejudice on sex or socioeconomic status against any participants in the system (Pennsylvania Supreme Court Committee, 2001; p. 286). Despite this clear mandate, different kinds of bias wreak havoc with fairness in courtrooms.

It is widely understood that stereotypes, preferences, and biases on gender or race are highly predictive of judgments or behaviors (Miller, 2019). In fact, a study done by Miller (2019) suggests that judges may be even more biased than the general public in deciding court cases. Explicit outward bias is easy to identify. In contrast, implicit bias occurs when bias is expressed unconsciously on some level. It is a powerful driver of discriminatory behavior (Bertrand et al., 2005). Implicit bias drives judges' decision-making (Bienias et al., 2017). If a jurist does not recognize his own bias, and no one else is policing for it, all hopes of correcting it are dashed. Implicit bias is the cancer of the court system. Often undetected and untreated but silently and slowly eroding the fundamental principles of fairness and justice.

Two particular types of bias were especially on display in the courthouse. The attribution bias causes people to make more favorable assessments for those "like" them. Hence, women lawyers reporting they were not given the same second chances and benefit of the doubt as male lawyers by male judges. The "affinity bias" causes persons to gravitate toward and develop relationships with people who have the same interest and background (Bienias et al., 2017, p. 4). Hence, older white male judges seeking young white males for clerkships and male lawyers for socialization, and the male lawyers "hanging out" in the judge's chambers. The affinity bias, a form of favoritism, is so prevalent in the legal system that researchers have deemed the legal profession a true "mirrortocracy" (Nalty, 2016).

BIAS FOR CASES OF INTERPERSONAL VIOLENCE

In 2010, I would return to my roots as a prosecutor in this rural area. I would get to see firsthand the changes that had been made in the decade after the blistering 2001 report. For the next eight years, I would represent female crime victims in court before mostly old white male judges. What was being done differently to root out and prevent the serious gender biases identified? I would quickly learn almost nothing in the reverent atmosphere that continued to surround and protect judges.

On my first day in the courthouse as a senior supervisory prosecutor, a soon-to-be president judge called me down to his office first thing to congratulate me on my new position. After returning to my office, I heard the judge appear at our window and ask for me. The secretary buzzed him in. He poised himself at the end of the hallway and, in front of everyone, tossed me keys I had accidentally left on his desk. With a smirk on his face he stated, "Here, you left these under my bed last night." People were speechless. My office manager came to my office to share with me that this judge had sent her shirtless pictures that embarrassed her. Yet she begged me to tell no one because she needed her job. I did not, having been conditioned to know better myself.

In every courthouse, a president judge (PJ) is the powerful boss. The PJ decides the fate and schedule of other judges. The PJ handpicks many of the court employees and conflict attorneys, engendering loyalty. During the next eight years, this PJ would exhibit unchecked sexism and gender bias in a host of ways. He set the tone and it trickled down the chain. No one dared challenge him. On the contrary, many male attorneys behaved as if they revered or feared him, possibly both. Our local newspaper would raise his profile to an exceptionally "great guy."

The 2001 report detailed disturbing findings about domestic violence cases and the handling of protection from abuse (PFA) proceedings. To my dismay, many of the dominating factors at play that worked to disenfranchise women from the 1990s continued to exist unchecked. The PFA Act was passed to protect victims of domestic violence, mainly women and children, through enforcement of court orders that prevent an abuser from having contact with his victim. PFA proceedings are civil but violations are criminally punishable by six months in jail and/or fines.

Women are at the highest risk of death directly after separation (Campbell et al. 2003). Despite the high stakes, there is no right to counsel for abuse victims in the PFA context or family law context. Many women must file complex legal pleadings on their own (Pennsylvania Supreme Court Committee, 2001, p. 394). The report confirmed when fashioning protective PFA orders, male judges failed to use provisions allowing them to fashion interim custody and support orders, leaving female litigants without immediate financial support. In turn, this forced survivors to deal directly with their abuser to work out custody and pay bills (Pennsylvania Supreme Court Committee, 2001, p. 389). Women sometimes felt pressured to withdraw valid cases due to threats to the children or custody being withheld by the abuser (Pennsylvania Supreme Court Committee, 2001, p. 392). If weapons were involved in the abuse, judges were required to check a box on the final order to prohibit the abuser's gun possession for the eighteen-month length of the PFA. Unfortunately, public hearings in 2001 confirmed that male judges went to great lengths to avoid imposing this condition on male abusers. Judges simply were not checking the box when required to. This practice was still occurring ten years later. Why would they do this? Because if a man cannot buy or own guns for eighteen months in central Pennsylvania, this man cannot engage in one of the most revered pastimes of rural white males—hunting. The strong hunting culture and higher rates of gun ownership in rural communities increase the likelihood that a woman will be threatened, intimidated, controlled, or harmed by abusive men with guns (Hall-Sanchez 2014). The judges refused to provide this protection to women despite the fact that weapons access by abusers increases a victim's risk of death by fivefold (Campbell et al., 2003) and that nearly half of all female homicide victims are killed by an intimate partner (Hall-Sanchez, 2014). Hall-Sanchez's study of rural separation/divorce and sexual assault revealed a pervasive hunting culture among rural men that appears to often be accompanied by a dangerous and disturbing "normalization" of casual use of firearms to control, frighten, and intimidate domestic partners.

In 2021, (DeKeseredy, 2021) compiled the causal factors for this "normalization." The major drivers are

- violent rural men are protected by a "good o' boys" network consisting of criminal justice officials (DeKeseredy, 2021).
- widespread acceptance of woman abuses and community norms prohibiting women from seeking social supports (DeKeseredy, 2021).
- a strong rural patriarchy and high rates of male pornography consumption (Hall-Sanchez, 2014; DeKeseredy et al., 2019).

Abusive rural men count on other males, including police officers and judges, to support their violent patriarchal status quo while counting on these same individuals to keep them safe in their community.

Male judges, often born and raised in the rural towns they preside over, are a crucial part of this network. Since enforcement of any principle of law is simply a function of a judge's discretion, the consequences are severe if the judge presiding over domestic violence cases has been part of this "male code" their entire life. Scant levels of fear or accountability can be generated in abusers if authority figures and social buddies operate by the same man code. When a judge incorporates these rural patriarchal norms into his decision-making, that judge is placing women's lives at risk daily through ignorance or arrogance, maybe both. I would personally witness this practice cost women their lives, predictably without consequence.

The president judge in our county was an avid hunter. His chambers were replete with animal heads of personal kills. He drove a stereotypical pickup with a gun rack. This judge was loath to enforce the weapons provision. This judge would criticize the PFA Act's "imposition" on the Second Amendment in front of the petitioner. The practical consequence of his personal feelings, openly expressed, bullied vulnerable women into sacrificing important protections. Years of zero accountability for the courts led to a predetermined outcome—her lawyer would forewarn the victim that she likely will have to "give in" on that issue to get what she wants. The judge's expectation from both parties was clear: The woman would agree to give up the weapons ban, and in turn, the abuser would consent to "stay away." The twisted justification? Her concession would improve her abuser's goodwill towards her, diminishing his desire to want to hurt her "again." She needed to conform to not "deserve" further abuse. This message was widespread and widely known. His attitude was a license for other mostly male judges, including magisterial district judges (MDJ), to follow suit. The judicial message to male abusers was, "We got your back."

Rural women were subjected to the dangers of overlapping prejudices of classism, racism, and sexism. Rural women are at greater risk of nonlethal intimate violence than are their urban and suburban counterparts (DeKersedy, 2019). Rural women have fewer social support systems and inadequate public transportation (DeKeseredy, 2021). Men can more easily isolate partners, contributing more to the victim's dependence, fear, and isolation (DeKeseredy & Joseph, 2006).

Rural women have always been disproportionately affected by poverty (Agarwal, 1989). I would see poverty be an unwitting facilitator of discrimination. When gender and poverty bias combine, the oppression is severe. I would witness survivors of violence with higher socioeconomic status have greater resources at their disposal. They unquestionably garnered more sympathy and respect across the board. Poorer survivors were accorded less credibility, less sympathy, and coarser treatment. Judges allowed more hostile and questionable cross-examination when these survivors testified. Poverty has been defined as a root cause of sexual victimization. While being victimized jeopardizes a person's economic situation, the worse housing and financial security get, the risk of being exposed to sexual violence increases. It is cyclical. PCAR Poverty and Sexual Violence: Building Prevention and Intervention Responses judges who participated in the 2001 study acknowledged their "ivory tower" problem of having "very little understanding" of "poor minority litigants" (Pennsylvania Supreme Court Committee, 2001, p. 319). Our PJ was an older white man who came from a politically connected life of privilege. Stereotypical attitudes about rape and women were still in the minds of some judges, defense attorneys, and police officers. The biases were most apparent in rape cases in which the survivor knew the perpetrator. Many survivors felt like some judges and attorneys seemed to hold them responsible for offenses perpetrated against them by acquaintances (Pennsylvania Supreme Court Committee, 2001, p. 422). Offenders in acquaintance cases were often given lower bail amounts and shorter sentences versus when parties were strangers (Pennsylvania Supreme Court Committee, 2001, p. 425). I would witness these exact biases routinely play out, victimizing domestic and sexual abuse victims in the worst ways.

In 2007, our gun-loving PJ presided over a PFA from a woman who had been abused and threatened multiple times by her estranged husband. Her husband favored a deadly combination of alcohol and violence and had a proclivity for guns. He had recently threatened her with a gun while riding in a car, pulled the weapon, and fired it. After she left him, he began threatening to kill her and her family. She sought protection from his ongoing abuse and threats by filing for a PFA. She would obtain a PFA against her estranged husband, and he would immediately violate it. Instead of giving him a jail sentence, the president judge merely fined him $300 and told him to not do it again. Despite the husband's volatile history involving weapons and an immediate violation of the order, when issuing the final order, the PJ struck the weapons ban. Shortly thereafter in April 2007, this thirty-six-year-old woman met her estranged husband at a gas station to exchange custody of their three-year-old daughter. In broad daylight in public, he pulled his gun and shot her dead before killing himself. The three-year-old lived. This judge was reported to the Judicial Conduct Board for this failing, his history of manipulation of the PFA law, and his discriminatory behavior. No corrective or punitive action was ever taken against him by the agency that allegedly polices judges, the Judicial Conduct Board. After her highly publicized murder, this judge would smartly pronounce himself the face of a new "custody exchange" center for our county, in her name. The center would allow parents to have custody exchanges at a set location manned by employees who assisted in the transfer between parents. Newspapers and the public crowned the judge as hero.

I prosecuted a violent attacked on a woman in her home by her estranged husband, a newly retired state trooper. A different older white male judge presided. The husband tied her up, held a gun to her, and threatened to kill her. She escaped out the door and her life was only spared when a passerby saw a man dragging a hysterical woman across the yard back towards the home. Troopers from the station this man recently retired from had responded to the scene. Despite that he barricaded himself inside with a gun, uttering irrational, and paranoid statements. He was treated with kid gloves by his longtime co-workers and fellow troopers. After transporting the victim back to the barracks instead of calling an ambulance for her injuries, the police asked the victim to meet with her estranged husband in person, so he could "apologize." This is male code for work it out privately. Her sister instead took her to the hospital. Already troubled by this, I learned the judge who arraigned him had not confiscated his weapons and was considering letting him out of jail. Did I mention the judge was a former state trooper? Or that this judge was a close political crony of our PJ? Both grew up locally and were aligned in policy matters. I convinced him to wait until the hearing to hear both sides. The victim arrived at the hearing visibly shaking from fear and detailed a long history of extreme violence and threats with a gun. Despite a steep decline in his mental health, she reported his fellow police always covered for him, and she felt hopeless. She told me, "If he gets bail, he will kill me." Confident with all this information, we appeared in front of the judge and strongly opposed any bail changes, and sought an order confiscating his weapons. Instead, the judge let him out of jail. As a consolation prize, the judge turned to me wink-wink, and promised he would "personally call the defendant's sister," whom he knew, to make sure she "took his guns out his home."

While furiously drafting an emergency petition to override his decision, we learned we were too late. Shortly after the hearing, out on bail with access to his weapons, wearing a disguise, and hiding a shotgun under his trench coat, he would enter her place of employment in a grocery store. She would realize it was him and run for her life. He would hunt her down in an upstairs office, find her hiding under a desk, and execute her with his shotgun while she pleaded for her life. I told the press that the system and the judge had failed her. I urged judges to start listening to victims who know their abusers best. My office thought there would surely be blowback from the public, consequences for the judge, and changes to the system. Nothing occurred of note other than an increase in perception of me as a troublemaker. The judge suffered no investigation consequence or even corrective action by the agency that governs his conduct.

The treatment of sexual assault survivors was equally discouraging. Some estimates indicate nearly 75 percent of sexual assault survivors do not report their attack (Samuels & Thacker, 2000). If you have ever worked in the system, you know why. When the criminal justice system is involved, survivors rightfully fear not being believed by those in the system supposed to help them. Rape culture, victim-blaming, empathizing with perpetrators, assuming the victim's consent, and unreasonably questioning the victim's credibility as the norm (Baum et al., 2018). The country would see it pushed into the headlines in the Steubenville rape case where the public and press seemed more supportive of the boy athletes who filmed their gang rape of an unconscious sixteen-year-old girl than they did for the girl. The country would see it in the Brock Turner case, where Turner was convicted of raping an unconscious woman near a trash dumpster. The world was outraged when Turner received six months in jail but was released after three. The judge was recalled due to widespread outrage over the sentence. However satisfying, this is not the norm. Most victims who are mistreated take what the system gives them and "move on" as best they can.

I would contend with rape culture from judges, police officers, and defense attorneys. I prosecuted a shocking stranger rape case where a man traveled to our community to celebrate St. Patrick's Day to get blackout drunk. The bars opened at 8 am on Friday with lines around the block. College students from other schools came by the busload. This visiting partier exited a house party and broke into a home occupied by a group of women he did not know. He entered the bedroom of one of the sleeping women and raped her. He was caught nearby after fleeing. Unfortunately for the victim, the judge assigned to her case was the same sexist judge who presided when I represented the wife of the lawyer. In accordance with his long history of open disdain for women, he was immediately skeptical of the survivor. He made snide remarks about the victim's request for a continuance related to her schooling. With zero basis to disbelieve her, he remarked that if he found out she was lying about why she needed a continuance, there would be severe consequences for her and the Commonwealth. Her attacker eventually pled guilty to burglary and stranger rape. At sentencing, the judge continued to express his disbelief that the parties did not know each other. He suggested it was near impossible that a man would enter a stranger's home and rape her unless she invited it, particularly a young male college student. He believed strongly there was "more to the story." The message was clear: women cannot be trusted, they are somehow to blame, and the man was getting railroaded. She had to be complicit. And if they had a prior relationship, this was not a "real rape."

This judge later presided over a case in which a young woman was attacked while walking home after midnight from her shift work. Two men would stalk her from a car, choosing her as their victim as they cut her off. One of them attacked her, beating her down in the street. He brandished a gun and tried to drag her into the vehicle. Her screams were so loud, officers a few streets over could hear it and responded, catching him at the scene. The woman was permanently traumatized, testifying she felt sure she was going to be raped, kidnapped, and killed once she saw the gun. The facts were so solid, the defendant pled guilty. Early on, the judge evidenced scorn and repeatedly questioned the story of the young woman, wondering aloud "why she was walking by herself so late at night when nothing good happens?" The court refused to impose a required gun enhancement on the defendant's sentence and refused to impose the lengthy prison sentence required by law. Despite troubling psychological assessments of the defendant, he imposed an illegally short county prison sentence to "protect the offender from the harshness of state prison." Did I mention this defendant was the son of a local lawyer? We appealed this illegal sentence, and the appellate court rejected the judge's outrageous behavior. They remanded the case, requiring the judge to impose the weapons enhancement and an appropriate state prison sentence. The fallout for this judge and these repeated flagrant abuses all centering on sex bias? Absolutely nothing again.

In 2001, our PJ presided over a rape trial of two African American Penn State athletes accused of raping a fellow Caucasian student (*Commonwealth v. Celestin*, 825 A.2d 670 (Pa.Super. 2003)). The victim consumed alcohol to the point she was barely conscious. Two wrestlers invited her back to their room to sleep it off. The victim testified that she came to while they both were taking turns raping her as she faded in and out of consciousness. The wrestlers invited others to watch while they took turns with her and then bragged to others how they had "run a train" on the victim. She only summoned the courage to report the crime after a few weeks of counseling. She was instantly rewarded with harassment from athlete groupies who blamed her and aggressively confronted her on campus. One defendant violated a bail condition by showing up at her dorm but was allowed to remain free. The victim began to attempt suicide. She attempted suicide a second time after PSU refused to discipline the athletes, allowing them to wrestle. At trial, the defense attorney was permitted to dutifully exploit all things rape culture, including this white woman's association with other "black men." One athlete was convicted of sexual assault. Despite all the controversies evident in the case, including racial tensions, athlete privileges (which requires its own book), and gang rape, it made no real news. While the victim had been forced to quit school due to the ongoing harassment, the judge graciously deferred sentencing so her rapist could finish his political science degree.

Pennsylvania's sentencing guidelines for sexual assault require a sentence of three to six years in state prison. Multiple people, including top-level Penn State administrators and coaches, sent character letters to the judge on behalf of the defendant. The judge slashed the three-to-six-year sentence to six months after gushing about the defendant's "accomplishments." The Commonwealth appealed. On appeal, our Superior Court issued a scathing opinion, criticizing the judge and rejecting the unreasonable 400 percent downward deviation from the required sentence. This was Brock Turner before there was a Brock Turner. The PJ attempted to justify the low sentence by finding, although the defendant was "obviously intimately and centrally involved" in the sexual assault of the victim, "his involvement was brief" (N.T. Motion to Modify Sentence, 12/17/01, at 25:3). Our Supreme Court balked, declaring, "We are offended by the trial court's suggestion that the brevity of the criminal act here justifies a lenient sentence. Such a proposition finds no support in the law or the guidelines." The Court required the PJ to resentence the rapist in accordance with Pennsylvania law (*Commonwealth v.*

Celestin, 825 A.2d 670 (Pa.Super. 2003)). In a word, this rebuke was scathing from an appellate court. The judge's response to the appellate court's blistering of him? Complete defiance. He hung it beside his desk, and during legal conferences, he referred to it and mocked it as absurd. It seemed to some that he posted it more as a badge than an irritant. Eventually, the wrestler would be awarded a new trial due to shortcomings by his lawyer. The victim had long moved out of the country to start over from this harrowing experience and a new prosecutor would withdraw the case. After a long and painful struggle, in 2012 this survivor would succeed in taking her own life. Her death certificate stated she suffered from "major depressive disorder with psychotic features, PTSD due to physical and sexual abuse (and) substance abuse" (Setoodeh, 2016).

Then and now our local paper was very deferential to the judges. I would frequently see the white male reporter sitting covering criminal court in the PJ's office laughing it up. The thought they would scratch the surface of these important issues or publish anything slightly critical of the judges was laughable. They all but ignored the glaring issues exposed in this case. Despite the deliberate indifference locally, the case would be forced into the national public eye when the one defendant became famous for writing the acclaimed film *The Birth of a Nation* in 2016. His co-writer for the movie? His co-defendant in the rape case. News media discovered the writer's past and sentiment towards him cooled and, in some cases, turned very negative. The victim's story would engender more sympathy from anonymous movie buffs than ever shown by her "impartial" trial judge. This judge was reported to the Judicial Conduct Board when the news highlighted the case and nothing came of it even though he was still handling full dockets, including rape cases. Every one of these white male judges decided the ultimate fate of innumerable female litigants over many decades. It is hard to estimate how far their toxic reach spread, but there is no question that at times, it cost actual lives.

BIAS INSTITUTIONALIZED

This continuing lack of accountability for judges twenty years after the 2001 report is indefensible since implicit biases and attitudes can indeed be measured. The widely used implicit association test (IAT) measures implicit mental processes. The IAT was developed in 1998 (Greenwalk et al., 1998). While people may try to hide their bias for moral reasons, the IAT requires a quick response, reducing the ability to drive results. In other words, it is hard to fake. Not only is this not being used as any type of diagnostic tool, but it also is not even being used as an "educational tool" in our court system. The complete failure to make any efforts to discover jurist bias before they wreck lives is very telling.

The legal system's total reliance on victim reporting to root out judges' gender bias, as opposed to using a reliable diagnostic tool in concert with a review of the judge's past decisions and behaviors, has the single purpose of protecting bad judges. They know they are powerful, safe, and immune. This lack of progress over the last twenty years is not just my observation; recent studies confirmed the legal profession lags behind other professions in gender, race, and ethnic diversity (Chambliss, 2018). Despite women encompassing close to 50 percent of law school graduates, the percentage of women among firm partnerships has barely budged over a decade. In 2017, women comprised only 21.5 percent of all firm partners and 17.4 percent of firm equity partners (Chambliss, 2018). Ongoing studies, efforts, and recommendations by diversity committees have made little progress (Bell, 2016).

Very little has changed in the two decades after the 2001 report. Will we ever be able to count on our state Supreme Court, the ultimate authority over the Judicial Conduct Board, to effectively police its own to ensure gender equality? Sitting Supreme Court Judge Justice Seamus McCaffery "retired" from our Supreme Court in 2014 after revelations that he had exchanged more than two hundred pornographic emails. In 2016, a trove of highly offensive emails sent to and from then sitting Supreme Court Judge Eakin, containing sexism, racism, and bigotry, was discovered. They were sent to and from male prosecutors and officials across the state over the years, revealing the extensive scope of the statewide "Old Boys Club" in the legal field. The emails were misogynistic and mocked minorities and gays. At first, the Judicial Conduct Board cleared Judge Eakin of any charges, referring to his emails as "unremarkable." After they were released, public outrage forced a second look. This time, the judge was charged with misconduct. He responded by resigning and was permitted to keep his generous pension. Settling his case this way meant there would be no public hearing and no peek behind the curtain of the courts. The court quickly assured the public that the rampant bias shown in the judge's emails did not affect his judicial opinions over the years, even though such a premise directly contradicts universal findings that such biases greatly influence decision-making. That way, women litigants from his prior cases would have no opportunity to question his prior rulings.

Recently in September 2020, a twenty-four-member Pennsylvania Interbranch Commission for Gender, Racial, and Ethnic Fairness penned an urgent letter to Supreme Court Chief Justice Saylor. He is the most powerful member of the Supreme Court—the top watchdog. The letter detailed shocking and ongoing offensive and discriminatory behavior across the state by various Pennsylvania judges. The incidents outlined detailed how a particular male judge referred to a potential juror as an "Aunt Jemima" and remarked she goes home to her "baby daddy who is also slinging heroin." He also berated a woman criminal defendant at sentencing, referring to her husband as a "flea-infested dog" with whom she had "laid down with." He also mocked her for failing to use contraception, available in "any rest stop bathroom."

In August 2020, another judge brazenly mocked a PFA petitioner as a "little blond honey" who was "too dumb to leave." The letter had a pressing tone of emergency and shock. The letter declared that it was clear that some Pennsylvania judges and staff still "feel free to publicly engage in racist, sexist, homophobic conduct." It was written as if the extreme nature of these incidents were a brand-new revelation. This commission demanded tangible consequences for the judges and annual implicit bias training for judges in areas of racism, sexism, and homophobia. Precisely like the ineffectual 2001 report did nineteen years earlier, although now this commission was high-lighting existing racism and homophobia in our courts. Can the commission expect Chief Justice Saylor to step up and take charge? Exactly one month before this letter was sent demanding swift reform, our chief justice himself was accused of seeking out another male judge and asking him to assist in a disciplinary investigation against a former member of the bench, a Black woman. It is virtually unprecedented for one judge to report another, particu-larly when the reported judge sits at the very top of the judicial power para-digm. In a sworn affidavit, the reporting judge asserted the chief justice said this female judge "caused us a lot of trouble when she was on the Supreme Court with her minority agenda" (McCoy 2020). This is the man the com-mission is counting on for immediate reform in rooting out gender and racial bias in our courts. He sits on a court where two other male members have been recently forced off the court due to scandals dubbed "Porngate." One of those expelled judges received troves of emails from prosecutors containing homophobic, racist, and misogynistic content during the time he presided over cases with litigants of all races, sexual orientations, and genders (Pitt et al., 2016). Six months later there has been no additional news about the allegation against our supreme court justice . . . One can almost guess how this might end.

CONCLUSION

Not all judges harbor sexist views about women. The problem is many still do. In rural communities especially, one sexist judge can set the tone for the entire system. The issue has been studied ad nauseam across the country if not the world, and the unyielding conclusion is that gender bias is the norm in courtrooms. There exists a large body of literature offering effective solutions to uncover and combat such bias. In response, Pennsylvania courts have supplied a twenty-year stretch of lip service, neatly documenting pervasive systemic bias in repetitive reports with lofty recommendations for change yet barely a dent has been made. Swift consequences still do not occur even when judges blatantly express bias on the record.

It might seem like a foregone conclusion the legal profession would feel a unique responsibility to combat unconscious bias because lawyers enforce and judges interpret gender bias laws. Instead, it is painfully clear the legal profession will not police itself in a system that requires self-destruction as the cost. The hope that authority figures will force change is bleak considering some are also prime offenders. If change can only come from outside the old boys' clubs, outside the "governing" agencies who protect these judges, who holds the power to force reform in our courts? Persons traditionally without power recently proved they had immeasurable power by acting in concert during the #Metoo movement. Cancel culture exploded on the scene in 2017 to combat sexual harassment, abuse, and assault. People joined together to take down Hollywood offenders because the authorities charged with policing the issue were part of the problem and cover-up (Carlsen et al., 2018).

Whether cancel culture is a crucial tool to provoke accountability or dangerous unchecked online harassment, it gets results. Cancel culture's power shift quickly spread to other matters of social justice, including racism and policing. It is sporadically but successfully rearing its head in the legal world such as in the highly publicized Brock Turner case. Even though we cannot settle for relying on the press to identify offenders in the legal profession, and we cannot stand by as only select publicized cases get justice, it appears we are currently relegated to this type of grassroots accountability to effectuate real change. Only when the collective public voice becomes loud enough to force the courts to make the changes society demands will equality become a reality for women.

REFERENCES

Agarwal, B. (1989). Rural women, poverty and natural resources: Sustenance, sustainability and struggle for change. *Economic and Political Weekly*, WS46–WS65. Retrieved August 19, 2021, from http://www.jstor.org/stable/4395522.

Baum, M. A., Cohen, D. K., & Zhukov, Y. M. (2018). Does rape culture predict rape? Evidence from U.S. newspapers, 2000–2013. *Quarterly Journal of Political Science*, *13*(3), 263–289.

Bell, J. (2016). Why law is the least diverse profession. *Law 360*. Retrieved from https://www.law360.com/articles/795764.

Bertrand, M., Chugh, D., & Mullainathan, S. (2005). Implicit discrimination. *The American Economic Review*, *95*(2), 94–98.

Bienias, E., Stout, S., Lynch, C., Pham, T. T., Polsinelli, R. R., & Rosenwald, L. (2017). Implicit bias in the legal profession. Intellectual Property Owners Association. Retrieved from https://ipo.org/wp-content/uploads/2017/11/Implicit-Bias-White-Paper-2.pdf.

Campbell, J. C., Webster, D., Koziol-McLain, J., Block, C., Campbell, D., Curry, M. A., & Laughon, K. (2003). Risk factors for femicide in abusive relationships: Results from a multisite case control study. *American Journal of Public Health*, *93*(7), 1089–1097.

Carlsen, A., Salam, M., Cain Miller, C., Lu, D., Ngu, A., Patel, J. K., & Wichter, Z. (2018, Oct. 29). #MeToo brought down 201 powerful men. Nearly half of their replacements are women. *The New York Times*. Retrieved from https://www.nytimes.com/interactive/2018/10/23/us/metoo-replacements.html.

Chambliss, E. (2018). IILP Review 2017: The state of diversity and inclusion in the legal profession. Retrieved from https://www.theiilp.com/resources/Pictures/IILP_2017_Demographic_Survey.pdf.

Commonwealth v. Celestin, 825 A.2d 670 (Pa.Super. 2003).

DeKeseredy, W. (2021). Male-to-female sexual violence in rural communities: A sociological review. *Dignity: A Journal of Analysis of Exploitation and Violence*, *6*(2), Article 7. https://doi.org/10.23860/dignity.2021.06.02.07.

DeKeseredy, W. (2019). Intimate violence against rural women: The current state of sociological knowledge. *International Journal of Rural Criminology*, *4*(2), 312–331.

DeKeseredy, W. S., Schwartz, M. D., Harris, B., Woodlock, D., Nolan, J., & Hall-Sanchez, A. (2019). Technology-facilitated stalking and unwanted sexual messages/images in a college campus community: The role of negative peer support. *Sage Open (January–March)*, 1–12.

DeKeseredy, W., & Joseph, C. (2006). Separation and/or divorce sexual assault in rural Ohio: Preliminary results of an exploratory study. *Violence against Women*, *12*(3), 301–311.

Frontiero v. Richardson 411 US 677 (1973).

Greenwalk, A. G., McGhee, D. E., & Schwartz, J. L. K. (1998). Measuring individual differences in implicit cognition: The implicit association test. *Journal of Personality and Social Psychology*, *74*(6), 1464–1480.

Hall-Sanchez, A. K. (2014). Male peer support, hunting, and separation/divorce sexual assault in rural Ohio. *Critical Criminology*, *22*, 495–510.

McCoy, C. (2020, July 23). Pa. Supreme Court chief justice complained about a Black justice and her "minority agenda," former judge says. *The Philadelphia Enquirer*. Retrieved August 19, 2021, from https://www.inquirer.com/news/pa-chief-justice-thomas-saylor-cynthia-baldwin-minority-agenda-reprimand-20200723.html.

Miller, A. L. (2019). Expertise fails to attenuate gendered biases in judicial decision-making. *Social Psychological and Personality Science*, *10*(2), 227–234. https://doi.org/10.1177/1948550617741181.

Nalty, K. (2016). Strategies for confronting unconscious bias. Colorado Bar Association. Retrieved from https://kathleennaltyconsulting.com/wp-content/uploads/2016/05/Strategies-for-Confronting-Unconscious-Bias-The-Colorado-Lawyer-May-2016.pdf.

Pennsylvania Supreme Court Committee (2001). *Pennsylvania Supreme Court Committee, 2001 of the Pennsylvania Court Committee on Racial and Gender Bias in the Justice System.* Retrieved from http://www.pa-interbranchcommission.com/_pdfs/FinalReport.pdf.

Pitt, B., Kessel, M., Martz, G. (2016, June 21). Pennsylvania attorney general exposed 1000s of pornographic, racist government emails. ABCnews. Retrieved from https://abcnews.go.com/US/pennsylvania-attorney-general-exposed-1000s-pornographic-racist-government/story?id=40030106.

Samuels, J. E., & Thacker, S. B. (2000). *Full report on the prevalence, incidence, and consequences of violence against women: Finding from the national violence against women survey.* U.S. Department of Justice. Centers for Disease Control. Retrieved from https://www.ojp.gov/pdffiles1/nij/183781.pdf

Setoodeh, R. (2016, August 16). Nate Parker's rape accuser committed suicide in 2012: Her brother speaks out (EXCLUSIVE). *Variety Magazine.* Retrieved from https://variety.com/2016/film/news/nate-parkers-accuser-committed-suicide-in-2012-her-brother-speaks-out-exclusive-1201838508/.

Chapter 13

From Trauma to Healing

Aboriginal-Led Solutions for First Nations Justice-Involved Communities in Australia[1]

Carly Stanley and Keenan Mundine

To be a survivor means to acknowledge the interconnected and diverse pathways of trauma. For some communities, trauma is not only an individual experience, but one that is collective—reflected within a community in terms of intergenerational and structural victimisation. Experiences of trauma and the role of the legal system in perpetuating these harms has framed much of the colonial history for Aboriginal[2] communities in Australia. There are many stories that can be shared about the experiences of First Nations people in the justice system, all of them a stark and distressing reminder of the legacy that many young First Nations people have inherited due to colonisation, intergenerational trauma, disadvantage, loss of culture, and dispossession. This chapter begins with a brief review of the modern history of Australia and the effects of colonisation on Aboriginal communities. The chapter then focuses on our personal stories and highlights the nexus between trauma, poverty, racism, and incarceration. We conclude with a discussion on the ways that we have used our experiences as survivors to advocate for repair, reform, and support for First Nations people in Australia.

SURVIVING COLONISATION AND
INCARCERATION: A BRIEF HISTORY

Australia's love of prisons and punishment dates back to colonisation. While Australia had been home to a diverse group of First Nations communities for thousands of years, it was not until Captain James Cook's "discovery" of Australia in 1780 and the landing of the First Fleet in 1788 that led to the emergence of Australia as a penal colony. For the next eighty years, over 160,000 convicts would be shipped to Australia from England, Ireland, Scotland, and Wales, instead of being sentenced to death (Sood, 2012).

With the introduction of the Penal Colony in 1788, a foreign system of law was imposed on First Nations people without any consideration of the current systems of lore that existed for Aboriginal people. In Western Australia, the imprisonment of Aboriginal people was a key element of the early development of the state. In 1840, a prison specifically for Aboriginal people on Rottnest Island was built, deepened by the 1902 amendment to the Criminal Code with a provision that summary jurisdiction could be applied in the case of any 'Aboriginal native' with a guilty plea to a charge for a noncapital offence. The magistrates could impose a custodial sentence of up to three years imprisonment, despite their usual limit of two years (Australian Law Reform Commission [ALRC], 2018).

The protection era paved the way for further control and regulation on the lives of First Nations people. Beginning in the late 1800s to early 1900s, a policy of 'protection' was enacted for Aboriginal peoples, which entailed complete government control over all aspects of the lives of Aboriginal people including the removal of First Peoples from their Country and homelands onto missions and reserves. It is clear that while our First Nations people were being controlled by the government under the ruse of 'protection,' our people were not yet intimately acquainted with the criminal justice system. Police however, played a key role in enforcing protection legislation. This would damage relationships between Aboriginal people and police, damage that is still evident today. One of the central roles of police during the enforcement of the protection and assimilation regime was to remove Aboriginal children from their families. The forcible removal of generations of Aboriginal children from their families as a result of various government policies became known as the Stolen Generations. The policies and practices of child removal were rooted in racist beliefs where children only needed to be born to an Aboriginal parent to be considered neglected. These practices left a legacy of grief, loss, and trauma that continues to impact First Nations people, families, and communities today (Commonwealth of Australia, 1997, Cunneen and Porter, 2017).

Throughout the protection regime, there was a reduced need to control Aboriginal people through imprisonment. While the historical era of 'protection' had been dismantled, such controls manifested in new forms. The racially driven and carceral nature of missions and reserves was gradually superseded by the institutional growth of the child protection, youth justice, and criminal justice system (ALRC, 2018). Currently, First Nations people are seventeen times more likely to be under child protection supervision than non-Aboriginal families (Australian Institute of Health and Welfare [AIHW], 2018) and the numbers of Aboriginal children in out of home care is projected to double in size by 2028 (Family Matters, 2019). Rates of incarceration in Australia have soared, and today we imprison a greater share of the adult population compared to any point since the late nineteenth century (Leigh, 2020). First Nations people of Australia bear the burden of this legacy. Not only are First Nations people arrested at unacceptably high rates, but our people are imprisoned at the highest rate in the world (Anthony, 2017).

Although Aboriginal and Torres Strait Islander adults make up around 3 percent of the national population, they constitute 27 percent of Australia's national prison population (ALRC, 2018). In 2018, around 43,000 Australians were in prison, a rate of 221 for every 100,000 adults. Among First Peoples, the 2018 incarceration rate was 2481 per 100,000 adults (Leigh, 2020). While the overall rates are lower in Australia compared to those in the United States, the United States has seen a decline in imprisonment. In 2018, America's imprisonment rate fell to 431 per 100,000 adults, the lowest rate in over twenty years. The rate of incarceration for blacks had also decreased 28 percent in the prior decade (1,134 per 100,000) (Carson, 2020). Meanwhile Australia's numbers have swelled over the same period and First Nations people are more likely to be incarcerated than African American people. These disproportionate rates of imprisonment have continued to rise despite declining rates of crime (Leigh, 2020). In 2016, Aboriginal people were 12.5 times more likely to be in prison than non-Aboriginal people. Aboriginal women are the fastest growing prison population as they are 21.2 times more likely to be in prison than non-Aboriginal women. 80 percent of these women are mothers (Ketchell, 2019).

In 1987 a Royal Commission into Aboriginal Deaths in Custody (RCIADIC) was established in response to a growing public concern from the Aboriginal community about the frequency and explanations for deaths in custody of Aboriginal people. In 1991, a report (RCIADIC) established that Aboriginal people in custody *do not die at a greater rate than non-Aboriginal people in custody.* The disparity instead lies within the rate at which Aboriginal people are imprisoned compared to the general community (RCIADIC, 1998).

While the primary drivers for mass incarceration are often external to the justice system, where extreme levels of poverty, disadvantage, and trauma contribute to the elevated levels of justice system involvement for First Nations people and communities, the system is also to blame. Structural bias and systemic racism is prodigiously apparent at every single aspect of the justice system and disproportionately affects First Nations people. At every distinct step we take, Aboriginal people progress through the justice system unfairly in comparison with our non-Aboriginal counterparts. Aboriginal people are much more likely to be questioned by police. When questioned we are more likely to be arrested rather than proceeded against by summons. If arrested, we are much more likely to be remanded in custody than given bail. Aboriginal people are much more likely to plead guilty than go to trial, and if we go to trial, we are much more likely to be convicted. If convicted, we are much more likely to be imprisoned, and at the end of their term of imprisonment we are much less likely to get parole (Commonwealth of Australia, 2016).

Understanding the history of justice and Aboriginal people since colonisation, as well as the correlation between racism, structured segregation, and government modes of control and regulation, is critical to addressing the mass incarceration of Aboriginal peoples in the contemporary justice system. The RCIADIC found that a multitude of factors, both historical and contemporary, intersect to cause the over-representation of Aboriginal people in custody. The RCIADIC reaffirmed the significance of history *'because so much of the Aboriginal people's current circumstances, and the patterns of interactions between Aboriginal and non-Aboriginal society, are a direct consequence of their experience of colonialism and, indeed, of the recent past'* (ALRC, 2018). In our search for reform and repair, we cannot overlook the effects of systemic racism and the interconnected, harmful impacts that colonisation and dispossession have had on our First Nations people, families, and communities (Commonwealth of Australia, 2016).

KEENAN'S STORY

Keenan Mundine is the youngest of three boys and is a proud Aboriginal man. Keenan's mother is a Biripi woman from Taree (New South Wales—NSW) and his father a Wakka Wakka man from Cherbourg (Queensland). Keenan grew up in Louis St Redfern (which is an inner-city suburb in Sydney, notoriously known as "The Block" on Gadigal land). "The Block" was a central meeting place for Aboriginal people across Australia with roots in political activism, when landlords in the area conducted a campaign of evicting all Aboriginal residents. In 1972, the Aboriginal Housing Company started to purchase houses that would serve as low-cost housing for Aboriginal people. During this time, many Aboriginal people were facing increased levels of discrimination in the private rental market and Redfern became a gathering place for Aboriginal people and families from across Australia. The Block is typically described as a zone in Redfern bordered by Eveleigh, Louis, Caroline, and Vine Street in Sydney, Australia. The Redfern region was described as the 'heartland of urban underprivilege', and Louis Street, where Keenan was raised, was the 'heart of that heartland' (Koori History, n.d.).

Despite all the challenges that were going on in my community and the negative lens the wider public viewed us through, this was also my home and the only place I felt safe and connected. Even though each dwelling was occupied by families outside of my own, I had family everywhere and I remember being able to walk into anyone's home and have a feed.—Keenan Mundine (recalling his time on The Block)

Keenan's parents both relocated to Redfern from their Country lands before Keenan and his brothers were born; Keenan and his brothers were all born in Sydney and raised on The Block with their mother and extended families. Despite the strong community and cultural foundations of The Block, there were also a number of challenges that plagued the community. Most notable of these challenges was the wide presence of drugs and alcohol. Both of Keenan's parents battled with their drug and alcohol use. The community also experienced high levels of violence, mental health, crime, and over-policing by the local authorities.

Keenan lost both of his parents before the age of eight. His mother, Corrina, suffered a drug overdose in 1993, and his father, Keith, took his own life by suicide in 1994. His father's suicide occurred across the road from where Keenan had to attend school every day. Following the loss of both of his parents, Keenan and his brothers were placed in the care of a family member and remained on The Block. However, the placement was not a healthy environment as they were subjected to extreme physical violence and neglect. This guardian also struggled with addiction and the house was one of severe poverty and disadvantage. After a year or two, Keenan was separated from his brothers and placed in the care of another family member. This separation had a detrimental effect on Keenan as a young boy—he had lost his parents and brothers within the space of four years. Keenan was removed to another community in the eastern suburbs of Sydney while his older brother Jai moved to Taree and his other older brother Keith moved to Brisbane to reside with family on their paternal side. Jai had been Keenan's protector throughout his childhood and would even step in to circumvent physical abuse against Keenan by their carer.

Keenan's new placement was also fraught with physical abuse by a non-biological family member, and this time he did not have his brother Jai to help shield him from the violence. Keenan describes this time as particularly difficult without the care and protection of his older brothers. From the ages of nine to fourteen Keenan remained in this placement with very little contact from his brothers. Meanwhile, his brothers were experimenting with drugs and alcohol while getting involved in criminal activity. Keenan recalls his guardians using his brothers' experiences as a warning to him about his own challenging behaviours. As time progressed and Keenan entered his adolescent years, he started to question the lack of contact with his brothers and disengaged from the few prosocial outlets that he had, such as football. Keenan's trauma manifested in ways that he had not yet experienced and he began experimenting with drugs and alcohol.

Given the significant disruption and trauma he had suffered throughout his childhood, Keenan's experiences of education were not positive ones. Whilst his memories of his childhood are scant, Keenan recalls the difficulties he encountered at school. It is of no surprise that Keenan quickly disconnected from his education in his early adolescence. School placed extra pressures on Keenan to conform to their structures and frameworks without support or recognition of his cultural needs as a young Aboriginal person or of the upsetting life events he had been exposed to at such a vulnerable and key developmental phase of his childhood.

It is now recognized that there is a strong correlation between school suspension, poor behavioural outcomes, academic failure, and dropout. School disengagement is a key element of what is known as the 'school-to-prison pipeline' (Hemphill, Broderick, and Heerde, 2017). The school-to-prison pipeline illustrates a pathway that commences when students experience considerable difficulties in the early years of school. Punitive, systemic practices such as disciplinary policy and procedures place disadvantaged young people, particularly Aboriginal young people, on a pathway to prison. Historically, the Australian education system has been adopted from colonial England and has been dominated by white, heterosexual, middle-class, female teachers, who neglect to check their own cultural bias and privilege and maintain indifference for Aboriginal culture. Cultural differences between educational institutions, teachers, and students result in differing expectations for students at school and in the classroom. Lack of cultural safety and competence by institutions and educators often causes detrimental results for diverse students and families. Educational stakeholders frequently blame paradigms of cultural differences as both the basis and resolve for inconsistencies in the education of Aboriginal students. "By assuming that classrooms are neutral, apolitical spaces, schools risk pushing the same colonial agenda that Aboriginal education was founded on" (Gebhard, 2012, 1).

As a result of Keenan's unresolved and ongoing trauma, he made some poor decisions in his adolescence. Keenan found belonging and protection with other older boys from Redfern who were friends of his older brothers and who he had family connections to. These boys were also dealing with their own trauma, poverty, and challenges in coming from a community with many disparities. Keenan was taught to look after himself by committing crimes. At the same time, his experimentation with illicit substances continued. As his drug use increased so did his need to support this habit.

Keenan was only fourteen when he first spent time in custody. In many ways, this was not unusual as his experience mirrors the data on the disproportionate confinement of First Nations youth. Aboriginal young people (aged ten to seventeen years) in all Australian states and territories are detained in youth detention facilities at a higher rate than non-Aboriginal young people (AIWH, 2020). Countless studies have demonstrated the long-lasting effects of early contact with the criminal justice system on children, families, and communities. The younger a child is when they are first sentenced, the more likely they are to continue to offend and end up in an adult prison before their twenty-second birthday (Allam and Murphy-Oates, 2021). NSW has the largest number of young people in detention compared with other states and territories (AIHW, 2017). 48 percent of children and young people in custody in NSW are Aboriginal (Just Reinvest NSW, 2018) and in the Northern Territory, 100 percent of children in custody are Aboriginal (Vita, 2015). On an average night in the June quarter 2019, young Aboriginal people made up about half (500 or 53 percent) of all those in detention, despite making up only 6 percent of the youth population. These numbers increase to 78 percent for young people between the ages of ten and thirteen. Nationally, on an average night in the June quarter 2019, 31 per 10,000 young First Nations people aged ten to seventeen were in detention, compared with 1.5 per 10,000 young non-Aboriginal young people (AIWH, 2020). This means that First Nations children (aged ten to seventeen) were twenty-two times as likely as young non-Aboriginal children to be in detention (AIHW, 2019a). Research also reveals a stark correlation between the children who have experienced out of home care and time spent in juvenile detention. From 2014 to 2019 more than half of the Aboriginal youth who had been in the justice system also had statutory involvement from child protection services (AIWH, 2019b).

By the age of fifteen, Keenan was addicted to heroin; by the time he was seventeen he was injecting heroin with a $500 a day habit. Keenan continued to cycle in and out of juvenile detention, each time released back into the community with no support for his substance abuse, no identification, no cultural support, no financial support, and significant unresolved trauma. Still an adolescent, trying to find his way in the world, it is of little surprise that he would continue on this journey up until eighteen. At eighteen, Keenan caught his first charge as an adult and spent two years on remand in an adult prison.

Once again, none of my trauma was identified and I was thrown into the prison yard with other people from all walks of life. I was eighteen in a cell with a fifty-year old man. Although I was highly anxious and hyper alert about my new environment, many of the boys and men from my community had already been through this process—including my two older brothers and it felt like an initiation into adulthood.—Keenan Mundine (recalling his first time in adult prison)

This experience continued Keenan's lengthy involvement in the criminal justice system which would see Keenan spend more than half his life behind bars. From the age of fourteen to twenty-eight, Keenan spent more of his birthdays in custody than he did in the community. Keenan often refers to the lack of appropriate and culturally responsive support available for him to successfully transition back into society after being released from prison.

In July 2012, Keenan committed an offence while under the influence which landed him back in jail at the age of twenty-five. One day, he was talking with some of the older Aboriginal men who were also in custody with him. A few of these men casually joked and remarked that they were collectively sentenced more than seventy years between them. There was a casual acceptance amongst the men that their future was one centered around incarceration. This was a turning point for Keenan as he realised that this was not how he wanted his life to continue. He had also met Carly during his short stint in the community (six weeks) after being released in May 2012. Keenan was sentenced to a term of imprisonment to be completed in the Compulsory Drug Treatment Correctional Centre (CDTCC) in Parklea, located within the western suburbs of Sydney. While in custody at the CDTCC, program participants are expected to participate in and complete a compulsory drug treatment program (CDTP). The CDTP is a treatment and rehabilitation program of judicial care, stabilisation, case management, educational and vocational support, and rehabilitation and supervision, intended to manage offender risk and meet the needs of the program participants. Each individual participant has a structured case plan that is closely monitored by staff at the CDTCC and the Drug Court and revised where necessary. The aims of the CDTP are to 'reduce drug use, reduce re-offending, promote community reintegration and provide judicial oversight.' The CDTP is conducted in three custodial stages and two community-based stages:

1. closed detention within the CDTCC,
2. semi-open detention involving detention within the CDTCC and access to specified programs in the community,
3. community custody (residing under supervision in the community),
4. parole, and

5. voluntary post-sentence case management in the community (Corrective Services NSW, 2013).

A significant deficit of the compulsory drug treatment program was the lack of cultural competence and safety. However, the flexibility in allowing Keenan to plan for his own recovery and reintegration slowly was fundamental in his rehabilitation. The therapeutic aspect of the CDTP provided Keenan with the opportunity to understand his trauma and recognize how his trauma enabled his substance abuse and criminal justice involvement, while Carly provided a cultural link for him. He often discusses the important role that she played in this process and that without solid, culturally safe community support, he would not have been able to complete the program satisfactorily.

Though Keenan had acquired skills and tools to aide in his recovery, his challenges were far from over. Research has noted the significant challenges that the formerly incarcerated must manage during the reentry process. As a First Nations man with a significant criminal history, Keenan's prospects of employment were limited. Keenan had identified that he wanted to work with the community, particularly in providing support to people with similar circumstances to him. Keenan began volunteering with a children's program at a local community service provider. The staff of this non-Aboriginal organisation observed Keenan engaging with some of the Aboriginal young people and immediately recognized the value Keenan could bring with his lived experience in working with these kids. Many of the children accessing the service shared similar experiences to Keenan as a child and Keenan's innate ability to engage these kids on an intrinsic level was invaluable. While the premise of this idea made sense, Keenan's quest to give back to his community and find healing in sharing his story and experiences would be easier said than done.

Federal discrimination laws in Australia are designed to protect people from discrimination in employment on the basis of their criminal record. However in practice, finance, socioeconomic opportunities, and employment inequalities are the consequence of a multifaceted amalgam of ongoing discrimination, historical bias/racism, and deep-rooted structural problems. Entrenched inequalities in the criminal justice system for First Nations people and communities contributes to the unequal socioeconomic position of First Peoples. In order to continue to work with the children's program, Keenan was required to obtain a Working with Children Check (WWCC).[3] This process is quite onerous and difficult for people with a criminal record. Although Keenan had never been charged or convicted of any offences of a sexual nature or any offences involving children, his initial application to obtain a WWCC was denied. The denial was issued despite the fact that he had been employed with the organisation on a casual basis for two years working directly with children. The negative impact that this process had on Keenan was immense and left him feeling that the system is not designed to give people a second chance—once you enter the realm of the injustice system, the punishment is incessant and ever-evolving. While he was eventually successful in appealing the decision, the process had a damaging effect on his healing and wellness. Unequipped to provide the right type of support at the time, his treatment by the organisation further fueled his destructive behaviours. Ultimately Keenan relapsed and, as a result, was ostracised by the agency he was working for at the time. The pressure and realisation that Keenan might not succeed were significant threats to his journey of rehabilitation.

For Keenan, connecting with Carly was key in his reform. For the first time, he had a safe and stable, drug-free home to return to. He was also able to find culturally safe community support. This allowed him to stay connected to his community while engaging in his healing and making positive connections between his Aboriginal identity, acknowledge the social and structural trauma he had experienced as a child, and find a path towards stability, sobriety and rehabilitation.

CARLY'S STORY

Carly, a proud Wiradjuri woman (Western NSW), was born and raised on Gadigal land in a large Aboriginal family. Carly's family identified with the local Aboriginal community of Redfern as her grandmother lived in the areas of Newtown and Erskineville. Carly had several family members who were involved in the justice system. Some of her earliest justice-centered memories included visiting her aunty and cousins in the local police cells (which was permitted in NSW in the 1980s) or making the trek with her grandmother to visit her uncle in NSW Correctional Centres. Carly recalls the over-policing of her community and family and was often present when the police would raid the family home in their search for other family members. Although some aspects of Carly's upbringing were traumatic, there were also positive memories, particularly when it came to her grandmother. Carly recalls a time when her staunch grandmother (all five foot of her) refused entry to the police into the family home without a warrant. Due to her early trauma and family's involvement with the system, it is fair to conclude that Carly grew up as an at-risk young person.

Like Keenan, Carly also disengaged with education in her teenage years. While she had suppressed the trauma she had experienced throughout her early childhood, it manifested into destructive behaviours. She engaged in drug use and criminal activity as an adolescent, though she was fortunate enough to not ever be charged, despite being arrested. She also discovered she was pregnant at seventeen. Despite these struggles, Carly was committed to changing the narrative of her trajectory. Carly enrolled at a vocational college and signed up for a course in Aboriginal studies. For this first time, she began to understand her upbringing and the position of her people. It was at this precise moment that Carly committed to working towards change and the betterment of her people. Carly commenced her professional journey working with a local health service, providing harm minimisation services and information to the Redfern community. Over the next two decades, she worked across a variety of fields within the community services sector, but was particularly drawn to supporting justice-involved people, families, and communities. This included also working for government agencies including juvenile justice, justice, and corrective services NSW. Carly also continued to study and completed an undergraduate and master's degree in criminology. While her experiences extended to working directly in a number of men's correctional facilities providing therapeutic programs and ad hoc welfare support to men in custody, their families, and communities, she realised that change was not going to happen from the inside. The structural barriers were too great to effect change where it was needed most.

THE BIRTH OF DEADLY CONNECTIONS

The culmination of both Keenan's and Carly's both lived and professional experiences, coupled with the ineffectiveness of the current colonial systems that are in place, inspired them to create an organisation to address the effects of trauma, disadvantage, and poverty on the mass incarceration and over-representation of First Nations people in the justice and child protection systems. *Deadly Connections Community & Justice Services Limited (DC)* was established in September 2018 to provide culturally safe (individual and systems) advocacy, support, information, referrals, and programs for First Nations people, families, and communities—particularly those who are system impacted. In Aboriginal English, 'deadly' means excellent or really good. The name of our organisation also recognises the importance of 'connection' in breaking cycles of disadvantage, oppression, intergenerational grief, loss and trauma, and systems involvement.

Deadly Connections programs and services are developed by the community for the community, and in collaboration with elders, people with lived experience, and professional support services. Our management, staff, and volunteers are *"credible messengers"—people with backgrounds and characteristics like the populations they serve, who develop robust relationships with program participants built upon authentic shared experiences and understanding.* Not only does the hiring of local Indigenous community members help to root our services in a culturally-relevant manner, but it also promotes the development of a workforce within our community. Together, these features create opportunities for Indigenous-led organisations to be changemakers for First Nations people, families, and communities.

The key principles in our approach include

- *Self-Determination*—Aboriginal people, families, and communities are experts of their own lives, with solutions to the challenges we face and their own agents for change.
- *Healing-Centered Engagement*—this holistic healing model and framework adopts Aboriginal culture, spirituality, community action, and collective healing.
- *Life Course*—we recognize the connections across all stages and domains in life and that intervention and change can occur at any stage of a person's life span and have programs to support everyone in the community—families, parents, children, and individuals.
- *Lived Experience*—we have developed an intervention model that combines lived experience with professional support to ensure a holistic approach to transforming lives.
- *Holistic*—we believe that individual health and well-being encompass the whole community throughout the entire life course. It includes collective issues like social justice, equity, and rights, as well as traditional knowledge, traditional healing, and connection to culture. The Aboriginal concept of health includes mental, social, physical, cultural, and spiritual health.
- *Cultural Connections*—as a community who has often been forcibly separated from its cultural roots due to the ongoing process of colonisation, the experiences of colonisation have continued through the present day via practices such as the incarceration of children, the excessive use of child removal from Indigenous families, systemic racism, and mass incarceration. At an individual level, we work to provide practical support for the community and individualised case care. At a systemic level, we advocate for social policy change around issues that have disproportionately impacted our communities and perpetuate grief, loss, and trauma.

As an Aboriginal community-controlled organisation, *Deadly Connections* focuses on promoting healing and justice by implementing alternative justice solutions that focus on transformative justice and community-driven initiatives. Our work aims to positively disrupt the intergenerational disadvantage, grief, loss, and trauma of First Nations people by providing holistic and culturally responsive services. As the DC ambassador, Keenan shares his personal story to spread awareness for the issues facing Indigenous Aboriginal people, families, and communities—particularly those impacted by the child protection and justice systems. On a policy level, our efforts call for using custody as a last resort versus the primary option. We also advocate for the divestment from prisons and the investment in community organisations to keep First Nations people from entering the child protection and justice system/s. Our vision is to break these cycles of system involvement so that First Nations people of Australia can thrive, not just survive. Indeed, true lived authentic experiences, culture, healing, self-determination, and a deep community connection must be the heart and soul of all work with First Nation communities.

FROM SURVIVOR TO ADVOCACY

We stand in solidarity with our mob to elevate their voices, challenge systemic inequalities, and assist them to create a brighter future for themselves through advocacy. A key component in our transformation from survivor to advocacy is our focus on the decolonisation of our child welfare and criminal justice systems. Decolonisation involves a paradigm shift from a white-centric society, to one that involves Indigenous culture through the transformation of existing systemic structures. Indeed, countless studies have demonstrated the long-lasting effects of early contact with the criminal justice system on children, families, and communities. The younger a child is the first time they're sentenced, the more likely they are to reoffend violently, to continue offending, and to end up in an adult prison before their twenty-second birthday (Sentencing Advisory Council, 2016).

In 2018, Keenan travelled to Geneva to speak to the United Nations Human Rights Council (UNHRC) about Australia's practices of youth incarceration, which has led to the detention of Aboriginal children as young as ten years old. In his speech, Keenan addressed the UNHRC urging them to pressure Australia to raise the age of criminal responsibility from ten to fourteen and to acknowledge the disproportionate effects of such policies on First Nations communities (Human Rights Law Centre, 2018).

STATEMENT AT THE 38TH SESSION OF
THE UN HUMAN RIGHTS COUNCIL

2 July 2018
Item 9: General Debate
Speaker: Keenan Mundine

Mr President.

I have spent more than half of my life behind bars.
I can still smell the prison cell I was locked in as a child. A tiny, cold cell. My first night in that cell was the loneliest of my life.
Mr President, right now, children as young as ten are being locked away in prisons across Australia.
This year alone, around six hundred children under the age of fourteen will be taken from their families and communities and locked up.
Most of these children are Indigenous—like me.
This council and many UN bodies have urged Australian governments to raise the age of criminal responsibility.
In joining this Council, the Australian government promised to champion the rights of Indigenous peoples.
But, for as long as Indigenous children are twenty-five times more likely to be imprisoned than non-Indigenous children, these will be hollow promises.
I have travelled from across the world to address this Council because I want my two sons to live in a country that treats them fairly.
This Council should demand that all Australian governments raise the age of criminal responsibility.
All Indigenous children deserve what I was denied—equality and freedom.

CONCLUSION

Keenan is living proof of the reality for many First Nations people. His story brings life to these statistics of disproportionate minority confinement for Aboriginal individuals. Too often people discuss the numbers, failing to recognise that behind these numbers are living, breathing people, families and communities. Keenan has used his voice to speak out against deaths in custody, police brutality, and family separations, issues that perpetuate the never-ending cycle of grief, loss, and trauma for First Nations communities. Such traumas are not just about his community—they are personal. Two of Keenan's brothers have lost their lives at the hands of the NSW police. Both T. J. Hickey and Patrick Fisher, members of the local community whom Keenan had grown up with, lost their lives as a result of police pursuits in Redfern. Keenan remains committed to using his platform to amplify the voices of those impacted by the justice and child protection systems, their families, and the countless others who have lost loved ones by the hands of the criminal justice system. By standing as a survivor, despite the structural obstacles, he continues to serve as a voice for change. Keenan and Carly utilize Deadly Connections as a platform for individual and systemic change.

True lived experience, culture, healing, self-determination, and a deep community connection must be at the heart and soul of all work with First Nations people and communities.

BIBLIOGRAPHY

Allam, L., & Murphy-Oates, L. (January 17, 2021). Australia's anguish: The Indigenous kids trapped behind bars. *The Guardian*. Retrieved at https://www .theguardian.com/australia-news/2021/jan/18/australias-anguish-the-indigenous -kids-trapped-behind-bars

Anthony, T. (2017, June). Factcheck Q&A: Are Indigenous Australians the most incarcerated people on earth? *The Conversation*. Retrieved at https://theconversation .com/factcheck-qanda-are-indigenous-australians-the-most-incarcerated-people-on -earth-78528

Australian Law Reform Commission (ALRC). (2018). *Pathways to justice—inquiry into the incarceration rate of Aboriginal and Torres Strait Islander peoples,* ALRC Report 133. Retrieved at https://www.alrc.gov.au/publication/pathways-to -justice-inquiry-into-the-incarceration-rate-of-aboriginal-and-torres-strait-islander -peoples-alrc-report-133/

Australian Institute of Health and Welfare (AIHW) (2017). *Youth detention population in Australia 2017*, Bulletin 143. Commonwealth of Australia, Canberra. Retrieved athttps://www.aihw.gov.au/getmedia/0a735742-42c0-49af-a910-4a56a8211007/ aihw-aus-220.pdf.aspx?inline=true

Australian Institute of Health and Welfare (AIHW) (2018). *Young people in child protection and under youth justice supervision: 1 July 2013 to 30 June 2017*, Data linkage series No. 24. Commonwealth of Australia, Canberra. Retrieved at https:// www.aihw.gov.au/getmedia/bdcab5ea-2009-4c44-95ff-8225f5171c4a/aihw-csi-26 .pdf.aspx?inline=true

Australian Institute of Health and Welfare (AIHW) (2019a). *Indigenous community safety*. Snapshots. Retrieved at https://www.aihw.gov.au/reports/australias-welfare /indigenous-community-safety

Australian Institute of Health and Welfare (AIHW) (2019b). *Young people in child protection and under youth justice supervision: 1 July 2014 to 30 June 2018.* Data linkage series no. 25. Cat. no. CSI 27. Commonwealth of Australia, Canberra. Retrieved at https://www.aihw.gov.au/reports/child-protection/young-people-in -youth-justice-supervision-2014-18/contents/table-of-contents

Australian Institute of Health and Welfare (AIHW) (2020). *Youth detention population in Australia 2019,* Bulletin 148. Retrieved at https://www.aihw.gov.au/ getmedia/c3ba6d29-7488-4050-adae-12d96588bc37/aihw-juv-131.pdf.aspx?inline =true

Carson, E. A. (2020). *Prisoners in 2018*. U.S. Department of Justice, Bureau of Justice Statistics. Retrieved at https://www.bjs.gov/content/pub/pdf/p18.pdf

Commonwealth of Australia (1997). *Bringing them home: National inquiry into the separation of Aboriginal and Torres Strait Islander children from their families*. Retrieved at https://humanrights.gov.au/sites/default/files/content/pdf/ social_justice/bringing_them_home_report.pdf

Commonwealth of Australia (2016). *Aboriginal and Torres Strait Islander experience of law enforcement and justice services.* ISBN 978-1–76010–469-6. Retrieved at https://www.aph.gov.au/Parliamentary_Business/Committees/Senate/Finance_and _Public_Administration/Legalassistanceservices/Report

Corrective Services NSW. (May 2013). *Review of the Compulsory Drug Treatment program and the Compulsory Drug Treatment Correctional Centre pursuant to the Crimes Administration of Sentences Act 1999.* Retrieved at https://www .parliament.nsw.gov.au/tp/files/3510/Review%20pursuant%20to%20Crimes%20 (Administration%20of%20Sentences)%20Act.pdf

Cunneen, C., & Porter, A. (2017). Indigenous peoples and criminal justice in Australia. In A. Deckert & R. Sarre (Eds.), *The Palgrave handbook of Australian and New Zealand criminology, crime and justice* (pp. 667–682). Palgrave-Macmillan. https: //doi.org/10.1007/978-3-319-55747-2.

Family Matters (2019). *The Family Matters report: Measuring trends to turn the tide on the over-representation of Aboriginal and Torres Strait Islander children in out-of-home care in Australia.* Retrieved at https://www.familymatters.org.au/the -family-matters-report-2019/

Gebhard, A. (2012, Sept/Oct). Pipeline to prison: How schools shape a future of incar-ceration for Indigenous youth. *Briarpatch.* Retrieved at https://briarpatchmagazine .com/articles/view/pipeline-to-prison

Hemphill, S., Broderick, D., & Heerde, J. (2017). Positive associations between school suspension and student problem behavior: Recent Australian findings. *Trends & Issues in Crime and Criminal Justice,* no. 531. Canberra: Australian Institute of Criminology. https://www.aic.gov.au/publications/tandi/tandi531

Human Rights Law Centre (2018). *Statement at the 38th Session of the UN Human Rights Council 2 July 2018 Item 9: General Debate. Speaker: Keenan Mundine.* Retrieved at https://www.hrlc.org.au/news/2018/7/2/former-youth-prisoner-at-the -un-calls-out-turnbull-government-for-failing-indigenous-children

Just Reinvest NSW (2018). *Policy Platform NSW Election 2019.* Retrieved at https: //www.justreinvest.org.au/wp-content/uploads/2018/10/Policy-Platform-2019-.pdf

Ketchell, M. (2019). Aboriginal mothers are incarcerated at alarming rates—and their mental and physical health suffers*. The Conversation.* Retrieved at https: //theconversation.com/aboriginal-mothers-are-incarcerated-at-alarming-rates-and -their-mental-and-physical-health-suffers-116827

Koori History (n.d.) *A condensed history of The Block in Redfern.* Retrieved at http:// www.kooriweb.org/foley/images/history/1970s/1973/block/blockdx.html

Leigh, A. (2020). *The Second Convict Age: Explaining the return of mass imprison-ment in Australia.* IZA Institute of Labor Economics, No. 13025. Retrieved at http: //andrewleigh.org/pdf/SecondConvictAge.pdf

Royal Commission into Aboriginal Deaths in Custody (RCIADIC) (1998). *Reports of the Royal Commission into Aboriginal deaths in custody.* Retrieved at http://www .austlii.edu.au/au/other/IndigLRes/rciadic/

Sentencing Advisory Council (2016). *Reoffending by children and young people in Victoria.* Victoria State Government. Retrieved at https://www.sentencingcouncil.vic.gov.au/publications/reoffending-children-and-young-people-victoria

Sood, S. (2012). Australia's penal colony roots. *BBC Travel.* Retrieved at http://www.bbc.com/travel/story/20120126-travelwise-australias-penal-colony-roots#:~:text=New%20South%20Wales%2C%20a%20state,being%20given%20the%20death%20penalty

Vita, M. (2015). *Review of the Northern Territory Youth Detention System report.* Retrieved at https://correctionalservices.nt.gov.au/__data/assets/pdf_file/0004/238198/Review-of-the-Northern-Territory-Youth-Detention-System-January-2015.pdf

NOTES

1. This chapter is written using Australian English, which retains the 'u' in words such as 'behaviour' and the 'ise' ending in words like 'colonisation' and 'organise', instead of the American use of 'ize.'

2. The term 'Aboriginal', 'First Nations', and 'Indigenous' are used interchangeably. The term 'Aboriginal' is also inclusive of both Aboriginal and Torres Strait Islander people, families, and communities.

3. The Working with Children Check (WWCC) is a requirement for anyone who works or volunteers in child-related work in NSW. It involves a National Police Check (criminal history record check) and a review of reportable workplace misconduct. The outcome of a check is either a clearance to work with children or a bar against working with children. If cleared, the check will be valid for five years, however applicants are continuously monitored.

Conclusion

Looking Forward

Kimberly J. Cook, Reneè Lamphere, Jason M. Williams, Stacy L. Mallicoat, and Alissa R. Ackerman

The work of survivor criminology is not easy; it is a paradigm shift in how we think about criminology and our professional commitments. We appreciate these contributors for their vulnerability, grace, and strength in sharing their lived experiences. We encourage you to consider survival, survivor criminology's place in academia (in terms of our scholarship, our teaching, and our activism), and students' needs. We end this volume with some resources for support and exploration.

WHAT DOES IT MEAN TO SURVIVE?

Survival. To continue to exist or be despite traumatic events or conditions. Throughout this volume, we have explored what it means to persist beyond interpersonal, social, and structural violence. It was experiences with surviving trauma that led us to criminology, seeking to make sense of trauma, and to find meaning. We learned about conditions that threaten survival, where trauma is institutionalized, including within criminology and academia. Finally, we may still question what it means to survive, and whether we have. We see multiple pathways towards and within survival and wonder: Is one ever done with surviving? Surviving is a multilayered process, as trauma is often unacknowledged, and thus rendered irrelevant by silencing and dismissal. The process of survival continues indefinitely. We start by acknowledging the harmful impacts of conditions and circumstances that were beyond our control. We move into another layer, often wondering what we did to bring it about—because we live in a victim-blaming culture, this layer can be very thick, dense, and impenetrable. To work through that layer, we need resources, and we need new ways of thinking about our experiences, such that we can understand the powerlessness we felt in those close encounters with trauma. Another layer of survival may emerge that pushes us to make meaning and engage in a "survivor mission" (Herman, 1997, p. 207). We may find that mission in the classrooms where we learn about patterns, theories, and strategies to study and combat these persistent social conditions. We seek opportunities for it to matter, because we have been told too many times that it does not matter. Against that backdrop of irrelevance, we strive to heal our wounds and that requires connection to compassionate companions.

Survival also means battling against the institutionalized structures that are designed to limit, restrict, and disempower individuals and groups. Criminological scholars/activists expose the root causes of social inequalities such as systemic racism, sexism, classism, and heterosexism. We know solutions must tackle both cultural and social structures to reduce the patterns of harm we document so well in criminology. We also know that one program on its own is insufficient to undo centuries of accumulated structural power, and powerlessness. We aim to reveal the impacts of that powerlessness by giving it voice and creating counternarratives that embody resilience, determination, and grit. Our survival depends on it.

Survival is not healing, however. Healing can be part of the survival process where we use our lived experiences to fuel research and teaching commitments, despite obstacles or mentors who urge us to keep quiet. Trauma can never be erased from our lens of knowing. While pursuing healing, we have also experienced compounded harms such as gaslighting, trauma triggers, ignored PTSD, emotional abuse, and other challenges. Healing acknowledges the harms, honors them, seeks to make them purposeful, and thereby diminishes the harms' impacts. Healing looks like a piece of wrinkled paper: when we ball up a piece of paper to toss it away (trauma), and then flatten the paper out again, the wrinkles remain. Regardless of how much you try and flatten the paper again, it will always show the wrinkles. We are the paper, and the harms of trauma are the wrinkles that remain always present within us, and also serve as object lessons for our teaching, research, service, and community engagement. We can, however, use that paper to (re-)write our stories and offer meaningful lessons.

Writing about survival promotes healing. Engaging in survivor criminology can be challenging and exposes a difficult duality. On one hand, giving voice to experiences is empowering. For some, their chapters offered space to control their narrative and reflect on the impact that it has on their trajectory within criminology. Still, revisiting traumas publicly is very difficult. These authors are vulnerable and brave. Criminologists are unaccustomed to using our lived experiences for insights as scholars; our systems of promotion and tenure, or other career paths, rarely support or acknowledge the strength of personal survival. As such, survivor criminology is a radical act of hope. We see students every semester who quietly seek our support, in the safe corners of the classroom after class is over, in the quiet corridors of our offices when we can have private conversations. We see our colleagues struggling with similar challenges, and because of the pressures of tenure track life, often remain silent for fear of ridicule or patronizing comments, or worse yet: fear of losing out on promotion and tenure. We chose to convert those quiet conversations into a louder platform, offering support to a wider audience by writing, and healing out loud, in this book. Coming forward for some of us did not risk structural security in our positions; coming forward for others of us exposed that risk. Rather than remaining silent and in the shadows of criminology, which claims expertise in our lived experiences, we have chosen to add our voices to the conversations in our field, in our professions, and in our communities. We hope that by doing so, others will be affirmed, inspired, and buoyed into persisting in their goals, because the opposite of trauma is not healing. "The opposite of trauma is power" (Sered 2019, p. 231). Being seen and heard is powerful.

UNEARTHING CRIMINOLOGY AS POTENTIALLY TRAUMAGENIC

We understand secondary trauma is perpetuated by the criminal justice system. We see that criminology can also be a space where trauma lives. The structural barriers discussed in several chapters expose that we must reckon with the traumagenic nature of academia and criminology. Criminology was established by white men, about white men, and failed to acknowledge diverse and intersectional communities that we study, and our community of scholars. Slowly, the discipline is evolving. Feminist criminology brought attention to the unique pathways of women as victim and offenders (Cook, 2016). Convict criminology illuminated the unique experiences of the formerly incarcerated and their impact on scholarship and policy (Ross & Richards, 2003). Queer criminology acknowledged the challenges that exist for LGBTQ+ populations within a discipline that has historically, and continues to perpetuate heteronormative structures and cultures (Buist & Lenning, 2016). Intersectional criminology acknowledges that race, class, gender, and sexuality co-create multiple trajectories towards crime and victimization, and aims to revolutionize the field (Potter, 2015). Each of these specializations offer powerful and valued perspectives to criminology. Survivor criminology adds to the conversations by highlighting our lived experiences as survivors of interpersonal, social, and structural trauma, to incorporate their voices.

Nonetheless, criminology can be dehumanizing and can perpetuate marginalization, as we have seen in several chapters of this book. Mainstream criminologists steer us away from excavating lessons from our lived experiences, and overlook the value of our experiences on the field. For many of us as students, we sought to connect with an area of study where we hoped to find answers to our questions, and where we hoped to find workable solutions to prevent others from the traumas we have endured. Sadly, this compounds our experiences of being silenced, and results in secondary traumas that we may feel academically worthless. Intersectionality and multiple traumas may expand into polyvictimization in a professional milieu not well-suited to acknowledging and healing these harms. But we did not know that at the start of our journeys into criminology. We may leave criminology feeling disappointed, dejected, and lost. This structural violence and institutional betrayal of academic life persist beyond our student experiences. It is replicated, often, in the professional settings of academic life; job searches, promotion and tenure, service obligations, and mentoring during the pre-tenure period are all mentioned by our authors in their journeys into and through criminology. We are left to wonder, for those of us who have prevailed such that we can contribute to this volume, how many more have left academic life with wounds they cannot give voice to? How many have left with a sense of failure or despair because the academy squandered the wisdom of their life experiences for our collective lessons? By creating brave spaces for these experiences to be shared, we hope to generate conversations that promote survival and healing.

FOR ACADEMIA: ADOPTING A
SURVIVOR CRIMINOLOGY LENS

Many of the contributing authors came to criminology and criminal justice seeking answers to deeply personal questions. Perhaps these experiences have resonated with students reading this book. As scholars, we learned that our questions were not always answerable through the discipline. Textbooks rarely reflect the lived experiences of marginalized people. Some professors may uphold the very system that continues to marginalize and dehumanize people. Sometimes simply asking the questions causes further trauma and isolation. Our hope is that through this book, students see the different ways to explore criminology. Lived experiences matter. Students will continue to seek those quiet conversations; we hope this book helps provide additional resources to connect students to criminology as a meaningful and compassionate field. We hope readers find value in the commitment to always be kind, being kind to oneself and others by listening, learning, and leading into a new type of academia. Become an ally and/or accomplice in the quest for racial, gender, and LGBTQ+ justice. To combat the systems of oppression that cause traumatic marginalization is a worthy goal for criminologists to embrace.

For faculty colleagues to embrace survivor criminology is to extend an avenue towards students and colleagues by cultivating safe, brave spaces that may support healing. Teaching and research are essential components of our work, and often create insights for students to grapple with their own experiences. We share these experiences, not so much for ourselves to be seen, but for our students to see that survival is possible, and the need for connection reveals who we truly are—simply human. Trauma is taught in many courses in U.S. colleges and universities (Carello & Butler, 2014). There are two main categories of trauma studies in the classroom: (1) those who engage in the analysis of personal, cultural, and historical trauma narratives, and (2) those who engage in helping students to create their own trauma narratives, typically through composition and writing-based course work. There are benefits of personal traumatic experience disclosure in classroom settings (Berman, 2001). Carello and Butler (2014) claim that effects of disclosing trauma in the classroom are unknown because "other than ethnographic accounts, no empirical research has been published outside of clinical disciplines" (p. 155). However, failing to teach about trauma may perpetuate feelings of shame, guilt, and secrecy that compound it (Becker-Blease & Freyd, 2007; Jolly, 2011). Integrating and discussing trauma where appropriate, educators should look to reduce the risk of retraumatization and secondary victimization for students exposed to traumatic materials (Carello & Butler, 2014).

Teaching with a survivor criminology lens should be trauma-informed, which is to understand how traumatic events create needs and vulnerabilities of survivors (Butler, Critelli, & Rinfrette, 2011). We encourage strategies that minimize the possibility of retraumatization, secondary traumatization, or a new traumatization by delivery of services (Carello & Butler, 2014). Strategies used by the contributors of this book are evident: using previously recorded lectures, creating safe space during office hours for deep conversation, and teaching about strength, survival, and policy reform. By opening these topics during classes, professors can indicate their own positionality with the issue, and give permission for heretofore silent students to begin pondering their own experiences. We acknowledge the risk of added emotional labor due to disclosure, and to prevent burn out or over exposure, some survivors may not (ever) be ready to disclose; no one is required to do this.

Faculty should be aware of trauma among college age students: lifetime prevalence rates of traumatic event disclosure for these students range from 65 to 85 percent (Frazier et al., 2009; Read, Ouimette, White, Colder, & Farrow, 2011). Exposure to sexual assault, unwanted sexual attention, and family violence is associated with distress and negative student outcomes (Anders, Frazier, & Shallcross, 2012). Avant, Swopes, Davis, and Elhai (2011) found that four out of five college students are exposed to at least one experience of psychological abuse while at college, 31 percent are exposed to physical abuse, and 36 percent to at least one incident of sexual abuse. Furthermore, Horsman (2000) argues that traumatic course content can result in students disclosing their own traumatic experiences to the professor. Whether invited, or not, many instructors are ill-equipped to handle traumatic disclosures among students. To be better prepared for these situations when they arise, instructors should learn about and utilize trauma-informed practices. These include things such as considering the emotional needs and safety of students, offering trigger warnings with potentially traumatic topics, and being prepared to make referrals to clinical care and other campus resources. It is important to recognize that while teaching about trauma is fundamental to understanding the human experience, educators should honor the dignity of trauma survivors and those who are learning about trauma survivors (Carello & Butler, 2014). For example, while teaching, we recommend using person-first language to prevent students with traumatic experiences feeling the impact of stigma that often emerges from our criminological concepts (i.e., "prostitute" or "delinquent," etc.). We also suggest that when students disclose to us, we stop the distractions around us (email, cell phones, etc.) and empathetically listen to them. We should also inform them about "mandatory reporting policies" that may be effective on our campuses. We can acknowledge their experiences, and we can point them to confidential services available to them on our campuses or within the community, and inform them that they are not alone.

We ask that scholars take seriously Hooks' (1994) philosophy about teaching to transgress as genuine praxis in their classrooms. Survivors often show up in our classrooms possessing "defiant" ontologies and epistemologies about the subject matters under discussion. Their way of exercising autonomy around academic debates in criminology is often counter, therefore, not welcomed. Yet the instructor's inaction or inflexibility around being inclusive to other equal ways of navigating academic terrain, especially curriculum and instruction, plays a role in reproducing trauma and inequality for many students, especially survivors. In this regard, honoring the lived experiences of survivors serves as an act of humanitarianism and also holds educational value. As an instructor, it matters to be present for all students in the classroom and allow the collective lived reality of all to transform and illuminate the learning experience.

As scholars engaging in trauma-related research, Connolly and Reilly (2007) viewed the research process as a confessional tale. Positionality is common practice in feminist methodology (Cook, 2016; Charmaz, 2014), though it is rarely done publicly. Unlike quantitative research, qualitative research encourages researchers to co-create information with their study participants (Maynard & Purvis, 1994; Vygotsky, 1987). Connolly and Reilly (2007) describe feeling like a repository for their participants' experiences of trauma. They felt compelled to "reassure, comfort, and share information that may be helpful to the participants" (p. 530). Their ethic of care guided them as researchers. Connolly and Reilly (2007) discuss reflexivity and different strategies a researcher can use when researching trauma. They suggest that reading research on trauma, as well as attending conference and paper presentations by researchers working in trauma, may be helpful for trauma researchers. "Hearing how these researchers have navigated through their own methodological issues and discussing the personal dilemmas that commonly arise . . . has proven to be an important reflexive practice in itself" (Connolly and Reilly, 2007, p. 532). Debriefing and other reflexive practices move their experiences from an emotional level to a cognitive level, allowing the researcher to reflect on the data and conduct the analysis in a less emotional manner. "It therefore becomes crucial for a person who is researching trauma to cultivate reflective alliances to not only debrief the research experience but to create a safe 'unloading zone' for the emotionality that emerges" (p. 534).This regrounds the researcher, allowing them to deepen their own understanding of the data and the role they play in a research context.

Added stress resulting from compassion fatigue may develop. Figley (1995) argues that compassion fatigue is known as "the natural consequent behaviors and emotions resulting from knowing about a traumatizing event experienced by a significant other—the stress resulting from helping or wanting to help the traumatized or suffering person" (p. 296). To combat compassion fatigue, Connolly and Reilly (2007) suggest spacing out interviews over a longer time period, and debriefing with colleagues following a difficult interview. Acknowledging that a researcher can be affected by the stories they hear helps trauma researchers and encourages self-care protocols.

SURVIVOR/SCHOLARS IN THE COMMUNITY

Survivor criminology reminds us that our commitment to this field extends beyond campuses. Community engagement is critical to serving others who have survived similar experiences to those we have navigated. It requires us to listen deeply and to use language that is meaningful to the communities with which we engage. Our survival and persistence in this field means that we have the ability to guide policy and practice. When we combine our lived experience with our professional expertise, it provides a foundation to make critical changes. These changes cannot and will not happen overnight, but they can happen. This book is proof that change can occur—that when we use our lived experiences and our professional expertise we can change lives.

Community engagement can look like many things. For some of us it might mean wearing our survivor criminologist "hat" at community meetings. It might mean using our experiences and expertise to participate in or lead conversations in community groups. It might mean being an invited keynote speaker where we share from both the personal and professional lens. Finally, it might mean calling attention to environments that are toxic or that lead to persistent traumatic stress. Just as we have called attention to the toxic and harmful nature of the academy, we must do a better job of calling attention to the places within our communities that are similarly problematic. Being a survivor scholar means we speak truth to power.

We also argue for pathways toward radical ontologies and epistemologies of survivorship within all spaces but especially criminology, where struggles against violence (of all kinds) are foregrounded and recognized as equally other forms of knowledge. Orthodox conceptions of criminological knowledge have long pursued knowledge as strictly a quantifiable pursuit. However, we argue that this process has not been some unassuming measure—that as a discipline, criminology has long engaged processes of erasure against the bodies and minds of those who have brought trauma with them to this project. To this end, criminology may be a site of tremendous violence, or it can be one of transformational possibilities. Through survivor criminology, we can imagine new publics and collaborations between the academy and everyday people. If the current order is one of oppressive and repressive logics, then the way forward must be through the liberatory direction from those who have survived the gauntlet of violence.

THE QUEST FOR HEALING: A RADICAL ACT OF HOPE

In addition to highlighting the resiliency of the authors of the chapters of this text, the title of this book is a call to action for all criminologists, survivors or not. Being a survivor is not a new experience: survivors have been around us and among us for as long as the academy has existed. It was simply easier for some to not hear the stories of their colleagues who were survivors as they did not have to take action on problems that to them did not exist. Survivor criminology removes the option for others to say the victimization of their colleagues does not exist. Now that we know better about survivors, we need to do better in helping survivors. There is also a great deal of value in collateral survival, allies, and accomplices in the journey towards survival. Because so much of our lived experience of trauma existed in a hermetically sealed bubble of silence, avoidance, and denial, we have frequently felt invisible, ignored, and insignificant. With allies who are not survivors, we hope to inspire collaboration in dismantling systemic oppressions; we hope to create relationships based on understanding, and "ride or die" dependability with and for each other. Because harm often renders us marginalized, survival is a celebration of connectedness. Please join us in the journey to transform criminology. We know that the master's tools will not dismantle the master's house (Lorde, 1984). This book offers survivors' tools: our tools, our goals, our discipline, our criminology. We claim our place in this field.

RESOURCES FOR SUPPORT

As we leave you with these stories and areas to explore, we want to acknowledge that some readers may be interested in additional resources on healing for individuals and communities. We offer the following national level resources for additional research and support on violence and trauma, and encourage you to also look within your local communities as well. This is not an exhaustive list and represents a place to begin your inquiry on programming, research, and policy on issues of violence and survivorship. We have also provided a reading and listening list of several works that have impacted each of us deeply as we consider what it means to be a survivor, and how that experience has impacted our journey as teachers, scholars, and advocates.

WEBSITES AND HOTLINES

- Rape, Abuse & Incest National Network (RAINN): https://www.rainn.org
- National Coalition against Domestic Violence: https://ncadv.org
- National Sexual Assault Hotline: 1.800.656.HOPE (4673)
- National Domestic Violence Hotline: 1.800.799.7233
- National Dating Abuse Helpline: 1.866.331.9474
- StrongHearts Native Helpline (Violence in Tribal Communities): https://strongerheartshelpline.org or 1.844.7NATIVE (1.844.762.8483)
- A Long Walk Home (gender and racial violence for Black communities): https://www.alongwalkhome.org/

- Ujima: The National Center on Violence against Women in the Black Community: https://ujimacommunity.org
- Center for the Pacific Asian Family (Violence in Asian/Pacific Islander communities): https://nurturingchange.org/ or 1.800.339.3940
- LGBT National Help Center: http://www.glnh.org or National Hotline 888.843.4564 / Youth Talkline 800.246.7743
- Ampersands Restorative Justice: https://ampersandsrj.org

BOOKS

- *Braving the Wilderness* by Brene Brown
- *The Body Keeps the Score: Brain, Mind and Body in the Healing of Trauma* by Bessel van der Kolk
- *Until We Reckon: Violence, Mass Incarceration and a Road to Repair* by Danielle Sered
- *Healing from Sexual Violence: The Case for Vicarious Restorative Justice* by Alissa R. Ackerman and Jill S. Levenson
- *Hope and Healing in Urban Education: How Urban Activists and Teachers are Reclaiming Matters of the Heart* by Shawn Ginwright
- *Pushout: The Criminalization of Black Girls in Schools* by Monique W. Morris
- *Shattered Justice: Crime Victims' Experiences with Wrongful Convictions and Exonerations* by Kimberly J. Cook
- *Life of the Mind Interrupted* by Katie Rose Guest Pryal

PODCASTS AND SOCIAL MEDIA

- Beyond Fear: The Sex Crimes Podcast: https://beyondfearpodcast.com
- Unlocking Us with Brene Brown: https://brenebrown.com/unlockingus/
- Survivor Criminology Facebook Group: https://www.facebook.com/groups/1380096445720480

REFERENCES

Anders, S. L., Frazier, P. A., & Shallcross, S. L. (2012). Prevalence and effects of life event exposure among undergraduate and community college students. *Journal of Counseling Psychology, 59,* 449–457.

Avant, E. M., Swopes, R. M., Davis, J. L., & Elhai, J. D. (2011). Psychological abuse and posttraumatic stress symptoms in college students. *Journal of Interpersonal Violence, 26,* 3080–3097.

Becker-Blease, K. A., & Freyd, J. J. (2007). The ethics of asking about abuse and the harm of "don't ask, don't tell." *American Psychologist, 62,* 330–332.

Berman, J. (2001). *Risky writing: Self-disclosure and self-transformation in the classroom.* Amherst: University of Massachusetts Press.

Buist, C., & Lenning, E. (2016). *Queer criminology: New directions in critical criminology.* New York: Routledge.

Butler, L. D., Critelli, F. M., & Rinfrette, E. S. (2011). Trauma-informed care and mental health. *Directions in Psychiatry, 31*(3), 197–212.

Carello, J., & Butler, L. D. (2014). Potentially perilous pedagogies: Teaching trauma is not the same as trauma-informed teaching. *Journal of Trauma & Dissociation, 15,* 153–168.

Charmaz, K. (2014). *Constructing Grounded Theory, 2nd Edition.* Thousand Oaks, CA: Sage.

Connolly, K., & Reilly, R. C. (2007). Emergent issues when researching trauma: A confessional tale. *Qualitative Inquiry, 13*(4), 522–540.

Cook, K. J. (2016). Has criminology awakened from its "androcentric slumber"? *Feminist Criminology, 11*(4), 334–353.

Figley, C. R. (1995). *Compassion fatigue: Coping with secondary trauma stress disorder in those who treat the traumatized.* New York: Bunner/Mazel.

Frazier, P., Ander, S., Perera, S., Tomich, P., Tennen, H., Park, C., & Tashiro, T. (2009). Traumatic events among undergraduate students: Prevalence and associated symptoms. *Journal of Counseling Psychology, 56,* 450–460.

Herman, J. L. (1997). *Trauma and Recovery.* New York, NY: Basic Books.

hooks, B. (1994). *Teaching to transgress: Education as the practice of freedom.* New York: Routledge.

Horsman, J. (2000). *Too scared to learn: Women, violence, and education.* Mahwah, NJ: Lawrence Erlbauam Associates.

Jolly, R. (2011). Witnessing embodiment: Trauma, narrative and theory at the limit in field research and in the classroom. *Australian Feminist Studies, 26*(69), 297–317.

Lorde, A. (1984). Sister Outsider: Essays and speeches. Trumansburg, NY: Crossing Press.

Maynard, M., & Purvis, J. (1994). Doing feminist research. In M. Maynard & J. Purvis (Eds.), *Researching women's lives from a feminist perspective* (pp. 1–9). Bristold, PA: Taylor & Francis.

Potter, H. (2015). *Intersectionality and Criminology: Disrupting and Revolutionizing Studies of Crime* (Key Ideas in Criminology Series). New York, NY: Routledge.

Read, J. P., Ouimette, P., White, J., Colder, C., & Farrow, S. (2011). Rates of *DSV-IV-TR* trauma exposure and posttraumatic stress disorder among newly matriculated college students. *Psychological Trauma: Theory, Research, Practice and Policy, 3(*2), 148–156.

Ross, J. L., & Richards, S. C. (2003). *Convict criminology.* Belmont, CA: Wadsworth.

Sered, D. (2019). *Until we reckon: Violence, mass incarceration and a road to repair.* New York, NY: The New Press

Vygotsky, L. (1987). *Thought and language* (A. Kozulin, Ed.). Cambridge, MA: MIT Press.

Index

About the Editors

Kimberly J. Cook, Ph.D., is a Professor of Sociology and Criminology at the University of North Carolina, Wilmington. She is the author of several academic books and peer-reviewed journal articles, including serving as a guest editor for the February 2006 special issue of *Theoretical Criminology* focusing on gender, race, and restorative justice, and a 2012 special issue of the *Albany Law Review.* She is a previous chair for the Division on Women and Crime.

Reneè D. Lamphere, Ph.D., is an Associate Professor of Sociology and Criminal Justice at University of North Carolina, Pembroke. Her areas of academic interest include corrections, mixed-methods research, sexual violence and victimization, family violence, and cyber and digital-media crimes. Dr. Lamphere has a particular interest in teaching and pedagogy and has published in the *Journal of Criminal Justice Education*, and her most recent research project examines the #MeToo movement and sexual assault disclosure among college professors. She currently serves as the President of the North Carolina Sociological Association. She also serves as a Guardian ad Litem for Robeson County, North Carolina, where she advocates for children in the foster care system due to abuse and neglect.

Jason M. Williams, Ph.D., is an Associate Professor of Justice Studies at Montclair State University. He has authored several books and articles and has co-edited a special issue for the *Journal of Criminal Justice and Law Review* that served to introduce the burgeoning new concept revolutionary criminology. He is also a guest editor for a special issue for *The Prison Journal* on the Black Lives Matter Movement and the broader carceral realities faced by marginalized people. He is also the book review editor for the *Journal of Decolonization of Criminology and Justice.* He has also served as the Secretary/Treasurer for the Division on People of Color and Crime.

Stacy L. Mallicoat, Ph.D., is professor of criminal justice and director of the University Honors program at California State University, Fullerton. Her areas of interest include feminist criminology, justice programming, capital punishment, and student success for criminal justice education. She is the author of five texts with Sage Publications and Carolina Academic Press, including *Women, Gender and Crime* and *Crime and Criminal Justice: Concepts and Controversies*. She has also served in leadership positions with the Western Society of Criminology, Academy of Criminal Justice Sciences, and the Division on Women and Crime.

Alissa R. Ackerman, Ph.D., is an Associate Professor of Criminal Justice in the Division of Politics, Administration, and Justice at California State University, Fullerton. She has served as a keynote speaker around the world. Her TEDx talk offers a new perspective on restorative justice and how it can help those who have suffered from sexual violence. She has authored or edited six books with various academic presses, including Rowman and Littlefield, Columbia University Press, and Carolina Academic Press and has also served as co-editor on a special edition of the journal *Sexual Abuse*.

About the Contributors

Babette J. Boyd, J.D., is a faculty member in the Department of Sociology and Criminology at the University of North Carolina, Wilmington. She is an attorney with specialization in prosecuting sex crimes, and other crimes against women and children. In 2016, Ms. Boyd was awarded a Fulbright Scholarship in Canada where she conducted a comparative study of Indigenous women and women of color in Canada and the United States, primarily in cases of sexual violence. Ms. Boyd's research interests include structural racism and sexism in criminal courts, voting rights, and social justice.

Steven Green is an undergraduate student majoring in criminal justice and public administration at California State University, Fullerton. His research interests include criminal justice policy reform, sentencing enhancements, rehabilitation and reentry, and life without the possibility of parole. He is a Project Rebound scholar and McNair Scholar and hopes to pursue a Ph.D. in criminology. He is also a community researcher with the Urban Institute and a member of the National LWOP Leadership Council with Human Rights Watch.

Monishia "Moe" Miller is a criminal justice scholar and childhood adversity expert. For more than twenty-five years, she has worked in the juvenile justice system. Her work focuses on bringing awareness to the issues surrounding social inequality and injustice on Black/African American youth in school, community, and justice systems. She completed her undergraduate work at University of California, Irvine, in sociology, and her master of science degree from California State University, Los Angeles in criminal justice administration. She is recognized as an Outstanding Lecturer in Humanities and Social Science at California State University, Fullerton, where she is currently faculty.

Toniqua C. Mikell, Ph.D., is a Black feminist and intersectional criminologist. She joined UMass Dartmouth in 2019 as an Assistant Professor of Crime and Justice Studies. Broadly, her work uses Black feminist criminology to understand the role of interlocking systems of oppression in explaining the victimization and social control of Black women, femme-identifying, and nonbinary individuals. Her research interests include queer criminology, prisoner reentry, sexual offending and victimization, and social justice implications of carceral state contact.

Keenan Mundine is the Co-Founder and Ambassador for Deadly Connections Community and Justice Services. He is a proud First Nations man with connections to the Biripi and Wakka Wakka Nation. His experiences of losing both parents at a young age and being separated from his siblings and placed in care, shaped his relationships with the child protection and justice systems throughout childhood and young adulthood. His lived experience is also highlighted in the documentary *Incarceration Nation* and the recent Amazon docu-series *Unheard*.

Jennifer Ortiz, Ph.D., is an Assistant Professor at Indiana University Southeast. Dr. Ortiz earned her Ph.D. in criminal justice from John Jay College of Criminal Justice. Her research interests center on structural violence within the criminal justice system with a focus on reentry post-incarceration. Ortiz maintains a firm commitment to civil service and activism. She serves as President of the New Albany, Indiana, Human Rights Commission, as an executive board member for Mission behind Bars and Beyond, a nonprofit reentry organization, and as Executive Counselor for the Division of Convict Criminology of the American Society of Criminology.

Stacy Parks Miller is a Pennsylvania lawyer who has practiced law in rural counties for the majority of her twenty-seven-year legal career. Stacy graduated from Duquesne Law School in 1994 and began her law career prosecuting crime in Clearfield County, Pennsylvania. She was the only female prosecutor in the District Attorney's Office during the decade she worked there. She would go on to become the first female elected District Attorney in Centre County, home of Penn State University. During her eight-year tenure, she would personally and successfully prosecute violent crime, domestic violence cases, rape, homicide, and child sex crimes.

Alexa D. Sardina, Ph.D., is an Assistant Professor at California State University, Sacramento in the Division of Criminal Justice. Her scholarship focuses on how restorative processes can be used to address sexual harm. Dr. Sardina has written and presented on research that combines her scholarly expertise on sexual harm and restorative justice combined with and informed by her personal experience as a rape survivor. She believes that "survivor scholarship" offers a critical perspective within the broader field of criminology. Dr. Sardina is a co-founder of Ampersands Restorative Justice and co-hosts the popular podcast *Beyond Fear: The Sex Crimes Podcast.*

Lauren J. Silver, Ph.D., is Associate Professor of Childhood Studies at Rutgers University-Camden. She is a feminist ethnographer whose work lies at the intersection of abolitionist praxis, queer kinship, and transformative child and youth studies. Her scholarship centers the lives of Black, brown, and queer young people who experience and resist structural violence; it is deeply connected to the urban places where she lives and works. Dr. Silver is the author of *System Kids: Adolescent Mothers and the Politics of Regulation* (2015, UNC Press). She integrates her beloved role as an educator with art, poetry, critical inquiry, healing, and activism.

Carly Stanley is the CEO and Founder of Deadly Connections Community and Justice Services (DC). DC provides holistic, culturally responsive interventions to First Nations communities in the Greater Sydney area, Australia. Carly is a proud Wiradjuri woman, born and raised on Gadigal land. She has spent the last twenty years working in both government and nongovernment agencies to improve justice and child protection systems, and to break the cycles of disadvantage and trauma so that First Nations people of Australia can thrive. She also holds a masters of criminology and is a 2020 Churchill Trust Fellow.

Meredith G. F. Worthen, Ph.D. (she/her/hers), is a Professor of Sociology and Sexualities/LGBTQ Studies scholar with key interests in stigma, prejudice, and crime. She is a social justice advocate for the LGBTQ community, especially through her creation of The Welcoming Project, and an advocate for survivors of sexual assault through her work as #MeTooMeredith. As a researcher, teacher, and activist, she dissects multiple dimensions of prejudice in efforts to cultivate understanding, empathy, and social change.

PRAISE FOR *SURVIVOR CRIMINOLOGY*

"This must-read volume does a masterful job of breaking the silence regarding the lived experiences of sexual violence, trauma, anti-blackness, and other abuses of so many criminologists and social scientists. There is hope. Times are changing, silence is breaking, and we are not alone in our lived experiences. Kudos to all the authors in this volume who are speaking up and making needed change."—**Callie Rennison, University of Colorado, Denver**

"This book challenges criminology to become a more humanistic and self-critical discipline. Drawing from intersectional feminism, the authors courageously document their experiences of violence, institutional discrimination, and broader social inequalities. *Survivor Criminology* is a hopeful book that will speak to students who bear their own scars of violence and injustice."—**James Ptacek, Emeritus Professor, Suffolk University**

"*Survivor Criminology* is the book that we as a society and a discipline need! It is filled with information that allows the reader to understand victimization but more importantly how people survive and go on to change the world!"— **Shelly Clevenger, Sam Houston State University**

"*Survivor Criminology* challenges the presumptive objectivity of social science research, adding a welcome experiential component to theory, methods, and practice. The contributors in this book provide lively and engaging reflections on how their personal experiences of victimization, their identity, and their social locations interact with canonical criminological themes. The result is a more holistic understanding of some of the most pressing issues confronting our society in addition to a roadmap of how resilience and insight contribute to the journey toward justice."—**Susan L. Miller, University of Delaware**

"*Survivor Criminology* is a beautifully collected anthology of narratives that speak of courage and resilience in the face of trauma and the call for a new approach to victims and victimization in the field of criminology—Survivor Criminology. The editors accomplished something incredible in creating the foundation for a much-needed shift in our discipline. The breadth and depth of experiences and the collective path navigating pain and recovery is palpable. This edited volume is a must-read for all, whether student, academic, practitioner, and/or survivor and anyone interested in poignant journeys of trauma, healing, and hope."—**Maria João Lobo Antunes, Towson University**

Made in the USA
Middletown, DE
22 August 2024